# THE BIRTH OF THE EURO

Today, 318 million people in 15 countries use the euro, which now rivals the importance of the US dollar in the world economy. This is an outcome that few would have predicted with confidence when the euro was launched. How can we explain this success and what are the prospects for the future?

There is nobody better placed to answer these questions than Otmar Issing, who, as a founding member of the Executive Board of the European Central Bank, was one of the euro's principal architects. His story is a unique insider account, combining personal memoir with reference to the academic and policy literature.

Free of jargon, this is a very human reflection on a unique historical experiment and a key reference for all academics, policy-makers and 'eurowatchers' seeking to understand how the euro has got to where it is today and what challenges lie ahead.

OTMAR ISSING is President of the Center for Financial Studies at the University of Frankfurt and Honorary Professor of the Universities of Frankfurt and Würzburg. He is a former member of the Board of the Deutsche Bundesbank (1990–8) and a founding member of the Executive Board of the European Central Bank (1998–2006).

# The Birth of the Euro

Otmar Issing

Translated from the original German
by Nigel Hulbert

CAMBRIDGE
UNIVERSITY PRESS

CAMBRIDGE UNIVERSITY PRESS
Cambridge, New York, Melbourne, Madrid, Cape Town, Singapore, São Paulo, Delhi

Cambridge University Press
The Edinburgh Building, Cambridge CB2 8RU, UK

Published in the United States of America by Cambridge University Press, New York

www.cambridge.org
Information on this title: www.cambridge.org/9780521731867

First published 2008

Printed in the United Kingdom at the University Press, Cambridge

*A catalogue record for this publication is available from the British Library*

ISBN 978-0-521-51673-0 hardback
ISBN 978-0-521-73186-7 paperback

# Contents

# Figures

# Tables

# Preface

The date 1 January 1999 marks a milestone in monetary history. Eleven national currencies – not least among them the D-Mark, held in such high esteem by the citizens of Germany – ceased to exist. Their place was taken by the euro, as the single currency for over 300 million people. In the meantime, the euro area has grown, and now encompasses a total of fifteen countries.

The birth of the euro is a unique event. Never before had sovereign states ceded their responsibility for monetary policy to a supranational institution. This constellation – on one side, a central bank (the European Central Bank, ECB) and a single monetary policy; on the other, nation states that largely retain their competencies in the areas of economic and fiscal policy – creates a particular kind of tension in the interrelationship. Quite a few observers, with probably the majority of economists to the fore, were more than sceptical as to the outcome of this experiment. To begin with, will the euro get off to a good start? Under the prevailing circumstances, how likely is it, if at all, that the euro can be a stable currency? And then: what about the future? Can European monetary union (EMU) survive in the absence of political union?

The subject has been comprehensively addressed both by economists and in the media. Since well before the start of EMU, and even more so afterwards, there has been a vast output of economic research. Hardly surprising, in light of the fact that the political decision presented economists with a special kind of experiment whose many different facets offer broad scope for in-depth theoretical and empirical studies. Among economists, as in the media, the pendulum has swung back from a predominantly sceptical assessment towards regarding the experiment as having been successful – initially with some surprise, but meanwhile almost as though it could have been taken for granted. After nine years, most observers pronounce the ECB and the euro to be an unqualified success. In so doing, they tend to forget just how difficult it was to prepare for the start of EMU, to build up the ECB as a new institution, and to lay the foundations for a single monetary policy.

This volume describes the road to the euro, and the setting-up of the ECB and of the single monetary policy, from the vantage point of one who was closely involved in a leading position. After leaving academia in October 1990 to join the Directorate of the Deutsche Bundesbank, I was appointed to the Executive Board of the European Central Bank on 1 June 1998, the date of its foundation, and hence placed at the centre of this unique event. Being responsible for the Directorates General for both Economics and Research, I was called upon to play a key role, in particular in the preparatory stages and the early days of the single monetary policy. To be confronted with what was in every way a special challenge, and at the same time to be granted the opportunity to help shape the response to it: what more interesting task could an economist ever hope to be given?

In this book, my aim is to let the reader share this experience of what is probably the most exciting event in modern monetary history. To that end, I analyse the gestation and birth of the euro from an economist's perspective, and at the same time describe the process of and background to the setting-up of such an important institution as the ECB. On the one hand, as a supranational institution, the ECB is a special kind of central bank; on the other, the ECB and its monetary policy can serve as the model of a modern central bank in general. The closing chapters look to the future, to the challenges that lie ahead for the ECB and European monetary union.

This mix of economic analysis and historical narrative determines the flavour of the book. Most chapters are quite approachable even for readers without any major grounding in economics. In certain sections, such as that dealing with the choice of monetary policy strategy, the need to consider the background of economic analysis and research is a determining factor.

The bibliographical references are for the most part to other works by the author. Their publication was largely contemporaneous with the processes described in the present volume and they serve to illustrate how every step, every decision taken was accompanied by intensive economic discussions within the ECB, in particular with my own staff. In turn, these publications contain extensive references to other literature. The book should therefore form a useful starting point for students and those wishing to pursue the topic further.

The present work is a reflection of the successful collaboration with my colleagues in the Directorates General for Economics and Research. I shall never forget the way in which they supported me in accomplishing my tasks through their outstanding professional competence, their commitment and their loyalty.

For their many valuable comments and criticisms, I should like to thank Marcel Bluhm, Vitor Gaspar, Hans Joachim Klöckers, Julian von Landesberger, Klaus Masuch, Wolfgang Modery, Wolfgang Schill and Volker Wieland, and also Ludger Schuknecht for individual chapters. Lars Svensson and John Taylor were kind enough to comment on passages relating to the choice of monetary policy strategy. Not least, five anonymous referees encouraged me in my project and at the same time made numerous suggestions, many of which I have followed. Wolfgang Modery took care of the figures and tables. My assistant Marcel Bluhm was an indispensable aid to me on all technical matters. Birgit Pässler untiringly transposed my manuscript into readable text. Chris Harrison guided the publication process at Cambridge University Press, and kindly offered to take charge of preparing the index.

In Nigel Hulbert I found the ideal German–English translator, and I am also grateful to him for a number of valuable suggestions concerning the text.

I dedicate this English-language version to my colleagues at the European Central Bank as an expression of my gratitude for their outstanding collaboration over the years.

Otmar Issing

# ONE

# The euro in 2008

Today, in 2008, the euro is the common currency of fifteen EU countries with around 320 million inhabitants, and most other member states are aiming to join the euro area in the near or not-so-distant future. With the issuance of euro-denominated banknotes and coins at the beginning of 2002, the former national currencies were taken out of circulation, their names henceforward consigned to the history books. The fact that isolated attacks by populist politicians fail to elicit much support for a return to the national currency only serves to confirm that the common currency has become an irreversible reality, and that going back is not really an option.

Globally, too, the euro has become firmly established as the second most important currency after the US dollar. By some measures, for example in terms of its share of global official reserves, the euro still lags a long way behind; but in other respects, notably in its role as currency of denomination for credit, the euro has more or less drawn level with the American currency. Investors all around the world put their faith in the euro and buy euro-denominated long-term paper. Confidence in the stability of the euro is reflected in inflation expectations that are firmly anchored at low levels, helping explain what are, historically, exceptionally low long-term nominal interest rates.

Over the nine years that have passed since its birth on 1 January 1999, the euro has been a striking success. With an average annual rate of inflation of around 2 per cent, it can deservedly be called a stable currency, both in historical terms and internationally.

This success story stands in marked contrast to many of the forecasts made before its introduction. The doomsayers either ruled out the currency union getting off the ground at all, or predicted its early demise, or at the very least thought it would lead to inflation – none of which actually materialised. So were all the concerns unfounded? Can one simply assume that the euro's success story will continue?

The fact remains that for sovereign states to cede their authority in the monetary sphere to a supranational institution, while retaining a greater or lesser degree of autonomy in other policy areas, is historically unprecedented. It is no coincidence, therefore, that observers speak of an experiment, an experiment whose outcome seems likely to remain uncertain for a considerable time to come.

The future offers excellent scope for speculation. But what are the reasons that lay behind the euro's good start and its success to date, and where do potential vulnerabilities lie? This book attempts to provide an answer to such questions.

# TWO

# Historical background

## The rocky road to monetary union

The idea of creating a monetary union in Europe can be traced back
a long way. Indeed, in the first century AD, a merchant could pay with
the same money, the denarius, throughout his long journey from
Rome via Colonia Claudia Ara Agrippinensium and Lutetia
Parisiorum to Londinium – that is, via Cologne and Paris to London.
Sixteen centuries later, however, the same journey involved an
unending sequence of money changing and conversion. Trade was
heavily hampered by high tariffs between countries and even broke
down in the frequent times of war. In Germany alone, if one may call
it that, a hundred different territories exercised the right to mint their
own coinage. The number of customs borders in this region in 1790
has been estimated at some 1,800. It was only with the establishment
of the customs union in 1834 that most trade barriers disappeared in
Germany. And it was only following political unification within the
German Reich in 1871 that the multiplicity of coinages was fully
abolished and the Mark introduced as the common currency.

What lessons might we draw from comparing these epochs of
European history?

There were two conditions that characterised the common currency period:

- The stability of the currency was ensured by the natural scarcity of the metal.
- A common currency went hand in hand with political union under the Pax Romana.

The loss of monetary stability due to the persistent debasement of coinage and the disintegration of the Roman Empire undermined the old system. There was no single currency in Germany again until the adoption of the gold standard and the establishment of political union under the German Reich in 1871. Elsewhere, other nation states such as France and Great Britain had brought about a single currency much earlier. The notion of a common *European* currency was aired now and again by individual authors or groups, often in conjunction with ideas for the political unification of Europe. But for a long time, there were no serious, still less promising, attempts towards such an objective.[1]

It was only after the horrors of two world wars that the project of European integration was given a new and decisive impetus. This is not the place to depict the various stages in this process, starting with the establishment of the *European Coal and Steel Community* in 1952. If at all, the goal of a common currency played only a background role.

Just a few years after the start of the *European Economic Community* (EEC) in 1958, there were occasional suggestions that work should also be undertaken towards monetary integration. A concrete first step was taken by the heads of state or government assembled at the summit conference in The Hague on 1 and 2 December 1969. They agreed that 'on the basis of the memorandum presented by the

---

[1] In 1712 Abbé de Saint Pierre, for example, published an essay, 'Projet de traité pour rendre la paix perpetuelle entre souverains chrétiens'.
   On the history of money in Europe see F. Berger, *12 into One: One Money for Europe* (Frankfurt, 2001).

Commission on 12 February 1969 and in close collaboration with the Commission a plan by stages should be drawn up by the Council during 1970 with a view to the creation of an economic and monetary union'. In autumn 1970, the 'Werner Group', named after the then Prime Minister of Luxembourg who chaired it, presented its report, which essentially contained a plan for the establishment of economic and monetary union in three stages. A short time afterwards, it was considered that this project should be completed over a period of ten years.

This ambitious aim was basically doomed to failure from the outset. For one thing, the international environment was to be affected in the years that followed by major turbulences: the floating of the D-Mark on 19 March 1973 signalled the final collapse of the Bretton Woods system of fixed exchange rates, and the European partner countries differed markedly in their views on fundamental exchange rate issues. For another, although the Werner Plan was the first to elaborate on the need for progress on the economic and institutional front in parallel with monetary convergence, the positions taken were still relatively vague and marked by controversy. What was missing above all, however, was the political will to press forward with this parallel approach in a concrete manner.

The years that followed were dominated by exchange rate risks both at the global level and in the European context.[2] Following a Franco-German initiative to break the deadlock, the Council on 5 December 1978 concluded the agreement establishing the *European Monetary System (EMS)*, which came into effect on 13 March 1979. With hindsight, this date marks a watershed in the process of monetary integration, confirming as it did the 'monetarist position'

---

[2] For a detailed documentation of the process from its beginnings to Stage III of economic and monetary union, see H. Tietmeyer, *Herausforderung Euro* (Munich, 2005); A. Szasz, *The Road to European Monetary Union* (London, 1999).

For another perspective and a somewhat different assessment, see T. Padoa-Schioppa, *The Road to Monetary Union in Europe* (Oxford, 1994).

supported above all in French circles and based on the assumption that, with monetary agreements in place, consequences would follow in their wake. In a nutshell, the argument ran: once exchange rates are fixed, further monetary convergence is more or less bound to follow. The exchange rate crises that ensued, however – a seemingly never-ending series of revaluations and devaluations, generally combined with hefty political altercations – testified to the relevance of the 'economistic position', whose proponents included prominent politicians such as Karl Schiller as well as virtually all leading German economists. On this view, the (premature) fixing of exchange rates inevitably creates tensions that ultimately generate sudden, major exchange rate movements. Lasting exchange rate stability can only be achieved if at least national monetary policies are in proper accord.

For an understanding of the further development of monetary integration, it is important to note the following characteristics of the EMS:

1. The European Currency Unit (ECU), though formally at the heart of the system, played a much more limited role (as a unit of account, etc.) than originally intended by the French.
2. Exchange rates were determined between the member currencies (the 'parity grid').
3. Compulsory interventions were correspondingly tied not to the ECU, that is, to a currency basket, but to the parity grid.

It soon became apparent that the EMS was a system founded on the strongest currency; in short, it was a 'DM bloc'. In the wake of the strong price pressures exerted by the second oil shock in 1979/80, the consequences of this currency system quickly came to light. The Deutsche Bundesbank fought against the inflation risks with a clear, stability-oriented monetary policy, thereby sparing Germany a repetition of the sequence of inflation and stagflation that had marked the period after the first oil price shock in the 1970s. Those countries that were unable or unwilling to join in this disinflationary process were forced into repeated devaluations of their currencies as their attempts to defend the parities reached crisis point. Under this system, there was no other alternative than to align monetary policy with the Bundesbank or to devalue one's own currency.

The increasing tensions within the EMS then escalated in the crises of 1992 and 1993.[3] Unlike the oil price increase, German reunification caused an extremely asymmetrical individual 'German shock', to which the Bundesbank reacted in accordance with its mandate by pursuing a monetary policy that first quelled the upward price pressures and then gradually brought prices back towards stability.[4]

The prospect of future monetary union lent support to the Bundesbank in its stability-oriented policy course. I wrote at the time:

> If one takes seriously the timetable for establishing monetary union in Europe in the future with a single, stable currency, one should not delay in fighting inflation; from this perspective, the end of the decade is closer than it might appear from a glance at the calendar. In Germany in particular, the fears among the public that the future European currency might prove a less stable store of value than the D-Mark need to be allayed. Keeping the value of the currency stable is therefore more than ever not just in the national interest, but is at the same time an important and indispensable contribution towards realising monetary union in Europe.[5]

The experience of this period confirms the theory of the so-called 'uneasy triangle', according to which only two of the three goals of stable exchange rates, stable prices (or monetary policy autonomy) and free movement of capital can ever be attained at the same time. Since restrictions on capital movements are incompatible with common market principles – disregarding other major objections

---

[3] See Szasz, *The Road to European Monetary Union.*
[4] See O. Issing, 'Economic prospects and policy in Germany', Institute of Economic Affairs, *Economic Affairs*, 15:1 (Winter 1994).
[5] O. Issing, *Frankfurter Allgemeine Zeitung*, 16 January 1993.

such as the practicability of capital controls – the only choice remaining is between the other two objectives. The option of flexible exchange rates was never seriously entertained in the context of European integration.[6] However, the regime of fixed exchange rates that were nonetheless subject to sudden upward or downward revaluations, as embodied in the EMS, had over time proven to be so vulnerable to crises that it appeared to be only a matter of time before another crisis entailed even bigger abrupt changes in exchange rates. Both the magnitude and the flexibility of international capital flows went far beyond anything experienced in the past.

In the 1992–3 turbulences, the devaluation of the Italian lira by more than 30 per cent against the D-Mark had changed competitive positions in bilateral trade at a stroke, leading to serious discussion at national level on the need to take countermeasures. There was an increasing risk that the next exchange rate crisis might jeopardise major achievements of economic integration such as the free movement of goods, services and capital.

Thus, out of the set of three objectives, it was basically 'only' monetary policy that remained on the table.[7] The solution whereby one country's currency took the lead was obviously untenable in the long run. For one thing, there were political arguments against it. The larger EMS member countries in particular were unwilling to accept a lasting necessity to act more or less in lockstep with the monetary policy of the Bundesbank. For the Bundesbank, conversely, it was not possible to pursue a monetary policy oriented towards 'European objectives'. On the one hand, this would not have resolved the sovereignty issue for the other countries; on the other, the Bundesbank would not have been able to fulfil its national mandate under the law,

---

[6] On this discussion, see O. Issing, 'Integrationsprozeß, Währungspolitik und Wechselkurse in der EWG', *Kredit und Kapital* (1969).

[7] On this analysis, see O. Issing, 'Europe's hard fix: the euro area', *International Economics and Policy*, 3:3–4 (2006).

nor would there have been any reasonable political, empirical or theoretical basis for such a policy orientation.[8]

The logic of the process meant that ultimately the only possible solutions were basically the two 'cornerstones', either flexible exchange rates or the path towards a common currency. Thus the creation of the EMS in 1979 had indeed laid the foundations for a common currency. In that sense, the proponents of the system of fixed exchange rates who had this ultimate aim in mind from the outset may feel themselves vindicated. Admittedly, looking back at the crises of the 1980s and 1990s one can see what huge risks had to be overcome in the process. Nor, by any means, does entry into monetary union mean that all the reasons for past crises have been, as it were, automatically eliminated. At the outset, the setting-up of a supranational central bank and the communitisation of monetary policy only initially resolve the trilemma of the 'uneasy triangle'. For the common monetary policy to be successful and for monetary union to be safely preserved, further efforts are needed. But more on that later.

### The decision in Maastricht

The final decision on the shape and starting date of Stage III of European Economic and Monetary Union (EMU) was taken at the Maastricht summit on 9 and 10 December 1991. In the run-up to the summit, there had been intensive groundwork and negotiations at all levels, with two groups in particular playing a key role.

Firstly, there was the Committee of Central Bank Governors, composed of the governors of the central banks of the EU member states. Chaired by Bundesbank President Karl Otto Pöhl, the

---

[8] For a time, incidentally, those opposing the idea of a single supranational central bank discussed alternative solutions whereby monetary policy would remain with the national central banks but exchange rates would nonetheless be fixed once and for all, i.e. irreversibly. Such a 'system', if it may be called such at all, would have no anchor, and its inevitable consequence would be competition in inflation policies. The idea was therefore rightly dropped.

Committee of Governors had unanimously approved a draft statute for a European Central Bank that was modelled largely on the Deutsche Bundesbank Act. Inter alia, the Governors had advocated the principle of 'one person, one vote' in monetary policy matters.

Secondly, there was the so-called 'Delors Group', set up on the occasion of the Hanover summit on 27 and 28 June 1988. In addition to European Commission President Jacques Delors and the EU central bank governors, this group also included Alexandre Lamfalussy, General Manager of the Bank for International Settlements, Professor Niels Thygesen, Miguel Boyer, President of the Banco Exterior de Espagne, and Frans Andriessen, member of the European Commission. Unlike the Committee of Governors, the Delors Group was beset by controversy, in particular as regards the transition from the status quo to monetary union.

In its report of 5 June 1989, the Council of Experts at the German Federal Ministry of Economics (of which I was at the time an active member) summarised its reservations, which to a large extent mirrored the opinion of the vast majority of economists in Germany, as follows:

> The underlying idea of the Delors Committee regarding the path towards monetary union is for monetary policy in Europe to be gradually communitised. Many of the individual arrangements for the two preliminary phases during which the Community is to become ready for monetary union serve this end. With all due respect for the difficult task of giving the EC countries the necessary guidance (towards ever greater convergence in stability policy) during this readying process: the Council of Experts considers this idea wrong. In matters of monetary policy, the Community is presently being guided, and guided well, by the Bundesbank, as the Delors Committee also acknowledges. At a later date, the objective is that it shall be guided equally well by a European Central Bank. In the interim, it is unwise increasingly to entrust this guidance de facto to co-ordinating bodies at Community level, with the national central banks only formally retaining ultimate responsibility until the end of Stage II.

The division into three stages can be traced back to the Delors Report of 17 April 1989. Meeting in June 1989, the European Council decided on the following: Stage I in the implementation of EMU would begin with the removal of all obstacles to capital movements between member states on 1 July 1990; Stage II would be marked by the establishment of the European Monetary Institute on 1 January 1994; finally, Stage III would commence on 1 January 1999 with the transfer of responsibility for monetary policy to the European Central Bank. For the sake of simplicity and conciseness, we refer in what follows to the start of monetary union on this date.

In its statement of 19 September 1990, the Central Bank Council of the Deutsche Bundesbank had pronounced itself in favour of a European Economic and Monetary Union. At the same time, however, the Council pointed out that clear and binding conditions for monetary union needed to be agreed on beforehand in order to put it on a sound footing. Following the Maastricht Treaty, the *European Monetary Institute (EMI)* was established with the start of Stage II of EMU on 1 January 1994. The EMI was given no monetary policy powers; rather, it was intended to be the central institution for preparing the third stage of monetary union. Headed by Alexandre Lamfalussy and with a very small team, especially in the early stages, the EMI carried out sterling work. Not least, the staff of the EMI would later form the nucleus of the ECB's personnel.

To outsiders, the fixing in Maastricht of a latest starting date (1 January 1999) for entry into Stage III of EMU came as a complete surprise. It accorded with the desire not just of the French President François Mitterrand but also of Germany's Federal Chancellor Helmut Kohl to set an irreversible deadline for the start of monetary union. In so doing, the Maastricht Treaty reflected 'monetarist' principles, but at the same time it took account of 'economistic' considerations by laying down preconditions – the so-called *convergence criteria* – for entry: only those countries which were sufficiently prepared for a single monetary policy regime would be allowed to take part in Stage III.

The years between Maastricht and the start of monetary union on 1 January 1999 would be marked by the tense relationship between these two approaches. The more the convergence process created the conditions for a lasting, stable monetary union, the more its inception would come to resemble a coronation. The more remiss future members were in doing their homework, that is, in putting domestic policy on a lasting, stable footing and thereby mutually converging, the more their entry into monetary union would be premature from the 'economistic' standpoint, and hence the more the monetarist thesis – adjustment to the conditions of monetary union *post festum* – would be tested.

Without anticipating the analysis to follow, it can be said that, right up to the present day, these two explanations have conflicted with each other, or, more accurately, competed with one another in a dynamic process. The setting of a deadline for the start of monetary union inevitably triggered a process of adjustment. But the fact of monetary union has not in itself sufficed to ensure its optimum functioning. Nine years on, the necessary economic policy adjustment to the conditions of monetary union has by no means been fully achieved.

In its statement of February 1992, the Central Bank Council of the Deutsche Bundesbank expressed its satisfaction that the planned institutional design for the final stage, in particular the Statute of the future European Central Bank, was largely in line with the Bundesbank's recommendations. To successfully pursue a policy of stability in the monetary union, it was crucial that the convergence criteria be strictly applied in selecting the countries that would participate. At the same time, the Central Bank Council reiterated the comment in its 1990 statement to the effect that a monetary union is 'an irrevocable joint and several community which, in the light of past experience, requires a more far-reaching association, in the form of a comprehensive political union, if it is to prove durable'. The Central Bank Council continued: 'The Maastricht decisions do not yet reveal an agreement on the future structure of the envisaged political union and on the required parallelism with monetary union. Future developments in the field of the political union will be of key importance for the permanent success of the monetary union.' We shall be returning to this tense interdependence between established monetary union and rudimentary political union in due course.

## The convergence process

Under the *Maastricht Treaty*, only those countries that had made sufficient preparations for joining were to participate in Stage III of EMU, with their readiness being evaluated on the basis of the so-called *convergence criteria*. These criteria are set forth in detail in the Treaty and have been described many times over. Essentially, they boil down to demonstrating that candidates fulfil the following conditions:

1. A low inflation rate
2. Sound public finances
3. At least two years' membership of the fixed exchange rate system (EMS) without tensions
4. Convergence of long-term nominal interest rates towards the level of (at most) the three currencies with the lowest rates of inflation

In addition, there was to be an assessment of how far an individual member state's national legislation, including the statutes of the national central bank, was compatible with the terms of the Treaty, in particular as regards the independence of the central bank.

It goes without saying that only those countries that displayed a high degree of convergence in their actual behaviour as well as in their monetary policy convictions and the degree of price stability achieved

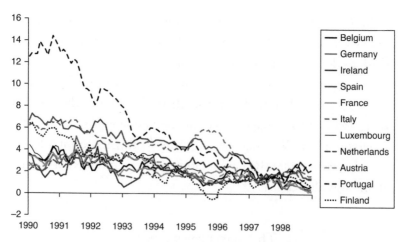

*Note:* Harmonised Index of Consumer Prices (HICP). Backdata estimated on the basis of national definitions of consumer price indices (adjusted in order to exclude owner-occupied housing for Germany, Ireland, the Netherlands and Finland).
*Source:* ECB calculations based on Eurostat data and data from national statistical institutes.

**Figure 1** Inflation convergence 1990–8 (annual percentage changes)

were supposed to join monetary union. The sizeable devaluations of certain currencies within the EMS were the inevitable consequence of widely divergent price trends compared with that of the anchor currency, the D-Mark. Whereas in the early 1990s there were still marked differences in inflation rates between the countries that would later join the monetary union, the subsequent convergence process was to result in inflation rates becoming aligned at what were – also from a historical standpoint – exceptionally low levels (see figure 1).

This evolution was helped by favourable exogenous factors such as declining oil prices, but the decisive element was the consensus on achieving stability supported not only by the central banks concerned, but also by fiscal and wage policy. The discipline exerted by the conditions for entry into monetary union came late in certain cases, but all in all it was timely enough. The threat of not being in at the start of monetary union because of not fulfilling the convergence criteria unleashed unsuspected forces, including in the sphere of fiscal policy

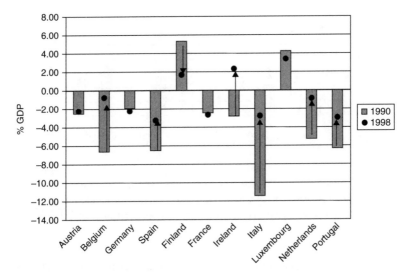

*Note:* Data for Germany in 1990 pertains to West Germany; 1990 data for Spain not available – chart presents 1995 data.

*Sources:* AMECO database (European Commission) and ECB. Net lending (+) or net borrowing (–): general government. Excessive deficit procedure (including one-off proceeds relative to the allocation of mobile phone licences (UMTS)). AMECO data deficit class: data at current prices.

**Figure 2** General government deficit 1990–8 (percentages of GDP)

– admittedly with grave exceptions as regards public debt levels. The 1990s saw often steep declines in budget deficits, albeit with the numbers massaged in certain instances by acts of 'creative accounting'. Such a violation of the spirit of the Treaty provisions was more than regrettable in the run-up to monetary union. As later became clear, it created precedents that significantly weakened discipline in applying the rules of the Stability and Growth Pact. All of this should not, however, detract from the appreciable efforts that were made to improve budgetary positions before the start of monetary union.[9]

As figure 2 shows, the reductions in budget deficits achieved during 1990–98 were impressive. Regarding the criterion of public sector indebtedness – the ratio of government debt to GDP at market

[9] On the Stability and Growth Pact, see chapter 5.

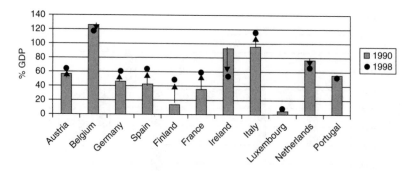

*Note:* Data for Germany in 1990 pertains to West Germany.
*Sources:* AMECO database (European Commission) and ECB.
**Figure 3** Government debt 1990–8 (percentages of GDP)

prices – the progress made, if at all, was much more modest (see figure 3). It really cannot be said that this criterion was strictly applied. The critical cases were undoubtedly Italy and Belgium. For both of these countries, founder members of the European Economic Community and in every respect at the centre of European integration, a major effort at interpretation and ultimately a political decision were required to enable their entry.

There being no provision for conditional entry, admission in such cases rested on a political undertaking to bring the level of debt down quickly and clearly towards the 60 per cent level. Subsequent developments showed that a country such as Belgium – not to mention a model case such as Ireland – finally got the message: reducing excessive levels of public debt was not only a requirement under a Treaty to which one was a signatory, but was also in one's own fundamental national interest. Nor was a corresponding policy of fiscal consolidation in any way detrimental to economic growth; if anything, the reverse was the case.

Stable conditions in the final stages of the EMS confirmed that the exchange rate criterion posed no real problem, although Italy and Finland were only able to satisfy the time-based condition – of at least two years – after the decision on accession was taken.

Bearing out what theory already suggested, the long-term nominal interest rate criterion did not present much of an additional obstacle. Given converging inflation rates, sound public finances and fixed exchange rates, there were unlikely to be major differences in long-term rates. Accordingly, all the candidates took this hurdle in their stride.

All in all, the convergence criteria fulfilled their function. Two aspects, however, merit a further comment.

The Treaty defined the conditions for entry – at least formally – exclusively in *nominal* terms. Among the eleven founder members there were, nonetheless, considerable differences in living standards and/or productivity. Thus the Treaty ducked the issue of how far a single monetary policy might pose problems for poorer countries in the catching-up process – an integral part of the whole project. With the enlargement of the European Union, and the still greater divergence in living standards between member states, this issue has taken on an extra dimension.

The second aspect concerns the convergence criterion for the budget deficit and total public debt. In the run-up to monetary union, numerous conferences were held to address this question. The chosen values of 3 and 60 per cent of GDP respectively were frequently criticised and even derided as being arbitrary.

Even if, given certain assumptions about nominal economic growth, there is a certain mathematical logic in the relationship between the two numbers, and the figure of 60 per cent roughly corresponded to the average level then prevailing in the EU, it is hard to defend the exact figures as such. But if it is accepted that concrete figures were needed as a guideline for fiscal policy and for purposes of monitoring performance, then the 3 per cent upper limit for the budget deficit does make sense. If the member states adhere to the central prescription of the Stability and Growth Pact, i.e. a balanced budget or budget surplus in normal economic conditions, then 3 percentage points of GDP offers a lot of leeway for an accommodative fiscal policy – essentially via the action of the automatic stabilisers. Most countries' fiscal policy in the past has tended not to need anywhere near the entire room for manoeuvre, let alone more. In any event, the Pact provides for exceptions in the event of episodes of particularly severe economic weakness.

The other focus of debate was on whether *institutional* arrangements to monitor individual countries' fiscal policy were necessary at all. It was felt by a good number of academics and bankers that this function should be left entirely to the market. Were a country to stray markedly from the path of fiscal policy virtue, there would very soon be a reaction in financial markets. Flight by investors would drive up interest rates on the long-term sovereign debt of the country concerned. Under the pressure of such a market reaction, policy-makers would soon need to abjure deficits.

This line of argument was countered by the experience that any such penalisation by financial markets, if at all, is very slow – too slow – to have an impact. As would soon become apparent, upon entry into monetary union a debtor country ceases to run the risk of devaluation of its own currency, and the crucial element for sanctions via the financial markets is therefore lost. Thus, all sovereign bonds denominated in the same currency (the euro) are to begin with differentiated only in terms of their liquidity, and the resultant interest rate spreads remain relatively low. Solvency risk remains; but a lot has to happen before a country actually goes bankrupt and ceases to service its debt.

In any event, the convergence criterion for budget deficits and total public debt proved to be absolutely essential. The decisive factor was how sustainable a sound fiscal policy was assessed to be. Would efforts towards consolidation weaken *after* entry into monetary union? Would countries revert to past patterns of behaviour when no longer disciplined by the need to meet the conditions for entry?

In response to a request from the German Federal Chancellor, the Central Bank Council of the Deutsche Bundesbank submitted an opinion concerning convergence in the European Union in view of Stage III of Economic and Monetary Union (published in the Bundesbank's *Monthly Report* of April 1998). This opinion was based largely on the analyses presented in the report produced by the EMI.

Public attention focused in particular on one sentence in this written opinion (page 38): 'Bearing in mind the progress in convergence which has been achieved in many member states, and after giving due consideration to the remaining problems and risks, entry into monetary union from 1999 appears justifiable in stability policy terms.' But immediately following this, still in the same paragraph, the Bundesbank had added: 'With regard to the requirement of a sustainable financial position, however, serious concern exists in the case of Belgium and Italy. This could only be eliminated if additional firm substantive commitments are undertaken.' This statement reflected major reservations – after all, the Bundesbank had always, as, for that matter, had the German Federal Government, called for the convergence criteria to be strictly applied. Indeed, in numerous places the written opinion underlined the Bundesbank's concern over sustainable policies for a successful monetary union, in particular in the area of the public finances.

The Bundesbank was, however, clearly aware of its own limited role in this process. Thus the opinion ends with the following sentences: 'Entry into monetary union will have significant economic implications which must be given careful consideration when the decision is taken. The selection of the participants ultimately remains a political decision, however.'

Previously, on 9 February 1998, 155 German economists had published an open letter entitled 'The euro is coming too early' that warned against entry into monetary union as from 1999 and called for an orderly postponement for a couple of years. The main reasons cited were insufficient progress in consolidating the public finances and the lack of flexibility in labour markets. Should the scheduled starting date be maintained, however, the convergence criteria

TABLE 1: *Conversion rates*

| Country | | 1 euro = |
|---|---|---|
| Belgium | Belgian francs | 40.3399 |
| Germany | Deutsche Mark | 1.95583 |
| Spain | Spanish pesetas | 166.386 |
| France | French francs | 6.55957 |
| Ireland | Irish pounds | 0.787564 |
| Italy | Italian lire | 1936.27 |
| Luxembourg | Luxembourg francs | 40.3399 |
| Netherlands | Dutch guilders | 2.20371 |
| Austria | Austrian schillings | 13.7603 |
| Portugal | Portuguese escudos | 200.482 |
| Finland | Finnish markkas | 5.94573 |

*Source:* ECB, *Monthly Bulletin*, January 1999.

would need to be applied as rigorously as possible with a view to sustainability. Despite this, the manifesto was not intended to call the monetary union fundamentally into question. In its opening paragraph, it stated: 'There is no alternative to European integration. The single currency will be part of it – at least for the core of Europe. However, the euro is coming too early.'

On 31 December 1998, the conversion rates between the euro and the individual currencies of the EU member states were irrevocably fixed, and thus with effect from 1 January 1999 the euro became the statutory unit of account. Table 1 shows the conversion rates between the euro and individual EU member states' currencies.

## Farewell to the national currencies

The transfer of responsibility for monetary policy from the national central bank to a supranational institution, the ECB, and the related loss of sovereignty represent a fundamental change in the structure of the state. For the ordinary citizens, this means first and foremost the abandonment of the respective national currencies, their names full of historical resonance. Not that citizens' experience with their national currencies had been uniformly positive. The past had been marked by repeated periods of high inflation.

This, in some cases, wide diversity of national experience naturally conditioned citizens' attitudes towards the new currency, the euro. In autumn 1995, for instance, 68% were for the euro and only 10% against it in Italy, whereas in Germany and Austria the respective percentages were 34% (23%) in favour and 45% (43%) against.[10] The least enthusiastic among the later eleven euro area countries was Finland, with 53% against and 33% in favour. In spring 1999, just after the start of EMU, approval ratings reached a peak, with figures (for/against) of e.g. 85%/11% in Italy, 55%/36% in Germany and 58%/30% in Austria. Only in Finland was a small majority (47%/49%) still against the new currency. In all cases, younger people were more positive about the euro than their elders.[11]

It was doubtless in Germany that resistance to EMU was the greatest. The decision to abandon the D-Mark required a great deal of political courage. Many surveys had only confirmed what people already knew: a clear majority of German citizens was opposed to such a move. Riding the wave of political sentiment, a 'Pro-DM' party was even created – although it was a resounding failure.

These survey findings were hardly a surprise. In no other country were the currency and the central bank in charge of it held in such

[10] On behalf of the European Commission, Eurobarometer has since 1973 conducted regular surveys on major EU issues. The findings quoted in the text are taken from surveys conducted in October/December 1995 and the Eurobarometer of April 2000 (Report no. 52). At the time, the figures for the three countries that did not join EMU in 1999 were (for/against): Sweden (29%/54%), the UK (32%/56%), Denmark (32%/60%).

[11] The surveys also cover other demographic features such as the split between men and women, and so on. More recently, the spring 2006 survey, published in January 2007, shows a sustained level of approval for the euro. The most enthusiastic country was Ireland, with a split of 87%/9% in favour. In Germany, the result was 66%/30%. In Finland, there had been a marked shift in favour of the single currency (78%/20%). It should be mentioned, however, that other surveys revealed a rather more critical attitude towards the euro.

high esteem as in Germany. Among the general public, the Bundesbank enjoyed more respect than almost any other public institution. The President of the Bundesbank was even sometimes referred to as an '*ersatz* Kaiser'. This high regard can only be understood against the backdrop of Germany's monetary history in the first half of the twentieth century: twice within a generation, the citizens of Germany had seen their financial wealth disappear as the currency became totally worthless.

In the hyperinflation of 1922–3, the monthly (!) rate of inflation ultimately reached the unimaginable figure of 32,000 per cent (October 1923). This destruction of the value of money meant the loss of their livelihoods for many people who, in the tradition of the gold standard (up to 1914), had placed their trust in the lasting value of their savings. Hyperinflation undermined the foundations of civil society. Stefan Zweig vividly described this turning point in German history:

> We must always remember that nothing rendered the German people so embittered, so full of hatred, so ready for Hitler as inflation. For however murderous the war had been, it had nonetheless given occasion for rejoicing with peals of bells and victory fanfares. And, as an irremediably militaristic nation, Germany swelled with greater pride at the temporary victories, whereas the inflation caused it to feel only besmirched, betrayed and belittled.[12]

Only twenty-five years later, the trauma of the demise of the national currency was repeated. The introduction of the Deutsche Mark in 1948, therefore, gave Germany its third currency within a generation.

And, quite unlike its predecessors, the D-Mark proved to be stable, coming in the 1950s to symbolise (Western) Germany's resurgence out of the ruins of the Second World War. The unprecedented esteem in which the currency was held was only possible in the vacuum created by the Nazi regime and the end of the war, and was

---

[12] S. Zweig, *Die Welt von Gestern – Erinnerungen eines Europäers* (Frankfurt, 1970), p. 359.

in a way a reflection of the pathological nature of the postwar German consciousness. The D-Mark was, so to speak, a substitute for the flag and other national symbols – in contrast to 2006, when Germany hosted the event, very few German flags were waved when the national team won the football World Cup in 1954.

Germany's central bank, first of all the Bank Deutscher Länder and from 1957 the Deutsche Bundesbank, won an unparalleled degree of respect among the German public as the guardian of the currency and guarantor of price stability through its clear, stability-oriented monetary policy stance. Internationally, too, the Bundesbank enjoyed incomparable prestige. 'Not all Germans believe in God, but they all believe in the Bundesbank', Jacques Delors is reported to have said. Whatever irony may have been behind the remark, it does reflect the worldwide esteem for Germany's central bank.

German reunification highlighted once more the special place occupied by the D-Mark in Germany's collective consciousness. It was not for nothing that, in their demonstrations, the citizens of what was then still the GDR expressed their desire to participate in nationhood by waving banners proclaiming 'If the DM doesn't come to us, we'll come to the DM.'

Without any doubt, a stable currency was to a very large extent the foundation that underpinned the economic reconstruction of Germany after the Second World War. After two catastrophic experiences in the first half of the twentieth century, Germans had come to appreciate the value of monetary stability. No wonder, then, that they saw little merit in the idea of abandoning their stable national currency.

In the event, however, Germans very soon adjusted to the new currency, the euro, even if their original concerns and fears regarding its stability still lurk below the surface. This can be seen not least in the controversy over the 'teuro' (a play on 'euro' and 'teuer', the German word for 'dear'): even though statistics clearly and reliably indicate that average inflation in Germany is at a low level not often matched in the days of the D-Mark, the impression persists that inflation has been especially high since the introduction of euro banknotes and coins. Not least, this perception can be explained by the fact that a range of everyday items actually did become a lot dearer. This *specific* finding is easily generalised and gives the impression that inflation is a lot higher *in general*.[13] That this is largely a question of psychology is borne out by tests in which subjects were asked to compare, amongst other things, restaurant prices. Even when the prices had been calculated at the exact conversion rate of $1 € = 1.95583$ DM, menus in euros were thought to be more expensive. This debate is illustrative of a general phenomenon, namely the possible discrepancy between the statistically correct rate of inflation and that which citizens actually perceive as the true rate. Price changes in frequently purchased goods such as food generally make a greater impression than those in items less often found on the shopping list. Moreover, price increases are more clearly registered than price cuts. Together, the two effects played a role at the time of the changeover to pricing in euros. The gap between perceived and measured inflation in fact narrowed significantly in Germany in subsequent years. More recently, in 2007, the gap widened appreciably again in the wake of sharp rises in petrol and heating fuel prices. According to surveys taken in 2007, roughly half of German citizens want the D-Mark back, while the other half are in favour of the euro. Viewed in the light of German history and given the conservatism that predominates in monetary matters in general, this is actually quite a positive result for the new currency, especially as 'back to the D-Mark' may presumably be regarded as part of that general longing for the 'good old days' that were allegedly always better than anything since.

There were two reasons in particular why Germany bade farewell to the D-Mark with a lot less trepidation than many had expected or feared.

---

[13] See in this connection ECB, *Monthly Bulletin*, May 2007.

First and foremost, the Statute of the European Central Bank agreed on in Maastricht is modelled so closely on the Bundesbank that there were persuasive arguments to back up the promise that the euro would be just as stable as the D-Mark. In addition, the German Chancellor Helmut Kohl had made it clear from the outset that Germany saw no acceptable alternative to Frankfurt am Main as the seat of the future ECB. The symbolism of the choice of location, in Germany and beyond, should not be underestimated.

Secondly, the proponents of EMU countered the widespread fears (especially in Germany) of fallout from other countries' fiscal deficits by pointing to the Stability and Growth Pact, which would act to ensure the soundness of the public finances in all the countries joining the monetary union.

## The countdown begins

### The decisions of 2 May 1998

There having long been no doubt as to the firm political will that monetary union should commence on 1 January 1999, it was now time to take the necessary decisions. This was scheduled for the *European Council* meeting in Brussels on 2 May 1998. Ironically, this date fell during the UK presidency, that is, the presidency of a country which had long since made it known that it would make use of its 'opt-out clause' and not join monetary union for the time being.[14] The heads of state or government had to make two kinds of decision: on the number of countries that would take part, and on the membership of the first ECB Executive Board.

The *European Commission* had proposed that eleven member states take part in monetary union at the outset. Belgium and Italy had

---

[14] In Maastricht, Denmark and the UK had secured for themselves the right not to participate in Stage III of EMU. These so-called 'opt-out clauses' are set down in relevant Treaty protocols.

committed themselves to make further efforts towards consolidating their public finances. (How much or how little such commitments are worth can meanwhile be seen – in a positive as well as negative sense – in both cases.) The Council had no difficulty in acceding to the Commission's proposal and including these eleven countries in the euro area: Austria, Belgium, Finland, France, Germany, Ireland, Italy, Luxembourg, the Netherlands, Portugal and Spain. The Council also agreed to fix the existing parities between these countries' currencies as the exchange rates for entry (conversion rates).

But while the decisions on which countries would participate were in a sense taken as read, those concerning the filling of positions proved to be – to put it mildly – extremely difficult. Under the Treaty (Protocol on the Statute of the European System of Central Banks and of the European Central Bank, Article 11),

> the President, the Vice-President and the other Members of the Executive Board shall be appointed from among persons of recognized standing and professional experience in monetary or banking matters by common accord of the governments of the Member States at the level of the Heads of State or of Government, on a recommendation from the Council after it has consulted the European Parliament and the Governing Council.

The Treaty provides for a non-renewable eight-year term of office for each member of the Executive Board. To avoid having the entire Executive Board leave office after the first eight years, it was decided to stagger the initial appointments, with the President being appointed for eight years, the Vice-President for four years, and the other Executive Board members for a term of between five and eight years. There was a long and bitter dispute over the appointment of the first President of the ECB. Previously, there had seemed to be agreement on the President of the EMI, Willem F. Duisenberg. France alone resisted this proposal and insisted on its own candidate, the Governor of the Banque de France, Jean-Claude Trichet. Following tense negotiations, the necessary 'common accord' was reached and

Wim Duisenberg was selected, after he had declared in writing that, in view of his age, he did not intend to serve the full eight-year term as President of the ECB; he would, however, himself choose the time at which he would prematurely relinquish his office.[15]

There do not appear to have been any problems whatsoever with the selection of the other candidates. Thus the composition of the first ECB Executive Board was decided on as follows:

Willem F. Duisenberg, President, eight years

Christian Noyer, Vice-President, four years

Sirkka Hämäläinen, five years

Eugenio Domingo Solans, six years

Tommaso Padoa-Schioppa, seven years

Otmar Issing, eight years

Without any doubt, those included in this list had the professional qualifications required under Article 11 of the Statute.

Willem ('Wim') Duisenberg (1935) already looked back on a long career as economist, IMF expert, university professor, banker and finance minister. His appointment as President of the EMI in June 1997, following on from his distinguished predecessor Alexandre Lamfalussy, made him seem the obvious candidate for the position of ECB President.

After studying law, Christian Noyer (1950) had attended the elite French institutions Sciences Po and ENA. He had held a number of posts as adviser and expert in the economics and finance ministry, including two years as Directeur du Trésor. He had gained international experience through membership of various bodies, not least as Chairman of the Paris Club of creditor countries.

Sirkka Hämäläinen (1939) had joined Finland's central bank after studying economics. After holding a variety of positions

---

[15] For an informative account, see Tietmeyer, *Herausforderung Euro*, who describes this episode under the heading 'Startschuss in Brüssel – vom Personalstreit überschattet' (Green light in Brussels – overshadowed by a dispute over people).

in the central bank, and a spell in the finance ministry, she had been appointed to the Board and then to the post of Governor. As well as being a member of numerous national and international bodies, she had lectured at the Helsinki School of Economics and Business Administration.

Eugenio Domingo Solans (1945) had studied economics and had held professorships in finance at a number of Spanish universities. Also a member of numerous national and international bodies, he had held several senior posts at Spanish banks. Alongside his professorship, he had latterly been a member of the Governing Council and the Executive Commission of the Spanish central bank.

Tommaso Padoa-Schioppa (1940), after studying economics, had pursued a successful career at Italy's central bank, rising to the position of Deputy Director General. For a time, he had held the position of a Director General in the Commission of the European Communities (1979–83). A member of numerous national and international bodies, he had latterly been President of the Italian stock market regulator (Consob).

Otmar Issing (1936) had followed his economics studies with a long career as university professor. Inter alia, he had been a member of the German Council of Economic Experts. From October 1990 he had been a member of the Directorate of the Deutsche Bundesbank.

Thus the first Executive Board of the ECB was made up of experienced members, most of whom in fact already knew each other.

### Early experiences in Brussels

On 29 April 1998, the Federal Minister of Finance, Dr Theo Waigel, had stated that, at the coming weekend's meeting of the heads of state or government in Brussels, Germany would nominate Professor Dr Otmar Issing as member of the Executive Board of the European

Central Bank. I had received the minister's telephone call asking whether I would be available for this position only a little while beforehand, at home late in the evening of 24 April.[16] There had been a debate in the German media over the question of 'the German candidate'. The consensus was that, following the decision on Frankfurt as seat of the ECB, the President could not be a German. On the other hand, it was inconceivable that there should be no German member of the ECB's first Executive Board.

The media saw two reasons why the Federal Government would on no account nominate Otmar Issing. For one thing, I was held to be largely responsible for the Bundesbank's rejection of the Government's idea of revaluing the (considerably undervalued) Bundesbank gold reserves and transferring the extra profit to the state in the run-up to monetary union. For another, following numerous articles I had published on the topic of the euro, I was held to be an economist who was at any rate sceptical about the 1 January 1999 starting date for monetary union, if not allegedly about the whole euro project.

Despite all objections, Bundesbank President Hans Tietmeyer finally persuaded the German Chancellor and Finance Minister to nominate me for the ECB Executive Board. Beforehand, he had urged me in the strongest terms to be ready to accept the post.

As it happens, Finance Minister Theo Waigel had nominated me eight years earlier as a member of the Directorate of the Deutsche Bundesbank. The fact that the Federal Government at that time gave no consideration to party-political issues, nor made any kind of approach to me beforehand, is a sign of its great respect for the Bundesbank and its independence. This time, too, the same objective detachment prevailed.

Next I had to clear the hurdle of a hearing in the *European Parliament*. All six candidates for the first appointments to the ECB Executive Board had been asked in advance to provide written

---

[16] It was around 10 p.m. when my wife brought the telephone to me in the sauna.

answers to a questionnaire with nineteen questions. In view of their fundamental significance, let me quote some of the questions and my answers:

Question 8: *Would you support the ECB being held accountable for realizing an explicit inflation target and over what time period? To what extent could a mixed targeting strategy (inflation target + money supply target) be defined and evaluated?*

The ECB is definitely accountable for the target of price stability. How this is formally achieved, whether with an embedded inflation target or an explicit inflation target, depends on the strategy that is still to be chosen. I have been involved in discussions on the strategy of the future European Central Bank from the outset, and have argued in favour of a mixed strategy whereby control of the money supply could be complemented by a wide-ranging analysis of the inflation outlook, including a model-based inflation forecast . . .

Question 10: *How would you seek to resolve the policy mix problems entailed in the combination of a centralized monetary policy and decentralized fiscal policies?*

It will be up to those responsible for national fiscal policies to take due account of the close interlinkages arising out of monetary union and to ensure the requisite policy coordination.

Question 12: *How do you envisage the ECB's role in establishing an appropriate exchange rate for the euro vis-à-vis third countries?*

An additional, separate exchange rate objective is not compatible with the ECB's mission under its Statute. A stable euro that enjoys the confidence of citizens and markets will play an important stabilising role in world financial markets and contribute to exchange rate stability. For the rest, I refer to Article 109 of the Treaty.

Question 15: *How do you see the distinction between ECB independence and its accountability, and what steps do you consider should be taken to ensure democratic accountability?*

In a democracy, one cannot view the independence of an executive body separately from its mission. The mission of the ECB is laid down in its Statute by the sovereign powers. Central bank independence is not an end in itself, but a means to achieve the objectives set by legislation. The ECB must be accountable for the decisions it takes to fulfil the objective. It has to communicate and justify how far the objective has been reached, what its monetary policy thinking is, and what monetary policy actions it is currently undertaking.

*Question 18: What steps should be taken to ensure transparency of the ECB's decision-making? Would you be prepared to publish minutes after decisions have been taken, and, if so, how long after and to what extent?*

It will be important for the ECB to keep the public fully informed about its policy. This applies first of all to the interpretation of its ongoing decision-making, where the ECB should provide wide information on its background analysis. It is also important to set out the reasons for the choice of monetary policy strategy. It is very much in the ECB's interest to be transparent about the basis for its decision-making, focusing on its prime responsibility for price stability.

The deliberations of the ECB Governing Council are confidential. Publication of detailed minutes is not provided for under the Treaty. Publishing minutes would jeopardise the openness of dialogue within the Governing Council that is essential for decision-making. Disclosing voting behaviour would personalise ECB decision-making, and might expose Council members to political pressure incompatible with the ECB's independence.

In my opinion, the ECB should regularly inform the public about its thinking on major issues and in particular about the decisions it takes. Institutional independence, transparency and public accountability need to support each other in a meaningful way.

My hearing before the European Parliament took place on 7 May 1998. After long years of relevant experience as an economist and latterly monetary policy-maker, I felt I was sufficiently forearmed for the verbal exchanges that might ensue. I did in fact have reason to expect stiff resistance, on two counts. Firstly, given my – publicly expressed – reservations about starting EMU too early and moreover with a large group of countries, I was hardly considered part of the 'europhoric' contingent. Secondly, my Bundesbank 'origins' meant that I was cast as a prominent advocate of a monetary policy that had come in for severe criticism in certain political circles, not least outside Germany. I was accordingly prepared to come under heavy attack.

Under the rules, each candidate – in their own separate hearing – was to deliver a brief opening statement. This is what I said:

> Mr President, Mrs Randzio-Plath, Ladies and Gentlemen, it is not just a duty but a great honour to be able to present my views on Economic and Monetary Union to the Members of the European Parliament gathered here today. In the written questions, you touched on important problems. I attempted to answer them suitably briefly. I should therefore like to take the opportunity of these opening remarks to explain my fundamental opinion regarding the significance of EMU. Let me begin by saying that, for me, EMU is by no means a purely technocratic project.
>
> My first impression of a monetary union dates from a time when I knew nothing about economics and was not even interested in the subject. The image I had was of a merchant who travelled from Rome to Colonia Claudia Ara Agrippinensium (today's Cologne) and throughout the long trip was able to pay using the same coin, the denarius. Incidentally, had he so wished, he could even have done so on the other side of the Channel. The Pax Romana ensured political cohesion, the scarcity of gold ensured the stability of the currency. And what did the centuries that followed hold in store for Europe?
>
> Someone born in 1936 like me, who walked to school through the rubble of his completely flattened home town, would later be able to see European borders open up, and take freedom to travel – at least in western Europe – for granted. He would be able to experience the wealth of European culture at its original sites, and to make friends in countries where according to his schoolbooks the enemy lived.
>
> This experience shaped my sense of history. Thus it was in fact quite logical that, when studying economics, I very soon turned to questions of European integration. The dismantling of all trade barriers, the free movement of persons – in short, the four great economic freedoms – were the grand objective that was achieved with the single market. I will not deny that I was more hesitant with regard to monetary union – not as regards the grand goal, which was always the culmination, the completion of integration, but rather out of concern about the great leap. Concern because I know, or think I know, what monetary union means, what its consequences are for many economic and political

spheres beyond the monetary one. This concern has been to a very great extent allayed in light of the major progress that the eleven member states have made on convergence over the last few years. To be frank, I would not have thought it possible that, before the start of monetary union, Europe – that is, the eleven countries we are talking about here – would attain virtual price stability and that Germany's inflation rate would be no better than the average! A few days ago, Eurostat released the March inflation figure: 1.2 per cent. Now that is price stability!

My concerns have not entirely disappeared, however, as Europe has not made similar progress with convergence in all areas of the economy. Here a lot remains to be done. For example, in its *World Economic Outlook* of last autumn, the International Monetary Fund – which is hugely enthusiastic about the project for monetary union – drew attention to the reforms that still need to be undertaken if the euro is to realise the great potential it contains. What is needed above all is action to bring down unemployment in Europe from its current dreadful high level.

The introduction of the euro will change the face of Europe. The introduction of the euro is the most significant event in the world of international money and finance since the end of the Second World War. The euro will only be able to play its intended role if it is a stable currency. To achieve this, the Maastricht Treaty gives the European Central Bank clear priority for the goal of price stability and endows its decision-makers with independence so that they can take the necessary decisions to achieve that end.

A currency lives by the trust of the population in monetary stability! Trust in stability and in the credibility of policy translates into low interest rates, greater investment and higher employment. That is the contribution that monetary policy makes. Gaining this trust is hard, and in the run-up to monetary union we can see that the euro has already gained a remarkable degree of confidence from the financial markets looking forward. We need to build on this capital. I am firmly convinced that, to help build or strengthen credibility, the European Central Bank needs transparency in its policy and communication of the reasons behind its decisions. The European Central Bank is accountable to the European public for the reasons underlying its decisions, for its strategy, and for its ongoing monetary policy measures – and where better to conduct that dialogue with the European public than with the European Parliament, the representatives of Europe's citizens?

For an economist there is no more fascinating job than to be able to contribute to the introduction, the creation, of a new currency. For myself, I cannot imagine a more fascinating job. I do not think I am under any illusion as to how difficult this job will be. I believe that, based on my career to date – combining economic theory with experience in a senior position in a central bank of no little importance – I can contribute to making the euro a success. I am at any rate willing to do my utmost to that end!

From the approximately two hours of questioning that followed I should like to quote a number of passages that are characteristic of the Parliament's ideas on the role of the ECB and also of subsequent debate in the Parliament and discussions with its representatives on numerous occasions.[17]

**Hendrick (Party of European Socialists):** This week's *Newsweek* has an interview with Alan Blinder who, as you may know, was Vice-Chairman of the Federal Reserve Board. When Mr Blinder was asked if he was the President of the European Central Bank what his first step would be, his response was that undeniably unemployment is too high in almost all the European countries. On the other hand, the brand new Central Bank, with its brand new currency, is going to perceive a need – and it is genuine – to establish its credibility as a serious central bank. Article 2 of the Treaty, as you know, talks about high levels of unemployment and Article 105 talks about supporting the general economic policies of the Community. Do you see any scope for the relaxation of monetary policy without prejudice to price stability in order to combat unemployment, and if not why not? You have partly answered the question by a study which you quoted but you made particular reference in that study to longstanding benefit. Do you see any short to medium-term benefits from this action?

**Issing:** Alan Blinder is a good friend of mine. He was Vice-Chairman of the Fed and he went back to Princeton University because he could not afford financially to stay any longer. The people there are paid shamefully. I had many discussions with him on this issue, we exchanged views as academics and later as central bankers.

---

[17] The record is available on the European Parliament website.

We always came back to the question of what is the trade-off between price stability and full employment or inflation and unemployment? Alan is always trying to convince me and I am trying to convince him. The main difference between the two of us is not about the long term or medium term, it is of course the short term, which you mentioned yourself. The main difference is that the Americans have no idea about our institutional environment, which is totally different. When thinking about labour markets and so many regulations they more or less automatically transfer their environment into the European one and see the ECB or the Bundesbank or Banque de France in the flexibility of American labour markets and a deregulated system. I think the main differences of opinion come from that. I wonder if Alan Blinder stayed for a while in Europe if he would still persist with his opinion but perhaps he is a lost case, I do not know. (*Laughter*)

**Hendrick (Party of European Socialists):** It would seem that Mr Blinder is not on his own. Mr Duisenberg said this morning once price stability has been achieved and established in people's minds, i.e. when the public no longer takes account of the actual prospect of inflation, there is room to gradually lower interest rates as long as this does not disadvantage price stability. That is Mr Duisenberg's view from this morning and Mr Duisenberg, as you would agree, is a European. Are you saying that you are at odds with Mr Duisenberg?

**Issing:** No, I am not at odds with him. We have, of course, had many discussions on that and my interpretation of this quote is that like me Mr Duisenberg was stressing the benefits of price stability for monetary policy. We have achieved price stability, which is reflected in the lowest interest rates we have seen for decades in Germany and the lowest ever since the Second World War in Italy and some other countries. This is the contribution of monetary policy; this is spurring on investment, this is especially fostering building because long-term rates matter the most and [low] long-term rates are only achieved if people, if savers, believe that price stability will continue in the future. This is the main issue; it is inflationary expectations and not just achieving a one-off situation. It is decisive to convince people that this situation will continue in the future and on that basis we will have lower real interest rates, and high inflationary expectations would increase real rates and be detrimental to investment.

**Funk (European People's Party, Christian-Democratic Group):**
Professor Issing, I would like to bring the discussion down to the level
of the citizens I have to do with every day. The question is this: there
is a group of people that is getting bigger every year, namely those
who live on their savings and are very worried about these savings
because they wonder whether afterwards they are not going to be
among those losing out under this monetary union. That is one
worry. The very wealthy will profit by it, but we ordinary people want
to live our lives for the next ten to twenty years with what we have
earned ourselves.

A second complaint we hear is that the big, globally active firms will
also benefit enormously from this big new currency, the euro. The
question to you is: what can be done so that citizens, European consumers, can get a share of these benefits?

**Issing:** I also try to stay in touch with the ordinary citizen. I have a
big family. My mother is over 90 and asks me almost every week 'Will
the euro be stable?' The fact is, the older the people, the more they are
worried about their small savings. It's probably quite understandable
psychologically, and you come across it a lot.

An important factor in Germany is that people even now have difficulty, unfortunately, in distinguishing between the introduction of a
new currency and the currency reform of 1948. It is very difficult, and
you have to realise that this opportunity, this potential, is being politically exploited by 'rabble-rousers' drawing false parallels. It's a very
serious psychological handicap, and in lots of speeches we try – as you
do, as all of us do – to draw attention in particular to this actually inex-
plicable effect, and how senseless the comparison is, but one needs to
take people's fears seriously and try to defuse them.

For the famous man in the street, all he will immediately gather is
that he can travel in Europe without having to change money – no
small thing for Europeans! Germans spend a net 60 billion DM and
more abroad every year, and in future a major share of that will be in
euros. That is what people will experience directly, and dealing with
such things is part of ordinary experience. If the economic situation
improves, ordinary citizens will certainly also gradually feel the
benefit of a bigger currency area, but these are things that take place
at an intellectual level rather than via direct experience, so there is
still a lot of work to be done to inform people. There I fully agree with
you.

**Berès (Party of European Socialists):** Mr Issing, you come from a country whose central bank must undoubtedly have served as a model in the creation of the European Central Bank, especially with its concept of independence. This concept is incorporated in an institutional framework including a federal government, a federal parliament (the Bundestag) and public opinion. Against this background, how do you personally, over and above the answers you were able to provide to our written questions, assess the situation in Europe? Does the balance currently provided for under the Maastricht Treaty appear sufficient to you, especially from the perspective of this institution, the European Parliament?

As you know, based on the report by our colleague, Christa Randzio-Plath, we have drawn up a whole series of proposals on which we would like to have your opinion over and above the written answers to our questionnaire, and would like to know how you view the possibility either of amending some of these points in the Maastricht Treaty or of inter-institutional agreements to improve the current situation, which would be in the direct interest of the independence of the Central Bank, which will only be independent if it does not become the scapegoat in public opinion.

**Issing:** The last thing you mentioned, namely the Central Bank becoming the scapegoat, is an important problem. However, there are two aspects to this problem, since being the scapegoat can also mean that a central bank may be held responsible for mistakes made in other policy areas. On the first point: it is true that when the Maastricht Treaty was drawn up the Deutsche Bundesbank, alongside one or two others, was the only major central bank to have the benefit, the advantage if you will, of independence. The Maastricht Treaty has now made central bank independence an important element in the institutional arrangements for European monetary policy under the single currency. However, that was not dictated by Germany but reflects the experience gained the world over. I am convinced that a decade ago this Statute of the European Central Bank would never have been approved by all twelve, and later fifteen, member states.

In the 1970s all the world's major economies had catastrophic experiences with inflation, the fight against inflation, stagflation and high unemployment. The 1980s were characterised by the fight against inflation and by major macroeconomic distortions, causing many countries serious problems. But the 1980s also saw a wealth of studies into the origins of the 1970s problems. Why was it that some countries had double-digit inflation and more? A large number of studies revealed that central bank independence and inflation outcomes are closely correlated. This experience informed the Maastricht Treaty. The conviction had spread to other countries, to all EU member states. It's not surprising that it takes some time to be able to live with this idea and this new arrangement. It didn't come out of the blue in Germany either. The German Chancellor Adenauer was not well-disposed towards the independence of the Bundesbank, and severely rebuked it in 1956 for raising the discount rate slightly! Politically it was a bone of contention, and support for this arrangement only grew over time – an arrangement which, incidentally, we owe to the Allies. In 1948 the Allies, so to speak, forced independence for the Bank Deutscher Länder on the Germans, albeit to our advantage. In 1957 the Bundestag enshrined this arrangement in a German law. The path of world history is not always the straightest, but if it produces good results then detours are also productive.

**Berès (Party of European Socialists):** I think perhaps I did not express myself clearly, as Professor Issing answered on the topic of central bank independence, which for me is not in dispute. The underlying point of the question I asked you was to know how this independence finds expression in dialogue with the European Parliament. But allow me to add another question, and I hope you can answer both: in your answers to the written questions you appear – as regards the interaction between monetary and fiscal policy – to have a strongly hierarchical concept of economic policy coordination. One gains the impression that monetary policy is the alpha and omega and that national policies merely have to adapt and subordinate themselves to the objectives set by monetary policy without any dialogue whatsoever. Is that your conviction? I would be grateful for an answer to the first question on relations with the European Parliament.

**Issing:** But of course! The central bank's relationship with the European Parliament starts today and tomorrow at the latest, and I am firmly convinced that such a dialogue is a useful way of exchanging respective positions so as to learn from them. It also gives the European Central Bank the opportunity to explain and where necessary justify its policy. In my view, the independence given to the ECB under the Maastricht Treaty is aimed at enabling it to take the decisions necessary to fulfil the tasks it has been set, with priority being given to price stability.

I don't think anyone can intend that the ECB's freedom of action as regards attaining these statutory objectives be constrained. For me, that is the crucial point. On all the rest, dialogue will evolve, that goes without saying, and we have not even reached the beginning yet. We find ourselves at the start of a learning process, whereby nobody knows precisely what flexible answers it will lead to in addressing a major problem.

On economic policy coordination, for myself I would like to say very clearly that I have no problem with euro member countries agreeing on a common economic policy– the sooner the better, and the more fully they do so, the easier it will be for the European Central Bank. That is not the problem; rather, the problem is that it is not so easy for economic policy in the individual countries to move towards this European dimension. For the ECB, a European objective has been laid down for the monetary union. The rate of inflation that expresses the objective, whatever it may be, is a European, a Community objective. It has no national element. A clear objective, a European objective, has been set by legislation, by the sovereign powers, and thus for me it is not a question of subordination but rather a question of how the other policy areas – economic policy, fiscal policy, the unions and employers with their policies – are integrated into this institutional arrangement such that ultimately we achieve good outcomes, not just in terms of price stability, but above all as regards employment.

**La Malfa (European Liberal, Democrat and Reform Party):** Professor Issing, I very much appreciated the broad policy sweep of your introductory remarks, and I should like to take advantage of your academic background to ask you two very precise questions.

The first is: what in your view is the mechanism linking the money supply and the price level, or, more exactly, how is a higher or lower rate of inflation reflected in higher or lower unemployment, and how does it happen in practical terms?

The second question: assume it is theoretically and empirically arguable that European labour market rigidity (a) has not increased significantly between the 1970s and today and (b) is not the main reason for unemployment – you cited a Nobel laureate, and I will cite Robert Solow, who recently maintained in a lecture that rigidities are not the reason for unemployment. Well, what policy means are still available to Europe to tackle the problem of unemployment?

**Issing:** I have already emphasised on a number of occasions that I do not see any medium- or long-term trade-off between inflation and unemployment, and that monetary policy can contribute most when it ensures low and stable inflation expectations and thus low real interest rates. That is the most important mechanism that I can see. There is no question at all that, given the frighteningly high levels of unemployment, the Europeans face a huge problem. Franco Modigliani urges central bankers to put a notice on their desks telling them to think about unemployment every day! I had a discussion with him a short while ago. I said, I do think about it every day! If somebody has to be reminded of that, they have no place in any official function in any European country. There is no disagreeing on that. What has to be discussed is the question of what is the right way to bring down unemployment . . .

**Katiforis (Party of European Socialists):** Regarding your friendly joke about Alan Blinder, given that economics is not physics, perhaps from a different perspective he thinks that you are a lost case and he may well be right with four and a half million unemployed in Germany.

In your opinion, for a central banker as opposed to an academic, is the personal characteristic known as intellectual arrogance an asset or a liability? Then a technical question, where do you put the non-accelerating rate of inflation and unemployment?

**Issing:** That part about Alan Blinder and the lost case was of course meant in a spirit of friendly irony. We both, like all of us involved in the debate, should not consider ourselves infallible. We try to learn from each other, we exchange arguments, we measure our own argument against that of the other person. We all have something to learn. I was once also of the opinion – at the time it was harmless, as I was only a professor and couldn't do any damage, except perhaps to people's heads, but not in actual decisions – that Milton Friedman's idea of letting the money supply grow by a constant percentage year in year out, that is, adhering to the famous 'k-per cent rule', was the solution to the problems of monetary policy. I have changed my mind since. The facts have convinced me that financial innovations alter the content of monetary aggregates economically. You have to bear that in mind, we couldn't foresee it at that time. You have to take account of the facts. Economics is not a matter of faith, but a science that has to be measured against real outcomes over and over. We have not come to the end of the debate, neither Alan Blinder nor I nor many others – they were only two names that happened to be picked out here – and there is no place for intellectual arrogance in a central bank.

In the academic world, one can hold extreme opinions. One can fight for one's positions, and I have often seen it happen that, at the end of discussions, the conclusion is: 'Further research is needed and next time we'll present another paper.' That is not possible in monetary policy. There one is accountable for one's decisions, and one has to realise – you were right to mention physics – that there are no final answers, that we are groping our way towards the right solutions. You have to take responsibility for what is ultimately decided on. There is always a gap – sometimes bigger, sometimes smaller – between what we know for sure and what reality obliges us to do: we can't wait until theory comes up with the definitive solution to individual issues; reality doesn't give us the time. That is the general problem between theory and decision-making, for example in a central bank.

As regards the inflation rate, I think the European Monetary Institute's preliminary idea of a range of 0 to 2 per cent is a reasonable level. Here we also need to discuss problems of measurement in Europe. To date, there are no comparable studies for other countries. That needs to be carefully considered. I think that that level is a starting point. As regards joblessness or employment, we have moved away from targets. Beveridge once said that 3 per cent is the full employment target. In my view – today we can only dream of such numbers – we must all act to bring down this frighteningly high level of unemployment, which is in double figures virtually everywhere in Europe. That's the objective. As to whether numerical targets are an aid to policy, I have my doubts.

**Torres Marques (Party of European Socialists):** Professor Issing is – as already mentioned – the only member nominated for eight years, and I note that, while practically the same age as President Duisenberg, he is prepared to serve out the full term of his mandate, which means that he will be the one to maintain relations longest with the European Parliament. For me, it is therefore very important to know his answer to the last question we asked in our questionnaire, that is, what weight he attaches to our vote. Here I don't see any answer. Professor Issing evades the question. I should like to put the question to him directly: will the political vote of the European

Parliament carry weight for you, given that we will hopefully be working together for eight years, yes or no?

Another question I should like to ask is the following. I think that being a member of the management of the Bundesbank will be rather different from being a member of the Executive Board of the European Central Bank, even if they are both independent banks: while Germany has [both] a federal government and a federal budget, we have neither government nor federal budget here. How much will you change your behaviour, Professor, if you leave the Bundesbank to become a member of the Executive Board of the ECB?

**Issing:** Concerning your first question: when I heard in the middle of the night that I was to be nominated, and moreover for eight years, I was surprised. Part of the reason for my surprise was certainly my advanced age, which you alluded to. From where I stand now, I do not intend relinquishing this position early. I hope I will have the strength to see it through and that you will help me so that I don't wear myself down in disputes with the European Parliament, but that we focus on the good results we produce. If you wish for us to work together for eight years, it is up to you to make it happen. It is not up to me.

Concerning the connection between the Bundesbank and the ECB, you are absolutely right. They are two different things. I don't see the ECB as a Bundesbank clone. In the law it looks like it in many respects – independence, price stability, a central bank council – and yet they are in part completely different. The ECB Governing Council is composed of governors from countries with different tax systems, welfare systems and labour market conditions, so it is not directly comparable. The task is different. In working at the Bundesbank I rested on the shoulders of the past, and lived off the reputation which that institution has built up over time. The ECB is a new institution that has yet to gain people's trust. It already enjoys the advance confidence of the markets; you can see that from long-term interest rates. But it then needs to justify that confidence through its policy. It needs to do that through transparency and through wise decisions. We all need to be aware that this is a difficult phase.

Let me conclude the extracts from the hearing there.

This dialogue with members of the European Parliament vividly illustrates the situation prior to the start of monetary union: high expectations, worries, scepticism – and, over and over again, arguments about the mission and role of the ECB's monetary policy. In the years that followed, I regularly appeared before the European Parliament. My perception is that I was increasingly able to clear up misunderstandings and to elicit understanding, even if not general approval, for the ECB's policy course.

As already mentioned, I was aware before the hearing that a considerable number of the Members of the European Parliament (MEPs) had an extremely sceptical, in some cases even hostile, attitude towards the monetary policy of the Bundesbank and the monetary policy philosophy behind it. (As I was to learn later, serious consideration was given to rejecting the 'German monetarist candidate'.) It was not within the realm of the possible to bring these MEPs round to my way of looking at things. All I could aim for was to set the 'technical hurdle' for rejecting me as high as possible without compromising on the issues. To judge by the overwhelming vote (56 in favour, none against, 3 abstentions), I appear to have succeeded.

## The euro area

### *The euro area economy*

By their decision of 2 May 1998 that eleven countries would participate in monetary union from its inception in January 1999, the heads of state or government created the world's *second-largest currency area* with, as it were, a single stroke of the pen. With a share of 15 per cent in world GDP, the euro area was second only to the USA (20.2 per cent), but well ahead of Japan (7.7 per cent), the previous number two. In terms of population, the euro area with its 292 million citizens even outdid the USA (270 million) (see table 2). At the same time, however, these numbers reflect the fact that living standards (as measured by per capita GDP) lagged behind the USA. There were also marked divergences in living standards between individual euro area member countries: as can be seen from table 3, Luxembourg, top of the league with per capita

TABLE 2: *Key characteristics of the euro area*

|  | Reporting period | Unit | Euro area | United States | Japan |
|---|---|---|---|---|---|
| Population | 1998 | mn | 292 | 270 | 127 |
| GDP (share of world GDP)[a] | 1997 | % | 15.0 | 20.2 | 7.7 |
| Sectors of production |  |  |  |  |  |
| Agriculture, fishing, forestry | 1993 | % of GDP | 2.4 | 1.7 | 2.1 |
| Industry (including construction) | 1993 | % of GDP | 30.9 | 26.0 | 39.2 |
| Services | 1993 | % of GDP | 66.7 | 72.3 | 58.7 |
| General government |  |  |  |  |  |
| Receipts | 1998 | % of GDP | 46.7 | 35.9 | 33.0 |
| Social security contributions | 1998 | % of GDP | 17.0 | 9.4 | 11.1 |
| Expenditure | 1998 | % of GDP | 49.1 | 34.5 | 38.6 |
| Current transfers to households | 1998 | % of GDP | 20.2 | 13.7 | 15.7 |
| Exports of goods[b] | 1997 | % of GDP | 13.6 | 8.5 | 10.0 |
| Imports of goods[b] | 1997 | % of GDP | 12.0 | 11.1 | 8.1 |
| Exports (% of world exports)[b] | 1997 | % | 15.7 | 12.6 | 7.7 |
| Bank deposits[c,d] | End 1997 | ECU bn | 4,657.9 | 3,953.4 | 3,663.4 |
|  | End 1997 | % of GDP | 83.9 | 55.3 | 98.8 |
| Domestic credit[d,e] | End 1997 | ECU bn | 7,128.5 | 5,881.5 | 4,710.8 |
|  | End 1997 | % of GDP | 128.5 | 82.2 | 127.1 |
| Claims on the private sector | End 1997 | ECU bn | 5,125.9 | 4,931.1 | 4,033.6 |
| Claims on the general government | End 1997 | ECU bn | 2,002.6 | 950.4 | 677.1 |
| Domestic debt securities | End 1997 | ECU bn | 5,002.4 | 11,364.0 | 4,015.2 |
|  | End 1997 | % of GDP | 90.2 | 164.7 | 108.5 |
| Issued by the private sector | End 1997 | ECU bn | 1,897.9 | 4,729.3 | 1,192.4 |
| Issued by the public sector | End 1997 | ECU bn | 3,104.4 | 6,634.7 | 2,822.9 |
| Stock market capitalisation[f] | Oct. 1998 | ECU bn | 3,190.9 | 9,679.7 | 3,300.9 |

TABLE 2 (*continued*)

|  | Reporting period | Unit | Euro area | United States | Japan |
|---|---|---|---|---|---|
| Real GDP growth | 1998 | % | 3.0 | 3.3 | −2.5 |
| CPI inflation[g] | Nov. 1998 | % | 0.9 | 1.5 | 0.8 |
| Unemployment rate (% of labour force) | Nov. 1998 | % | 10.8 | 4.4 | 4.4 |
| Broad money growth[h] | Q3 1998 | % | 4.4 | 7.4 | 3.3 |
| Three-month interest rate | End 1998 | % | 3.25 | 5.00 | 0.18 |
| Ten-year government bond yield | End 1998 | % | 3.94 | 4.70 | 2.02 |
| General government |  |  |  |  |  |
| Surplus (+) or deficit (−) | 1998 | % of GDP | −2.3 | 1.4 | −5.5 |
| Gross debt | 1998 | % of GDP | 73.8 | 59.3 | 115.6 |
| Current account balance[i] | 1997 | % of GDP | 1.1 | −1.7 | 2.3 |

[a] At constant prices and purchasing power standards in 1997; euro area: 1990 prices.
[b] Excluding intra-euro area trade; exports: f.o.b.; imports: c.i.f.
[c] Euro area: total deposits with MFIs (monetary financial institutions); United States: demand, time and savings deposits in banking institutions; Japan: demand and time deposits in deposit money banks.
[d] Euro area data for bank deposits and domestic credit are calculated on the basis of the irrevocable euro conversion rates announced on 31 December 1998.
[e] Euro area: MFI loans to and holdings of securities of euro area residents; United States and Japan: domestic credit.
[f] United States: the New York exchanges (NYSE and Nasdaq); Japan: Tokyo and Osaka exchanges.
[g] HICP for the euro area; national data for the United States and Japan.
[h] Euro area: M3 aggregate; United States: M2 aggregate; Japan: M2 and CDs.
[i] Provisional data for the euro area.

*Sources:* Eurostat (population, stock market capitalisation, real GDP, euro area data for exports, imports, inflation (HICP), unemployment and current account balance), European Commission – autumn 1998 forecasts (shares of world GDP, general government data (calendar year basis)), OECD (sectors of production), IMF (exports, imports, bank deposits, domestic credit, gross debt for the United States and Japan), BIS (domestic debt securities), national data (for the United States and Japan: CPI inflation, unemployment, broad money growth, three-month interest rate, ten-year government bond yield, current account balance) and ECB (for the euro area: broad money growth, three-month interest rate, ten-year government bond yield).
Reproduced from ECB *Monthly Bulletin*, January 1999.

TABLE 3: *Per capita GDP in purchasing power standards relative to the euro area average*

| Country | Year | Per capita GDP in purchasing power standards |
|---|---|---|
| Euro 11 | 1998 | 100.00 |
| Austria | 1998 | 106.83 |
| Belgium | 1998 | 106.83 |
| Finland | 1998 | 92.11 |
| France | 1998 | 92.61 |
| Germany | 1998 | 98.50 |
| Ireland | 1998 | 97.66 |
| Italy | 1998 | 96.40 |
| Luxembourg | 1998 | 175.05 |
| Netherlands | 1998 | 103.55 |
| Portugal | 1998 | 61.57 |
| Spain | 1998 | 76.80 |

*Note:* The volume index of GDP per capita in purchasing power standards (PPS) is expressed in relation to the average for the euro area member countries (euro 11) set to equal 100. If the index of a country is higher than 100, this country's per capita GDP is higher than the euro area average (and vice versa). Basic figures are expressed in PPS, i.e. a common currency that eliminates the differences in price levels between countries, allowing meaningful volume comparisons of GDP between countries.

*Source:* Eurostat.

GDP in PPS terms of 175.05 against the average of 100, lay far ahead of the tail-ender Portugal, with per capita GDP in PPS terms of 61.57.

The main features of this new currency area can be outlined as follows. While previously the member countries could be described as predominantly small, open economies, the euro area as a whole, with export and import shares (as a percentage of GDP) of 13.6 per cent and 12.0 per cent respectively, represents a large, relatively closed economic area (the comparable figures for the USA are 8.5 per cent und 11.1 per cent).

In terms of the structure of the economy, the differences compared with the USA were relatively small. What is striking, in contrast, is the significantly higher share of the public sector in the euro area, including state transfer payments to private households.

An extremely negative picture in comparison with the USA was painted by the high rate of unemployment, which, despite having fallen in the years before, still stood at 10.8 per cent (with large differences between countries). These numbers reflect on the one hand the faster economic growth in the USA, but on the other hand also the high degree of labour market rigidity in the euro area due to widespread state intervention. The divergence is also evidenced by the significantly higher participation rate (above all for women) in the USA.

What is of great significance for the ECB's monetary policy is the structure of the *financial system* in the euro area. The few comparative numbers given in table 2 suffice to show that, on both the deposit and lending side, and in the share of private-sector debt securities, the banking system predominates over the market financing that is typical of Anglo-Saxon countries in particular.[18]

Notwithstanding some differences between the individual member countries, the structure of the financial system in the euro area can be said to be relatively homogeneous.

The introduction of the euro and the single monetary policy was expected to lead to major changes in certain sectors, doubtless including the early emergence of a single money market. What was still an open question was how far the euro would act as a catalyst for integration elsewhere in the financial system.

### An optimum currency area?

Having the eleven chosen countries in at the start of monetary union was a *political* decision, and it was thus by no means clear whether this country group was also suited for a single currency on economic grounds.[19]

---

[18] Subsequently, the ECB published a whole series of studies on the financial sector. See, for example, ECB, *Monthly Bulletin*, April 1999.

[19] See O. Issing, 'Economic and monetary union in Europe: political priority versus economic integration', in J. Barens, V. Caspari and B. Schefold (eds.), *Political Events and Economic Ideas* (Cheltenham, 2004).

Obviously, bringing together countries with persistently wide inflation differentials in a monetary union would not hold out much chance of success. In that respect, the convergence criteria played an important role. But fulfilling these preconditions in terms of nominal variables is clearly not enough. Upon entry into monetary union, a country loses important instruments (monetary policy and the exchange rate) for responding to shocks, such as for example a decline in global demand for its exports. If such events occur after the start of monetary union, therefore, other economic variables need to take over the adjustment function.

The historical 'norm' is for the currency area to correspond to the national territory: one country – one currency. It accordingly came as a surprise when some economists began to ask in the 1960s whether this historical rule actually made sense in economic terms. Might economic links near the border between two (or more) countries not be so close that the existence of different currencies is a drawback, while in the interior of the countries concerned the differences are so great and economic linkages so small that different currencies do indeed make sense?[20]

This purely economic perspective breaks the link between national territory and currency area. In a series of groundbreaking studies, Robert Mundell, Ronald McKinnon and Peter Kenen analysed the criteria for an *optimum currency area*.[21] Basically, these criteria can be summarised under two aspects.

The ability to adjust to exogenous shocks requires a high degree of flexibility in the markets for goods and services so that prices can react as rapidly as possible to market changes. This flexibility is needed above all in the labour market, that is, wages must adjust to changing

---

[20] The latter case, for example, was discussed – albeit only in hypothetical terms – in connection with German reunification.

[21] R. A. Mundell, 'A theory of optimum currency areas', *American Economic Review*, 51:4 (1961); R. I. McKinnon, 'Optimum currency areas', *American Economic Review*, 53:4 (1963); P. B. Kenen, 'The optimum currency area: an eclectic view', in R. Mundell and A. Swoboda (eds.), *Monetary Problems of the International Economy* (Chicago, 1969).

market conditions to avoid a large, persistent increase in unemployment. High labour mobility, that is, the willingness to move to where the jobs are, is a further measure of the degree of adaptability. The more the price system (in the widest sense) bears the burden of adjustment, the less important is the loss of the national exchange rate and monetary policy instruments, and the greater the benefit of using a single currency. This benefit increases with the size of the currency area and the economic *interlinkages* between the areas forming a monetary union. This applies both to trade in goods and services and to financial market integration.[22] Greater homogeneity in the production structure and in consumer preferences reduces the likelihood of asymmetric shocks, that is, shocks that impact differently on the individual members of the monetary union.

In the 1990s, a number of studies attempted to ascertain which group of countries within Europe might best satisfy the conditions for an optimum currency area. The result was mostly a relatively small group of countries in a kind of 'DM bloc' which, firstly, had tied their exchange rates to the D-Mark for some time and, secondly, whose economy had close linkages to that of Germany. This was not shown to be the case for the group of eleven countries. In a word, the euro area that was to be created on 1 January 1999 fell quite a long way short of meeting the conditions for an optimum currency area.

Moreover, in the event of an asymmetric shock that, say, hits one region especially hard, public transfer mechanisms (via tax receipts and government expenditure, including the welfare system) generally come into play within a national territory to offset to a greater or lesser degree divergences in economic development between regions. This mechanism requires a commensurate central budget. In the EU, there is neither the funding nor the political will for such a compensatory mechanism. For the rest, it might be feared that such

---

[22] On this, see W. M. Corden, *Monetary Integration*, Essays in International Finance, no. 93 (Princeton, 1972).

a mechanism among euro area member countries could undermine individual efforts to surmount the problems arising. Any failure to meet the conditions for a functioning monetary union, therefore, impacts fully on the individual member states.

This state of affairs led many sceptics to foresee that the monetary union would have a difficult start, would encounter major problems, and even that it was destined to fail.[23] With many regarding the failure of monetary union as more or less of an inevitability, some authors also felt that it would destroy the basis for stability and peace in Europe.[24] The direst warning against EMU may well have been that sounded by Martin Feldstein, who went beyond economic reservations to invoke the risk of serious conflicts between the USA and Europe.[25]

Thus the majority of economists were agreed in their evaluation of the monetary union from the economic perspective: this group of eleven countries represented anything but an optimum currency area.

All that could be concluded from this, however, was that monetary union would start under extremely difficult conditions and that policy-makers would need to do their utmost to improve the chances of its lasting success. The criteria developed under the theory of optimum currency areas are, in any case, neither definitive nor complete. Conditions such as the necessary market flexibility can also be created *after* entry into monetary union. To that extent, the criteria are *endogenous*, that is, dependent on the process itself. Optimists were confident that with a single monetary policy the need for reforms to increase flexibility would become so obvious that policy-makers would be bound to react.

---

[23] Milton Friedman, for example, wrote to congratulate me on being appointed to an 'impossible job'. He went on to predict on several occasions that the monetary union would collapse within the next five years.

[24] B. Conolly, 'The case for a euro catastrophe', *The International Economy*, July/August 1998.

[25] M. Feldstein, 'EMU and international conflict', *Foreign Affairs*, November/December 1997.

The theoretical criteria for an optimum currency area are incomplete because they exclude the political aspect of monetary union even where necessary for it to function, examples being agreement on the primacy of price stability, and the need for sound public finances.

From the perspective of economic theory, the start of European monetary union marked the beginning of an *experiment* of truly historic dimensions. The few years that have passed since 1999 have already seen numerous studies in various disciplines, ranging from economics to political science, evaluating the initial experiences against the well-known theories.

# THREE

# The ECB and the foundations of monetary policy

## The Statute

### Tasks

The legal basis for monetary policy is usually laid down by national legislation. In the case of the ECB, as a European, supranational institution, an international agreement was needed. The provisions on European monetary union and the ECB are contained in the Treaty on European Union[1] (Articles 105ff.), with the further rules on the Statute of the European System of Central Banks and the European Central Bank being set out in a Protocol that forms an integral part of the Treaty.[2]

The *European System of Central Banks (ESCB)* consists of the *European Central Bank (ECB)* and the *central banks of the member states (national central banks)*. In choosing this wording, the Treaty authors had obviously assumed that all the EU member states would

---

[1] Hereinafter simply 'the Treaty'.

[2] On the legal and institutional framework, see: C. O. Lenz and K. D. Borchardt (eds.), *EU- und EG-Vertrag*, 4th edition (Berlin, 2006); C. Zilioli and M. Selmayr, 'The European Central Bank, its system and its law', *Yearbook of European Law* (Oxford, 1999–2000); H. K. Scheller, *The European Central Bank* (Frankfurt, 2004).

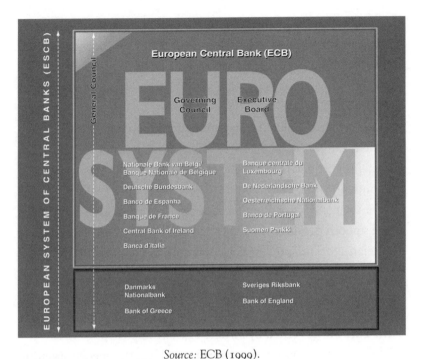

*Source:* ECB (1999).

**Figure 4** The Eurosystem and the European System of Central Banks (ESCB)

also be members of the monetary union. Because this is not the case, however, the text of the Treaty leads to terminological confusion, since by ESCB it means, on the one hand, the central banks of *all* EU member states together with the ECB but, on the other hand, in most places refers exclusively to the central banks of those countries that are actually members of EMU. Consequently, the ECB introduced the term '*Eurosystem*', comprising the ECB and the central banks of the countries belonging to the monetary union. The term 'ESCB', in contrast, always includes the central banks of all EU member states (see figure 4). Under Article 105(2) of the Treaty and 3(1) of the Protocol, the Eurosystem has the following basic *tasks:*[3]

[3] The text of the Treaty refers in each case to the ESCB, but it obviously means the 'Eurosystem' as defined by the ECB.

- to define and implement the monetary policy of the Community
- to conduct foreign-exchange operations consistent with the provisions of Article 111 of the Treaty
- to hold and manage the official foreign reserves of the member states
- to promote the smooth operation of payment systems

The ECB has a monopoly on the issue of banknotes, that is, it has the exclusive right to authorise the issue of banknotes within the euro area. It is also empowered to collect the statistical data necessary for the conduct of monetary policy. The Eurosystem contributes to the smooth conduct of policies pursued by the competent authorities relating to the prudential supervision of credit institutions and the stability of the financial system.

Other provisions govern, inter alia, how the system is to be represented externally. Questions of responsibility for the exchange rate of the euro are governed by Article 111 of the Treaty.

The set of tasks and their formulation reflect the special situation of the ECB as a new central bank in the context of a community of states where responsibilities are distributed across European and national levels in a process which – as the debate about a European constitution shows – is by no means complete.

The case of monetary policy, however, is cut and dried: there is only a *single* monetary policy for the euro area, which is set in a centralised decision-making process. This single monetary policy is the main focus of the present volume.

In legal terms, the monetary policy of the ECB rests on three pillars:

- Prohibition of monetary financing
- Central bank independence
- Primacy of price stability

### Prohibition of monetary financing

The prohibition of *monetary financing* is an obvious precaution when one bears in mind that virtually all lost currencies – and there are a lot of corpses in this 'graveyard' – can be laid at the door of government misuse. In the age of paper currency, governments – especially in wartime, but not only then – cranked up the printing press to finance public expenditure. If it was not itself part of the administration, the central bank was pressured into buying up unlimited volumes of government paper or granting direct credit to the public sector, thus constantly increasing the amount of money in circulation and fuelling inflation. Ultimately, there was frequently no alternative but to abolish the currency so as to avoid state bankruptcy. Citizens who had bought government securities trusting in the credit-worthiness of the state paid dearly for this policy with the loss of their assets.

Article 101 of the Treaty puts a stop to this by prohibiting the ECB and the national central banks from undertaking such transactions, thus banning the provision of credit to the public sector and the *direct* purchase of public debt instruments.[4]

Not only does the Treaty prohibit monetary financing of public expenditure, but it also contains provisions regarding the soundness of member states' budgetary policies (Article 104 of the Treaty and the related Protocol). The *Stability and Growth Pact* concluded in 1997 supplements the excessive deficit procedure (as set out in Article 104). We shall dwell in more detail on the relationship between monetary and fiscal policy in due course.

### Central bank independence

Article 108 of the Treaty governs the *independence* of the ECB and the national central banks.

> When exercising the powers and carrying out the tasks and duties conferred upon them by this Treaty and the Statute of the ESCB, neither

---

[4] In discussing the question of how far the ECB has the necessary instruments to combat the threat of deflation, it needed to be emphasised that in the conduct of its monetary policy the ECB can in principle buy unlimited amounts of securities – including government paper – on the secondary market.

the ECB, nor a national central bank, nor any member of their decision-making bodies shall seek or take instructions from Community institutions or bodies, from any government of a Member State or from any other body. The Community institutions and bodies and the governments of the Member States undertake to respect this principle and not to seek to influence the members of the decision-making bodies of the ECB or of the national central banks in the performance of their tasks. Each Member State shall ensure, at the latest at the date of the establishment of the ESCB, that its national legislation including the statutes of its national central bank is compatible with this Treaty and the Statute of the ESCB.

These rules go beyond what is customary in corresponding national legislation and forbid even any attempt to exert influence. As experience would later show, however, this prohibition cannot be said to have been very effective.

The independence of the central bank is of fundamental importance for its formulation and implementation of monetary policy.[5] A prerequisite for this is the independence of the persons involved. This independence of *personnel* is ensured via long-term contracts that cannot be prematurely terminated,[6] as provided for under the Statute of the ECB. Members of the Executive Board have a term of office of eight years, with renewal explicitly excluded.[7]

When the question of the Statute of a future European Central Bank began to be discussed in the late 1980s, Germany was basically the only country whose central bank, the Deutsche Bundesbank, enjoyed independence. How did it come about that ultimately all EU

---

[5] One way of nullifying central bank independence is to restrict the central bank's financial resources or interfere in its internal powers of organisation.

[6] Removal from office would only be possible for reasons that have nothing to do with the exercise of the functions, for example in the case of criminal conduct.

[7] Reference has already been made to the special arrangements for the appointment of the first Executive Board. Governors of national central banks are appointed for a minimum of five years. The actual arrangements – as regards reappointment, etc. – vary from country to country.

member states agreed to a Treaty that provided for the untrammelled independence of the future European Central Bank?

In political economy terms, an obvious answer would be: the overwhelming esteem for the D-Mark and the Bundesbank among the German public. In this, the independence of the central bank played a major role. German citizens were greatly concerned about monetary stability following any abandonment of the D-Mark. Under these circumstances, no German government could have dared take such a step without insisting on the European Central Bank having a Statute largely analogous to that of the Bundesbank (including the central bank's task of 'maintaining price stability').

Germany's position was well known to its European partners. But there was another decisive factor as well. In most countries, the performance of monetary policy in the 1970s had been disastrous: high rates of inflation in the wake of the first oil price shock, followed by stop-and-go policies lacking any sense of direction. At the end of the decade, stagflation ruled: inflation was still high, but the hoped-for benefit in the form of higher employment and growth had failed to materialise – on the contrary, the economy was stagnating.

This experience coincided with an increasing focus among economists on the role of *expectations* and of monetary policy *credibility*.[8] While the topic of central bank independence had hardly been addressed at all (outside Germany), there was an obvious connection with recent research findings on the importance of monetary policy credibility: how could a central bank hope to win confidence in its policy if in its policy decisions it was obliged to a greater or lesser degree to act on the instructions of the government, the latter being guided not least by considerations of electoral tactics?

---

[8] The literature on this topic has grown considerably over time. See, for example, A. Alesina and L. H. Summers, 'Central bank independence and macroeconomic performance: some comparative evidence', *Journal of Money, Credit, and Banking*, 25:2 (1993); O. Issing, 'Central bank independence – economic and political dimensions', *National Institute Economic Review*, 196, April 2006.

In Germany, central bank independence had originally been called for, not to say dictated, by the Allies (actually the Americans). It was not least thanks to Ludwig Erhard that, despite resistance at the time by the German Chancellor Konrad Adenauer, independence was enshrined in the 1957 Bundesbank Act.[9] Both then and later, the question of a possible 'democratic deficit' was raised again and again. Opponents of independence argued that such an important task as monetary policy could not be handed over to an 'Areopagus' of unelected bureaucrats unaccountable to parliament.[10] At the end of the constitutional debate, it was found unequivocally that it is within the power of the legislature to grant the status of independence to the central bank.

Politicians in other European countries also finally realised that subordinating monetary policy to government objectives, dominated as these were by short-term considerations, was the main reason underlying the unsatisfactory outcomes. Thus, in his statement of 20 May 1997 announcing that the government was making the *Bank of England* (largely) independent, the UK Chancellor of the Exchequer Gordon Brown said: 'The previous arrangements for monetary policy were too short-termist, encouraging short but unsustainable booms and higher inflation, followed inevitably by recession. This is why we promised in our election manifesto to . . . reform the Bank of England to ensure that decision-making on monetary policy is more effective, open, accountable and free from short-term political manipulation.'

The independence of the central bank is limited to the fulfilment of the task laid down in the law. Independence and a clear statutory mandate are mutually dependent. As the statement by Gordon Brown made clear, it is a matter of 'voluntary renunciation of power'

---

[9] On the constitutional aspects, see K. Stern, 'The note-issuing bank within the state structure', in Deutsche Bundesbank (ed.), *Fifty Years of the Deutsche Mark* (Oxford, 1999).

[10] On the question of independence see O. Issing, 'Central bank independence and monetary stability', Institute of Economic Affairs, Occasional Paper, no. 89 (London, 1993).

on the part of the politicians: an institution within the state structure is given a mandate and granted independence in order to fulfil it. This is exactly what later happened at the European level with the Maastricht Treaty. The Treaty was signed by all EU heads of state or government and ratified in all parliaments (and in some cases also confirmed by referendums).

Obviously, in a democracy, the legislature may amend or repeal such powers. In the case of the Bundesbank, that would have been possible by changing the law by a simple majority vote; in the case of the ECB and the Eurosystem, only by unanimous agreement following the same procedure as for conclusion of the Treaty.

The Bundesbank was regarded worldwide as the model of a successful policy of monetary stability. By pegging their exchange rates within the EMS, most EU countries had ended up by following the course laid down by the Bundesbank. In addition, both theoretical and empirical economic research yielded persuasive reasons why central banks should be independent. Coupled with the above-mentioned political economy argument, all these considerations together resulted in the necessary unanimity on an analogous ECB Statute.

With what degree of conviction the political leadership in the individual countries backed this Statute remained an open question.[11] Remarks made in France during the 2007 presidential campaign and afterwards evoked major fundamental reservations. In the United Kingdom, too, the approval of the Statute at the time was anything but enthusiastic during the period of the Maastricht

---

[11] Cf. the comments made by President François Mitterrand in a televised debate on 3 September 1992 in the run-up to the French referendum on the Maastricht Treaty: 'La Banque Centrale, la future Banque Centrale . . . elle ne décide pas . . . Les techniciens de la Banque Centrale sont chargés d'appliquer dans la domaine monétaire les décisions du Conseil Européen, prises par les douze Chefs d'Etat et de Gouvernement, c'est-à-dire par les politiques qui représentent leurs peuples . . . Or, j'entends dire partout . . . que cette Banque Centrale Européenne sera maîtresse des décisions! Ce n'est pas vrai! La politique monétaire appartient au Conseil Européen et l'application de la politique monétaire appartient à la Banque Centrale, dans le cadre des décisions du Conseil Européen.'

negotiations. But in any event, the ECB had a solid legal foundation on which to start conducting its monetary policy in a state of independence in 1999.

The counterpart to central bank independence in a democracy is policy *transparency* and public *accountability*. In view of the ECB's special status as a supranational institution in a European Union that is not comparable to a nation state, complying with this obligation is an extremely complex matter.[12] Under the Treaty (Article 113), the ECB addresses an annual report on its activities to the European Parliament, the Council and the Commission, and also to the European Council. The ECB also has to submit four quarterly reports. The task of presenting the reports to the European Parliament falls to the President of the ECB. At Parliament's request, the President of the ECB and the other members of the Executive Board may be summoned to hearings.[13] In communicating with the public, the ECB goes well beyond its statutory obligations, as is evidenced by its *Monthly Bulletin*, the press conferences held by the President and Vice-President, and a host of publications of various kinds. From the outset, the existence of a large number of official languages and the diffuse nature of the 'European public' posed huge challenges to the ECB's communication policy.

### The primacy of price stability

An institutional arrangement that grants the central bank independence cannot leave the central bank's objective open. Article 105 of the Treaty stipulates:

> The primary objective of the ESCB shall be to maintain price stability. Without prejudice to the objective of price stability, the ESCB

---

[12] See the two articles in ECB, *Monthly Bulletin*, November 2002.

[13] In the first few years, I was regularly invited to discussions of the relevant committee. Initially, our policy came under at times violent attack, but I was subsequently able to contribute to an increasingly better understanding of the ECB's policy.

shall support the general economic policies in the Community with a view to contributing to the achievement of the objectives of the Community as laid down in Article 2. The ESCB shall act in accordance with the principle of an open market economy with free competition, favouring an efficient allocation of resources, and in compliance with the principles set out in Article 4.

That the Treaty should have mandated the ECB primarily to ensure *price stability* is actually and above all self-evident: this is the real task of monetary policy. How should a central bank *not* be obligated to preserve the value of the money it puts into circulation? In times of low inflation (i.e. of stable money) it is, however, easy to forget the importance of this achievement or to take it for granted. That is why the case has to be made for price stability over and over again[14] – and it is rendered all the more essential by the fact that discussion of other possible objectives of the central bank frequently reveals such an (implicit or explicit) disregard for price stability.

The arguments on the importance of price stability are essentially 'symmetrical', that is, they apply both to a general rise in prices (inflation) and to a general decline (deflation). Generally speaking, the more pronounced and persistent these processes are, the greater the harm they do.

### The importance of price stability

The superiority of a market economy over any kind of central planning is based on the correct signals coming from prices for economic agents when making their decisions on production and consumption, investing and saving. These signals emanate from *relative*

---

[14] The first ECB conference was devoted to this topic. See the conference volume: A. G. Herrero, V. Gaspar, L. Hoogduin, J. Morgan and B. Winkler (eds.), *Why Price Stability?* (Frankfurt, 2001), in particular the paper by O. Issing, 'Why price stability?'. See also O. Issing, 'Challenges for sustained economic growth under changing economic, social and international environments', Bank of Japan, *Monetary and Economic Studies*, special edition, 22: S-1, December 2004.

prices: changes in relative prices signal changes in relative scarcity and thus guide the activities of market participants in the right direction. If prices change simultaneously owing to an *overall* rise in prices, agents will find it difficult, if not impossible, to distinguish shifts in relative prices from overall price increases. The signalling function of the price system is impaired, which means that the performance of the economy is below potential.[15] This misdirection affects firms' long-term investment decisions in particular, but also consumer spending.

If this distortion of the price system takes on greater dimensions, there are frequently increasing attempts to counter this shortcoming by indexation to nominal prices. In this sense, indexation is no more than an attempt at working 'as though money were stable'. Such attempts are never perfect. For the rest, they take up resources and therefore cause costs, and are hence an expression of a pathological state induced by the instability of money.

Inflation, and deflation too, leads to an arbitrary redistribution of income and wealth. In the book mentioned earlier, Stefan Zweig gave a graphic illustration of this in the extreme case of Germany's inflation after the First World War; and a large economic literature has provided both theoretical and empirical proof of this effect.

This redistribution effect is heightened considerably by the tax system (and, as the case may be, through transfer payments), which is generally based on nominal values and adjusted, if at all, only with a long lag to changes in the value of money. Empirical studies have shown that such effects can be substantial even at 'harmless' levels of inflation.[16]

---

[15] Edmund Phelps, the 2006 Nobel laureate, has made major contributions on this topic. A convincing – and at the same time graphic – description was already provided by K. Wicksell, *Interest and Prices* (New York, 1965; orig. pub. Jena, 1898, trans. pub. 1936), pp. 1ff.

[16] See, in particular, M. Feldstein (ed.), *The Costs and Benefits of Price Stability* (Chicago, 1999).

Not knowing whether prices will remain stable in the future causes uncertainty. Economic agents, be they investors or consumers, savers or borrowers, will attempt to hedge against such uncertainty, leading to corresponding increases in nominal prices, not least long-term interest rates. Accordingly, financing for investment becomes more expensive – and so does government borrowing.

### *Price stability and other objectives – a trade-off?*

The arguments in favour of price stability are basically undisputed. Under Article 105 of the Treaty, the Eurosystem is to support the general economic policies in the Community, with a view to contributing to the achievement of the objectives of the Community as laid down in Article 2, as long as this does not compromise the goal of price stability.

This reference to Article 2 of the Treaty is less than helpful insofar as that article contains a whole list of desirable objectives, from harmonious, balanced and sustainable development of economic activities to protection of the environment and so on.

Economically relevant in this context are only the 'high level of employment' and 'sustainable and non-inflationary growth', these being the focus of many debates on the ECB's monetary policy (see, inter alia, the hearing before the European Parliament, reported in part in the previous chapter).

It should be emphasised first of all that, according to the wording of the Treaty, price stability has absolute priority. Even were there to be a trade-off between price stability and employment, therefore, the ECB could not under any circumstances give it the slightest consideration.

Empirically, for the rest, the relationship between inflation and growth (and also employment) is pretty clear. In very general terms it can be summarised as follows: high inflation negatively impacts growth, and does so all the more, the higher it is. With low rates of

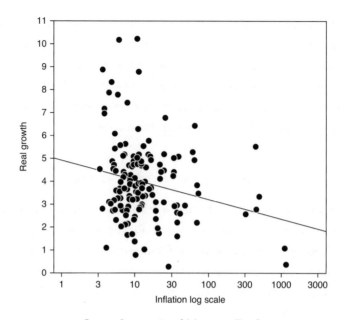

*Source:* International Monetary Fund.
**Figure 5** Inflation and real economic growth 1965–95 (annual average percentage rate changes)

inflation there is no measurable connection, with inflation and growth rates showing no clear correlation (see figure 5). However, there are also persuasive arguments why even single-digit rates of inflation have a harmful effect on employment and growth. For a low-inflation-rate scenario, the result can also be interpreted like this: price stability does not come at the cost of growth; it is a 'free lunch'.[17]

The wording in Article 105 of the Treaty, whereby the ECB is to support general economic policies insofar as this does not compromise the objective of price stability, gives rise to persistent controversy. The idea that a central bank can alter its policy, which presumably means lowering its interest rates, as soon as price

---

[17] See, inter alia, R. J. Barro, 'Inflation and economic growth', Bank of England, *Quarterly Bulletin*, 35 (1995). For further literature and on the effects of inflation and deflation in general, see O. Issing, *Einführung in die Geldtheorie*, 14th edition (Munich, 2007), pp. 233ff.

stability is achieved, is fundamentally mistaken. Ensuring price stability is not a matter for the current moment but must always be
forward-looking, oriented to the future. Today's price stability is the
outcome of yesterday's monetary policy – that is, of decisions taken
two years (and longer) before.

Accordingly, policy rates 'today' influence the evolution of prices
'tomorrow', again reckoned over a period of years. The level of
(policy) interest rates which from today's standpoint ensures price
stability in the future does not leave any leeway to pursue other
objectives. This observation is also borne out by the Tinbergen Rule,
named after the Dutch economist, whereby one can only ever
achieve *one* objective with *one* instrument.[18] If price stability is vulnerable to exogenous shocks, the central bank must examine over
what time horizon it wishes to achieve its objective. In doing so, it
will also need to take into account the time profile of economic
activity and employment.

Monetary policy should not be called upon to do more than it is
capable of. Maintaining price stability is difficult enough, and monetary policy cannot do more than that. By disregarding this fact,
monetary policy creates expectations it cannot fulfil and thereby
undermines its credibility, exposes itself to permanent political pressure and inevitably fails to achieve its actual objective.

A central bank that succumbs to the temptation of stimulating
growth and employment through a policy that is willing to tolerate
rising prices may certainly be successful in the short run – all the
more so, the more convincingly it has previously eschewed such a
policy. But any such success comes at a heavy cost in terms of a loss
of credibility. Ultimately, in order to nip the process of inflation
expectations triggered by such a policy in the bud, the central bank
will need to raise its rates above the level at which it would have set
them had it continued to pursue its policy of monetary stability

---

[18] J. Tinbergen, *On the Theory of Economic Policy*, 2nd edition (Amsterdam, 1952).

instead. On account of the loss of credibility, the interest rate level across periods is higher than with a constant monetary policy aimed solely at maintaining price stability. In the end, therefore, an inflationary monetary policy does not add up, and on balance society is worse off. Thus the long-run maintenance of price stability and correspondingly well-anchored inflation expectations are not only the best, but also the only way in which monetary policy can contribute to growth and employment over time. If the central bank deviates from this course, not only will it fail to make a positive contribution to achieving the 'other objectives', but – quite the reverse – it will also fail to fulfil its actual mandate.[19]

The above reflects current knowledge at the time the consultations and negotiations on the Statute of a European Central Bank got under way. Moreover, a weaker formulation of the mandate than in the Bundesbank Act was considered unacceptable, not only by the German side.[20] The wording of Article 105 of the Treaty, giving priority to price stability, represented the 'state of the art' in central bank legislation. Nothing has changed since then. Indeed, virtually all central bank legislation enacted since that time is geared to a greater or lesser degree towards price stability. It is chiefly in statutes enacted earlier and hence superseded by current thinking that the central bank is assigned a number of different objectives.

## The decision-making bodies

In accordance with Article 9(3) of the Statute, the ECB has two decision-making bodies, the *Governing Council* and the *Executive Board*, plus the *General Council of the ECB* (Article 45).

---

[19] These issues have been addressed from a variety of angles in the literature, in particular in the works of M. Friedman, E. Phelps, R. Barro, F. E. Kydland and E. C. Prescott.

[20] Over time, the Bundesbank had come to construe its statutory mandate to 'safeguard the currency' as meaning the maintenance of price stability. The ECB Statute from the outset avoids any uncertainty over whether 'the stability of the currency' refers to its 'internal' value (price stability) or its 'external' one (exchange rate stability).

## The Governing Council

The *Governing Council* is the ECB's highest decision-making body. It comprises the members of the Executive Board and the governors of the national central banks belonging to the Eurosystem. The Governing Council normally meets twice a month. Occasionally (generally in August) it makes use of the possibility of a telephone conference. Initially composed of 17 members, the Governing Council numbered 19 following the accession of Greece (2001) and Slovenia (2007). Including Cyprus and Malta (2008), the Governing Council currently numbers 21 members.

The President of the EU Council (the Council of finance ministers – Ecofin) and a member of the Commission (responsible for economic and financial affairs) may participate in meetings of the Governing Council, but without having the right to vote (Article 113 (1)).[21] Under an informal agreement, the President of the Eurogroup (of finance ministers of EMU member countries) takes on this task if the Ecofin President comes from a country that is not part of the Eurosystem.

The most important tasks of the Governing Council (Article 12 of the Statute) are to adopt the guidelines that are necessary for the performance of the tasks entrusted to the Eurosystem and to formulate the monetary policy of the Community.

In special cases, a two-thirds majority of the votes cast is required, while in certain financial matters (e.g. concerning the capital of the ECB) the votes are weighted according to the national central banks' shares in the capital of the ECB.[22]

Generally, and thus above all in questions of monetary policy, the principle of *'one person – one vote'* applies, and decisions are taken by

---

[21] The President of ECB is invited to participate in meetings of the EU Council when it is discussing matters relating to the objectives and tasks of the ESCB. Logically, the President is invited to meetings of the Eurogroup.

[22] For details, see Scheller, *The European Central Bank*, pp. 51ff.

a *simple majority* (with the President having a casting vote in the event of a tie).[23]

Upon entry into monetary union, responsibility for monetary policy passes from the national central banks to the ECB. The most important function of the Governing Council is therefore to take the necessary monetary policy decisions so to ensure that the objective of the ECB, namely maintaining price stability, is achieved. In the monetary union, with the euro as common currency, there can only be a *single monetary policy*. Hence the decisions taken by the Governing Council necessarily apply throughout the euro area. Likewise, the achievement (or otherwise) of the objective of price stability can only be measured in a single index for the whole euro area.

There was widespread concern, not to say scepticism, over whether the Governing Council would be up to the task. Would the governors of the national central banks not have in mind first and foremost the consequences for 'their' country in their monetary policy decision-making, and less so their 'European' mandate? Although the members of the Executive Board were presumed to be focused solely on the monetary union, the distribution of votes (initially, 6 to 11) suggested that national interests would predominate.

This reasoning was *flawed* from the outset in that any purely national interests would tend largely to cancel each other out. For example, if the economy was weaker than the average in some countries (which would therefore, on this argument, incline towards lower policy rates), in others it would necessarily be better than the average (and monetary policy preferences would be the exact opposite).

The deciding factor, however, would prove to be the Governing Council's own perception of its role. All the members of the Governing Council have the same task, namely to ensure price

---

[23] A new regime will come into effect once the number of governors of national central banks exceeds fifteen.

stability in the euro area. Thus the governors of the national central banks are members of the Governing Council in a *personal* capacity and not as representative of their own country. The national central bank governors consequently had to make it clear from the outset 'at home' that they would not take any form of instructions under any circumstances. For example, Hans Tietmeyer, the first Bundesbank President to be a member of the Governing Council, left no doubt regarding his independence vis-à-vis the Central Bank Council and the Directorate of the Bundesbank from the very beginning. The same is true of his successors as Bundesbank President.

The Governing Council's opening meeting on 9 June 1998 brought a first, highly symbolic test of its 'European' focus. As had been customary in the days of the EMI, the nameplates for the Governors had been arranged in order of their home country, and the members of the Executive Board had been placed next to each other in a block. Pointing out that the Governors were attending in a personal capacity to fulfil a common task, and that one should not even begin to imagine that the Executive Board was on one side and the national central bank governors were on the other, Hans Tietmeyer proposed that this arrangement be changed. Since that time, there has been a nameplate for the President as Chair (and next to him the Vice-President), and all other Governing Council members are seated by alphabetical order of their surnames.

Thought had also been given beforehand as to how Governing Council meetings should best be prepared and run so as to ensure a European focus and rule out any national leanings from the start. This was bound to be an important consideration in thinking about how monetary policy was to be formulated. Without a convincing strategy focused on the European mandate, the discussion risked fragmenting into individual standpoints in which, possibly entirely unintentionally, national aspects might also come to the fore.

## The Executive Board

The *Executive Board of the ECB* (Article 11 of the Statute) comprises the President, the Vice-President and four other members appointed following the procedure described earlier. The Executive Board is the *operational decision-making body* of the ECB. The Executive Board normally meets every Tuesday, with additional meetings being called as necessary. It is chiefly responsible for implementing the monetary policy defined by the Governing Council, and to that end gives the necessary instructions to the national central banks. It also prepares the meetings of the Governing Council.

Like the Governing Council, the Executive Board is a *collegial body*, with all members each having one vote (the President has the casting vote in the event of a tie). The Executive Board as a whole takes responsibility for its decisions. This principle does, however, leave open the question of how the Executive Board distributes the operational responsibilities.

One option would have been not to allocate specific responsibility for particular business areas of the Bank to individual Executive Board members. As I had expected, the Executive Board did decide to assign portfolios to individual members, namely:

*Willem F. Duisenberg*, President:
Directorates: External Relations; Secretariat; Protocol and Conferences; Internal Audit
*Christian Noyer* (Vice-President):
Directorates General: Administration and Human Resources; Legal Services
*Eugenio Domingo Solans*:
Directorate General: Information Systems
Directorates: Statistics; Banknotes
*Sirkka Hämäläinen*:
Directorate General: Market Operations
Directorate: Controlling and Organisation

*Otmar Issing:*
Directorates General: Economics; Research
*Tommaso Padoa-Schioppa:*
Directorates General: International and European Relations;
Payment Systems

These areas of responsibility came to be modified as the terms of office of existing Executive Board members expired in turn and new members were appointed. My areas of responsibility remained unchanged for as long as I held my position.

Being put in charge of the Directorates General for both Economics and Research was a weighty responsibility. In any central bank, these two areas are at the very centre of monetary policy-making. This is where the analyses on the real economy and monetary conditions are produced, macroeconomic projections drawn up, speeches on monetary policy drafted, and relevant public statements crafted. In-house research and the monitoring of the latest developments in economic studies outside are further indispensable elements.

Compared with the situation in an established central bank, the task took on still greater importance in a new institution like the ECB and in preparing monetary policy for a new currency. The ECB was faced with issues of fundamental importance: for example, the decision taken on a particular strategy would determine the course of monetary policy indefinitely.

Unsurprisingly, therefore, there was a great deal of advance speculation about who would be assigned this responsibility. There were two main reasons why the choice fell on me: on the one hand, my academic background as an economist specialising in the field, and on the other, the fact that I had occupied a similar position in the Bundesbank, that is, the central bank that had for many years determined the monetary policy course in Europe and was perceived to be a guarantor of monetary stability.

From the very beginning, I was under no illusion as to the difficulty of the task and the scale of the responsibility. It was also clear to me that the task could not be accomplished without a highly qualified, motivated and loyal staff. In this phase, placing the responsibility for these two Directorates General in one pair of hands was of the utmost importance. The two areas of economic analysis and research had to work closely together in an intensive process if the economists' expertise was to be exploited to the full, all the more so as – measured against the size of the task – we initially had only a very small number of staff.

The nucleus of the team, excellent economists all, had gradually come together at the EMI and hailed from all fifteen EU member countries. Nor were the 'newcomers' any less qualified. There was no doubt whatsoever about the quality and motivation of the staff – quite the reverse: never before had I seen such enthusiastic, boundless commitment. There was, however, only a relatively small proportion of experienced economists, and very few were familiar with dealing with concrete issues of independent monetary policy. Success would depend on constant dialogue, the mingling of theoretical and empirical knowledge on the one hand, and monetary policy experience on the other. Being called upon to lead this team was the most fascinating task an economist can be given.

As one consequence of this allocation of business areas, the major responsibility that was the ECB's *Monthly Bulletin* also fell to me. Soon after we had taken up our duties, I had a conversation with the President, Wim Duisenberg, about the ECB's future publications, following which he asked me to give the matter some thought. A central question was naturally whether we should publish a monthly report or content ourselves – like many other central banks – with a quarterly report, as called for by the Statute. Despite the pressure of time and the very limited resources available, I became convinced that, especially at the start of monetary union, we needed to keep the public informed with the highest possible frequency, that is, every month. On the one hand, it was a matter of making the public aware of the very existence of the single currency area and its particular characteristics. To that end, in close collaboration with the statisticians, the *Monthly Bulletin* was supplemented with a statistical section, which was expanded significantly over time. On the other hand, there was a need to supplement the regular reporting on the euro area economy with information and analyses on important topics such as monetary policy strategy, instruments and so on.

When I told Wim Duisenberg what I had concluded, his spontaneous reaction was: 'Otmar, monthly?' I replied: 'Yes, I know what it means. If I am to be responsible, this will spoil two weekends per month. But we just have to be present in public every month.' He then asked: 'When will you start, in June 1999?' To which I answered: 'No, in January next year with the start of monetary union.' Duisenberg: 'January! Can you make it?' Me: 'I am not sure, but we have to.'

I was thus given an extremely difficult task and a great responsibility. From my experience with the Bundesbank's *Monthly Report*, I knew how important this means of communication was, but also what it entailed in terms of the ongoing commitment and large amount of resources needed to make it a success. The Executive Board of the ECB bears a collegial responsibility for this publication (and others). But without this individual accountability, the undertaking would not have been practically feasible given the short time available, nor would it have been possible to shape the publication and ensure the consistency of its content over time. For my colleagues on the Executive Board, it was not easy to come to terms with the influence my responsibility gave me over the form and – even more so – the content of this crucial instrument of communication. There was inevitably the occasional conflict, but in the end it was time pressure, and above all competency, that prevailed – I was after all able to rely on the excellent staff of the two Directorates General: Economics and, on particular issues, Research.

There was little time left to prepare the first *Monthly Bulletin*, which had to be done as a sideline, as it were. I had been convinced from the start that the first issue had to appear in January 1999, that is, with the inception of monetary union. There was no time for lengthy reflections and discussions about the look of the publication. To design the cover, we enlisted the help of an expert from the Österreichische Nationalbank. In ordering the contents and structure, we had to make sure that the first *Monthly Bulletin* was such as to allow for continual improvements to subsequent issues without altering the basic framework for the analysis of the economic situation.

The staff involved in the preparatory work went about their tasks with a great deal of motivation, but most of them had no relevant experience. Only gradually were we able to put the necessary structures in place for the publication process, in particular to ensure the requisite level of quality throughout.

By a huge effort, we managed to prepare and publish the *Monthly Bulletin* for January 1999. Before long, the *Monthly Bulletin* would gain worldwide recognition as the ECB's communication 'flagship'. From the start, I had planned to adapt the look of the *Monthly Bulletin* to modern standards as soon as we had more time and had gained experience. The *Monthly Bulletin* was first published in its current form in January 2004.

## The General Council

The third decision-making body of the ECB is the *General Council* (Article 45 of the Statute). The General Council comprises the President and Vice-President of the ECB and the central bank governors of all EU member states. The other members of the Executive Board are thus not members of the General Council, but may participate – without having the right to vote – in its meetings. In practice, they – and their staff – make the major contribution to the meetings. The General Council normally meets four times a year, in March, June, September and December, on the dates of the second meeting of the Governing Council in those months. The General Council naturally has no monetary policy responsibilities, and largely assumes tasks previously performed by the EMI. Thus it chiefly provides advice to EU countries that have not yet joined monetary union in preparing for their accession. In this connection it issues the convergence reports that detail the progress made in this process. The General Council also oversees the functioning of the exchange rate mechanism (ERM II).

Following Greece's entry, only three of the fifteen EU countries at the time remained outside the monetary union, namely Denmark, Sweden and the United Kingdom. This constellation in itself indicates that in its early years the General Council did not play any major role. For example, only Denmark was a member of the ERM, without any problems arising. The General Council suddenly took on a completely different complexion, however, when another ten countries joined the EU in 2004. The majority of these *new EU members* had made the transition from centrally planned economies and dictatorships to a free-market economy (and democracy). But despite remarkable successes, a considerable process of adjustment was still needed. In their monetary policy, the euro played to a greater or lesser degree the role of anchor currency. Estonia, for example, had already pegged its currency to the D-Mark in 1992 under a currency board arrangement, and later transferred this regime to the euro.

All the new EU countries are planning to join the monetary union, and are obliged to do so under the Treaty, since none of them has an opt-out clause. This state of affairs leads to discussion of a wide variety of issues in the General Council, with an important role being played by the *convergence reports*. In the spring of 2006, for example, the report by the ECB (together with that from the Commission) attested that Slovenia had fulfilled the convergence criteria, thus paving the way for the country's entry into monetary union on 1 January 2007. In the case of Lithuania, in contrast, both reports raised serious reservations.

In the meantime, a further two countries – Bulgaria and Romania – have joined the EU. Accordingly, their central bank governors are members of the General Council. And, in the wake of the enlargement of the EU, the staff of the ECB now includes nationals from all twenty-seven EU member countries.

## Preparations for the single monetary policy

### Getting off to the right start

Following the establishment of the ECB in June 1998, no more than seven months remained in which to complete preparations for the start of monetary union. This task had to be accomplished at the same time as everyone's efforts were needed to build up the institution itself: the internal structures had to be put in place, cooperation with the national central banks in the Eurosystem had to be organised, and contacts had to be established with the 'outside world' – with the European Parliament and the EU Council; with other, national central banks (chiefly the US Federal Reserve, the Bank of England and the Bank of Japan); and finally also with academia, the media and the markets.

Preparations for the most important task, the start of the single monetary policy in January 1999, were an absolute priority. Although the EMI had done important groundwork, it had now become possible – and necessary – to decide on the future monetary policy. All observers were agreed that virtually no central bank in history had ever faced a challenge of this magnitude: preparing the monetary policy for a new currency and for an extremely complex and heterogeneous currency area – one, moreover, about which much remained unknown overall.

Scepticism was rife. There was no doubt that were the start and the first few months to be deemed a failure, confidence in the new institution and the new currency would be badly shaken. Investors and markets would react with suspicion, and a lack of trust in the stability of the new currency would be reflected in corresponding risk premia and hence rising interest rates. It would presumably take the new central bank a long time to repair such reputational damage. In a nutshell, the ECB had to get it right first time.[24]

It was therefore crucial that the initial phase, the transition from the national currencies to the euro, be made a success, and at the same time that monetary policy be geared to continuity from the outset. The empty space that was my just-finished office was a vivid symbol of 'zero hour'. In one of the contributions marking my retirement, a senior staff member borrowed Dante's words to describe what we felt at the time: *Lasciate ogni speranza voi ch'entrate* – 'Abandon hope, all ye who enter here'. Well, the ECB was not hell, and every day we drew strength from the hope that it would all come right in the end, or rather at the start. Yet we had no grounds for blind optimism: the situation we were setting out from was far from simple.

We had to make the most of every day we had in working on a blueprint for the future monetary policy. The first step was to correctly assess the starting conditions.

## Monetary policy under uncertainty – the situation of the ECB

Generally speaking, monetary policy produces its effect only with long lags. Monetary policy decisions, in contrast, have at times an immediate impact through their influence on economic agents' expectations; such an effect can even occur in advance if certain policy actions are expected and hence, for example, already

---

[24] The crucial institutional prerequisite for success from the start is the unrestricted transfer of monetary policy competence and responsibility to the new central bank, the ECB. This can be clearly seen, for example, from a comparison with the Federal Reserve Act of 1913. This failed to concentrate decision-making and control in a single authority. The result was infighting over power and control that was only ended with the Banking Act of 1935. The finance ministry (the Treasury) continued to retain its strong influence up until 1951. See the impressive, extensive monograph by A. H. Meltzer, *A History of the Federal Reserve*, vol. i, 1913–1951 (Chicago, 2003).

discounted in investment decisions. But the effects of monetary policy on economic activity and prices are felt only with a long delay. Econometric estimates suggest that it may take two to three years for a monetary policy decision to produce its full effect on the price level or the inflation rate. These lags are not only long, but also variable.

This lagged effect in itself implies a high degree of *uncertainty* for monetary policy, which can be compounded by other factors, such as data imperfections, and so on. A central bank should, therefore, never lull itself into a false sense of security as regards the impact of its policy, but on the contrary needs to make the awareness of uncertainty a fundamental principle guiding its actions.

The economic universe is constantly changing under the impact of events and shocks of all kinds. Even while market participants are still trying to adapt to past shocks, there may be new developments that entail renewed efforts to adjust one's own position in line with the new situation. To take but one example – albeit a particularly important one: globalisation is constantly posing new challenges to the economy at large, to firms and employees, investors and savers. While shocks generally occur sporadically, with highly variable timing and intensity, there are also one-off events. The reunification of Germany is one example: this brought a fundamental change in the economic structure of the country, east and west, and posed huge challenges to economic policy. Thus the Bundesbank was confronted not least with the question of how far it should modify, or even replace, its monetary policy strategy (based on a monetary aggregate target).

From the monetary policy standpoint in particular, the start of European monetary union presented a challenge several orders of magnitude greater.[25] It is difficult to overstate the uniqueness of this event, one without historical parallel. 'Sailing into uncharted waters' is how the challenge facing the ECB was commonly characterised.

---

[25] See O. Issing, V. Gaspar, O. Tristani and D. Vestin, *Imperfect Knowledge and Monetary Policy*, The Stone Lectures in Economics (Cambridge, 2005).

In the field of economics, one speaks in this context of a 'regime shift', a term applied in general to fundamental changes in policy. In a ground-breaking paper, Nobel laureate Robert Lucas highlighted the serious potential effects of such a regime shift.[26] His core finding is that individual economic agents' adjustment to policy changes can be associated with sizeable changes in macroeconomic variables such as the saving ratio or the correlation between output and employment. As a result, models based on historical data using empirical parameters become unreliable or simply useless. If policy ignores the influence of the regime shift and continues to rely on existing models or parameters, mistakes will inevitably result. As an economist, I was deeply impressed at the time by the reasoning in this paper, to which numerous publications by other authors lent support. What was needed now was to apply this knowledge correctly in practical policy-making.

Bearing in mind the situation that had previously faced the Bundesbank, as mentioned above, we had to make sure in preparing for the future monetary policy of the ECB that we never lost sight of the potential implications of the imminent – or already ongoing – fundamental regime shift. This awareness of the extreme degree of uncertainty became, as it were, the leitmotiv in preparations for the ECB's monetary policy.[27]

### The elements of uncertainty

There is a huge literature on the topic of 'uncertainty and monetary policy'.[28] Our initial task was, starting from the general theory, to

---

[26] R. E. Lucas, 'Econometric policy evaluation: a critique', *Carnegie-Rochester Conference Series on Public Policy*, 1 (1976).

[27] The first conference jointly organised by the ECB with the Center for Financial Studies (CFS) was logically devoted to this topic: European Central Bank, Center for Financial Studies (eds.), *Monetary Policy-Making under Uncertainty* (Frankfurt, 2000).

[28] See, for example, Federal Reserve Bank of Kansas City (ed.), *Monetary Policy and Uncertainty: Adapting to a Changing Economy* (Kansas City, 2003). The paper by C. Walsh in this volume provides a good overview with an extensive bibliography.

take account of the particular situation of the ECB. Basically, the literature distinguishes between the following types of uncertainty.[29]

### Uncertainty about the state of the economy

Before making decisions, economic policy-makers in general and the central bank in particular must gain a comprehensive and reliable overview over the prevailing economic conditions. This may seem trivial, but on closer examination it becomes clear how hard it is to actually satisfy this requirement. For example, it is frequently the case that only limited data are available, that their quality is unsatisfactory or even unacceptable, and that their timeliness leaves a lot to be desired. In addition, data are in part highly susceptible to subsequent revision. This is true of a lot of 'simple' data, but applies even more to complex, synthetic indicator variables such as the output gap or the equilibrium real interest rate. These are data that cannot be directly recorded or observed, but have to be estimated using models. Estimates for such variables often show wide divergences: frequently, the numbers are then subject to substantial revision, sometimes even years afterwards.

At best, therefore, such data are only reliable with a long lag, and thus are not available in that form at the time policy decisions are made. Consequently, if monetary policy relies on currently available data, it risks making serious mistakes.[30] In fact, the central bank needs to identify the nature, scale and persistence of any economic shocks. Is it a supply shock or a demand shock? Does it originate from domestic or foreign sources? Is it likely to be transitory or

---

[29] On this, see O. Issing, 'Monetary policy in a world of uncertainty', *Economie Internationale*, 92 (2002).

[30] In a series of studies, A. Orphanides identified serious policy mistakes that were made because the US Federal Reserve relied on real-time information on the output gap. See, for example, A. Orphanides and S. van Norden, 'The unreliability of output gap estimates in real time', *Review of Economics and Statistics*, 84:4 (2002).

longer-lasting? And how significant is it for individual sectors and for macroeconomic variables such as the inflation rate?

### Uncertainty about the structure of the economy

While our knowledge of current economic conditions is already subject to some degree of uncertainty, it is even more so for the structure and functioning of the economy. There are two dimensions to this uncertainty. Firstly, we have *model uncertainty*: experts use a large number of models to attempt to capture the 'reality' of economic relationships and to estimate the effect of monetary policy measures through simulations. These models differ from each other, in some cases markedly, and their respective advantages and drawbacks have yet to be definitively tested.[31]

Secondly, the degree of uncertainty depends on the strength and stability of the structural relationships within these models (what economists call *parameter uncertainty*). Even if there were a consensus on the 'right' model of the economy – which is not the case – there would still be uncertainty as to the strength and reliability of the relationships between the individual variables. These relationships may vary over time, particularly in connection with a regime shift. A major policy shift can therefore significantly widen the gap between estimation results and reality.

### Strategic uncertainty

This form of uncertainty relates to the interaction between private agents and policy-makers. The central bank faces a constant challenge in assessing the possible reactions of economic

---

[31] On this, see B. McCallum, 'Issues in the design of monetary policy rules', in J. Taylor and M. Woodford (eds.), *Handbook of Macroeconomics*, vol. 1C (Amsterdam, 1999).

agents – firms and households, savers and investors, and also the state (fiscal policy) – to its policy decisions, and some degree of uncertainty always remains. The same fundamentally applies to economic agents' own assessment of the direction, scale and timing of the central bank's monetary policy actions.

This uncertainty is increased on both sides if the economy is undergoing major structural changes, whereby developments in the financial sector are of particular relevance for monetary policy. Monetary policy impulses, such as changes in central bank interest rates, are transmitted via the financial sector, both via banks (e.g. through their lending) and via financial intermediaries (such as insurance companies) and markets. The financial sector plays a key role in the monetary policy transmission mechanism, that is, in the way that monetary policy measures affect output and prices at the macro level.

This ongoing mutual observation thus leads to an interaction between the central bank as policy-maker and the economic agents affected by monetary policy decisions – and, among the latter, financial market operators in particular.

### The data situation

Like any other central bank worldwide, the ECB is confronted with uncertainty in all its forms. However, the regime shift from the national currencies to the euro, and from the national central banks to the single monetary policy, was an additional factor that could considerably heighten all three forms of uncertainty.

First of all, this relates to the data situation. Anyone accustomed to the comprehensive, at times almost overwhelming flow of information in an established central bank was bound to find the situation that prevailed at the start of the ECB extremely worrying.[32]

---

[32] On this, see ECB, *Monthly Bulletin*, April 2001.

Some important data were simply not available at all for the euro area: for example, export and import price indices, or data on output in construction or the service sector, which accounts for no less than some two-thirds of total GDP.

Data sources for land and house prices, for example, were extremely heterogeneous, of variable quality, and did not lend themselves to aggregation in a single indicator for the euro area. As well, the timeliness of individual data was anything but satisfactory. For instance, compared to the USA there were differences of up to five months in the time needed for labour market data to become available.[33]

In some areas, the data situation was significantly better. With the Harmonised Index of Consumer Prices, Eurostat provided the most important indicator for the development of euro area prices on a timely basis. As for monetary statistics, the national central banks had prepared the ground well. The data on the various monetary aggregates, for example, soon proved reliable, and their timeliness was remarkable. The problem in this area was chiefly that, for econometric analysis of the relationship between the money supply and prices, for example, only synthetic time series were available for the period before the start of EMU. Thus, the 'European' monetary aggregate first had to be compiled on the basis of national data and adjusted as necessary for exchange rate changes. In addition, much of the work related only to a more or less restricted selection of the countries that would later join EMU. The results of such analysis therefore had to be interpreted with due caution.

In any case, the conversion to a common statistical base caused a discontinuity in the time series. It was, however, by no means easy to

---

[33] Not least owing to the EMU Action Plan launched in September 2000, there has been a marked improvement in the situation, although much still needs to be done in certain areas.

estimate the extent to which the new data constituted a break in the statistics.

### Consequences for policy preparations

Two factors played a major role in the uncertainty about the *structure* of the economy. Firstly, it remained unclear how far the regime shift associated with monetary union would affect – possibly fundamentally – individual structural relationships. At any rate, the ECB had to assume such structural breaks might occur. Secondly, the financial sector in the individual countries, and hence in the future monetary union as a whole, was undergoing a transformation, not least in the wake of the globalisation of financial markets. The transition to a common currency and to a single monetary policy could be expected to accelerate this process. Expectations diverged as to how far the euro would act as a catalyst, and there was a correspondingly large degree of uncertainty.

For its part, strategic uncertainty also raised difficult questions. How would economic agents react to the new currency? Of prime importance in this regard were medium- to long-term inflation expectations and the confidence (or possible lack thereof) in the new central bank. Thus the degree of strategic uncertainty depended in large measure on the ECB itself. Would the ECB be able to build up a fundament of trust before the start of monetary union, or would the general scepticism regarding its capacity to act and its commitment to stability prevail?

Against this backdrop, the ECB faced an enormous challenge. A blueprint for the future monetary policy had to take account of the high degree of uncertainty. At the same time, the ECB had to perform the delicate balancing act of being transparent vis-à-vis the public in this respect, as in others, while at the same time building confidence in its future policy.

Addressing these questions formed a large part of the work

undertaken in the Directorates General for Economics and Research. For the purpose of intensive, ongoing discussions, I had picked a group of excellent economists from the two areas. It was extremely important for us to discuss our thinking over and over with outside experts as well. In spite of the intensity of the work and the short time available, many seminars were held with leading economists from all over the world. In numerous bilateral discussions, I had the opportunity to respond to criticisms, and to weigh my own ideas against those of others and thus test them for their theoretical and empirical soundness.

Of particular value were the visits by prominent experts who combined an academic background with central bank experience. Despite their own heavy workload, they accepted my invitation and made themselves available for seminars on relevant topics. For instance, we were able to discuss the whole spectrum of issues relating to inflation targeting with one of its proponents, Mervyn King, from the design stage to the problems which arise in practice, including that of communication. Alongside monetary policy questions, we were particularly interested in the experience of the US central banking system, not least because of its comparable organisational structure, with the Federal Reserve Board in Washington and the individual Federal Reserve Banks. Don Kohn of the Board was the ideal interlocutor in these exchanges. Concerning the possibilities (or the drawbacks) of a monetary target, we were able to draw on the theory and practice of Bundesbank policy. But it was also helpful to be able to discuss the experience of the Swiss National Bank with its multi-year monetary aggregate targets. Again, no one could have done this better than the SNB's expert with responsibility for this area, Georg Rich.

These seminars were an important supplement to our own research and reflections. Over and above this, the mutual trust formed a basis for frank, in-depth personal discussions from which I learnt a great deal.

## Monetary policy options

### A *purely discretionary policy lacks credibility*

In the run-up to the start of monetary union, the ECB had to decide how it wished to shape its monetary policy and how it intended to communicate – if necessary in advance – the results of its deliberations. Should it point out to the public the extreme degree of uncertainty involved and simply say 'We know how difficult this task is, but we will do all in our power to achieve the goal of price stability'? Announcing such a 'let's do it' policy[34] would scarcely have helped overcome the general scepticism towards the new institution. Especially in the case of a new institution, any suggestion of a purely *discretionary* policy would have created uncertainty about its future behaviour and suspicion as to the strength of its commitment to pursue a stability-oriented policy – all the more so as purely discretionary policy had been discredited as a result of its past failures.[35]

For the ECB it was crucial to build *confidence* in its future policy and *credibility* for its course.[36]

Experience has shown that the central banks most likely to enjoy credibility are those that can look back on a successful policy of monetary stability. This the ECB could not do: as a new institution,

---

[34] On this, see: B. McCallum, 'Two fallacies concerning central bank independence', *American Economic Review*, Papers and Proceedings, 85 (1995).

[35] One problem to be noted in this context was that of dynamic or temporal inconsistency. See F. E. Kydland and E. C. Prescott, 'Rules rather than discretion: the inconsistency of optimal plans', *Journal of Political Economy*, 85 (1977). A. Blinder may have been correct in observing that this problem does not play any role in the central bank's considerations (see A. Blinder, *Central Banking in Theory and Practice*, Cambridge, Mass., 1998). The question, however, was whether the public and the markets would trust the new ECB not to spring a surprise and pursue an expansionary policy, which it might have been tempted to do. On how discretionary monetary policy compares with inflation targeting regimes, see, for example, V. V. Chari and P. J. Kehoe, 'Modern macroeconomics in practice: how theory is shaping policy', *Journal of Economic Perspectives*, 20:4 (Fall 2006), pp. 12ff.

[36] O. Issing, 'Die Europäische Zentralbank – das Problem der Glaubwürdigkeit', in D. Duwendag (ed.), *Finanzmärkte im Spannungsfeld von Globalisierung, Regulierung und Geldpolitik*, Schriften des Vereins für Socialpolitik, vol. 261 (Berlin, 1998).

it had no track record of its own to point to. Nor could one necessarily expect that the trust built up by the successful national central banks could be passed on to the ECB.

Some central banks recognised at an early stage the importance of monetary policy credibility and have consistently geared their actions to that end. Ultimately, by the 1990s all major central banks placed a high value on credibility.[37] For the ECB, the crux of the credibility problem was to convince the public in general, and the financial markets in particular, that it would pursue a policy of price stability under all circumstances, and would ultimately succeed. Pointing out that the ECB's primary objective of price stability and its independence were enshrined in its statute was a good start, but was unlikely to be sufficient to create the requisite confidence in its future policy. Before the start of monetary union, therefore, the ECB had to try to anchor *inflation expectations* at a level consistent with its price stability mandate. This called for a credible *undertaking* on the part of the ECB itself, a kind of implicit contract between the central bank and the public that would also spell out its commitment to a *high degree of transparency* and to *justification* of its monetary policy decisions.[38]

## Strict rules – not an option

The pros and cons of binding monetary policy rules are a longstanding topic in the academic literature. Henry Simons expressed the challenge in a nutshell in the title of a paper: 'Rules versus authorities in monetary policy'[39] – that is, rules versus a policy that

[37] See A. Blinder, 'Central bank credibility: why do we care? How do we build it?', NBER Working Paper, no. 7161, June 1999.

[38] On the fundamental considerations and how they stood the test of time, see V. Gaspar and A. K. Kashyap, 'Stability first: reflections inspired by Otmar Issing's success as the ECB's chief economist', in ECB (ed.), *Monetary Policy: A Journey from Theory to Practice. An ECB Colloquium in Honour of Otmar Issing* (Frankfurt, 2007).

[39] H. Simons, 'Rules versus authorities in monetary policy', *Journal of Political Economy*, 44 (1936).

leaves the door open to (possibly) arbitrary actions on the part of policy-makers.

While under the gold standard (and other binding currency arrangements) the hands of monetary policy are tied, this is not the case for today's ubiquitous paper currency. The bad experiences with depreciation in practice and with ultimately unsuccessful attempts to use monetary policy for purposes of economic management motivated liberal authors in particular to develop proposals aimed at tying monetary policy-making to strict rules. The best known of these is Milton Friedman's demand that the central bank should let the money supply grow – as steadily as possible – by a statutory fixed percentage each year (the so-called 'k-per cent rule').[40]

This strict *money supply rule* was never given any consideration by any central bank as a strategy for monetary policy. Friedman, and others, ascribed this to resistance on the part of central bankers, who feared for their prestige and did not wish to be downgraded to mere 'machines' bound slavishly to follow the instructions of a strict rule. Besides other objections, the following argument and actual experience provide grounds for rejecting this rule: the money supply in question has to be defined in terms of a specific monetary aggregate; changes in payment behaviour and the emergence of new payment instruments (e.g. credit cards) – in short, financial innovations of all kinds – can radically change the economic content of a concrete monetary aggregate and hence reduce the predetermined growth rate *ad absurdum*.[41] Other strict rules also call forth serious objections. Pursuing this analysis further[42] would transcend the scope of this book. However, the discussion surrounding *monetary policy rules* does highlight the problem that faced the ECB – just like other central

---

[40] M. Friedman, *A Program for Monetary Stability* (New York, 1959).

[41] See, for example, O. Issing, 'Geldpolitik im Spannungsfeld von Politik und Wissenschaft', in H. Albeck (ed.), *Wirtschaftsordnung und Geldverfassung* (Göttingen, 1992). In fact, Friedman himself later distanced himself from this idea.

[42] See ECB, *Monthly Bulletin*, October 2001. For an overview, see J. B. Taylor, *Monetary Policy Rules* (Chicago and London, 1991).

banks – in fulfilling its responsibility towards the public and lending credibility to its policy.

## Concerning the Taylor rule

In the discussion of forms of rule-based monetary policy, a special position is occupied by the *Taylor rule*, named after the US econo-mist John Taylor. Briefly put, this rule describes how the central bank reacts (by adjusting its policy interest rate) to changes in two macro-economic variables, namely the deviation of the actual rate of infla-tion from target, and the divergence of output from its long-term potential (the 'output gap').[43] Because of the way that changes in macroeconomic variables feed back on monetary policy, this is also termed a 'feedback rule'. With this rule, Taylor aimed to offer central banks a strategy that would enable monetary policy to overcome the drawbacks of a discretionary policy, reduce the fluctuations in infla-tion and real activity, and stabilise inflation at a low rate (2 per cent).

As a monetary policy strategy, the Taylor rule was out of the ques-tion for the ECB.[44] Among the general objections was the fact that different shocks may emerge that call for different monetary policy responses, which are not foreseen under the Taylor rule. In addition, applying the rule entails exceptionally high information require-ments (about non-observable variables such as the output gap and the equilibrium real interest rate). Nor was it possible for the ECB to dis-regard information on a number of other variables such as monetary and credit aggregates, exchange rates and so on in its policy-making. Applying the Taylor rule takes only indirect account of these vari-ables via their influence on actual inflation or the output gap.

---

[43] See J. B. Taylor, 'Discretion versus policy rules in practice', *Carnegie-Rochester Conference Series on Public Policy*, 39 (1993). For my colleagues and myself, it was extremely helpful to be able to discuss all the relevant issues in depth with John Taylor at the ECB.

[44] On the arguments, see ECB, *Monthly Bulletin*, October 2001, pp. 41ff.

Conceptually, the Taylor rule is nevertheless of great interest to central banks. For example, the Taylor rule can provide indications as to the current stance of monetary policy and to that extent act as a kind of guide.[45]

## Why not inflation targeting?

In the course of the preparatory work undertaken by the EMI, the experts had ruled out an *exchange rate strategy* for the ECB. A central bank can only pursue one objective, and thus cannot aim to achieve an exchange rate target at the same time as price stability. Besides, the future euro area was much too large to be made dependent on another currency.

That left, as it were, only two strategy options: *monetary targeting* and *inflation targeting*. At the time the discussion was taking place, the latter strategy already enjoyed a lot of support among academic economists, and could point to extremely successful practical models, in particular the policy pursued by two proponents, the Reserve Bank of New Zealand and the Bank of England. Inflation targeting was well on the way to becoming the 'state of the art' in central bank policy-making.[46] What could have been more obvious than to follow the example of these central banks and the urging of leading economists? There are persuasive reasons why the ECB at the time chose a different course.

Put simply, *inflation targeting* can be understood as a strategy with the following main elements:

---

[45] See O. Issing, V. Gaspar, I. Angeloni and O. Tristani, *Monetary Policy in the Euro Area: Strategy and Decision-Making at the European Central Bank* (Cambridge, 2001), p. 41. To that end, the ECB has regularly run Taylor rule estimations with a variety of coefficients, as well as using indicators that also take account of changes in exchange rates or financing conditions. Precisely under conditions of extreme uncertainty, I considered it very important to monitor such estimations in the background as a kind of benchmark against which to measure our policy.

[46] There is a vast amount of literature on the subject. For a good overview, see B. S. Bernanke, T. Laubach, F. S. Mishkin and A. S. Posen, *Inflation Targeting: Lessons from the International Experience* (Princeton, 1999); B. S. Bernanke and M. Woodford (eds.), *Inflation Targeting* (Chicago and London, 2004).

1. The central bank announces a *numerical target* (point target or target range) for the aimed-for rate of inflation.
2. The model-based inflation forecast serves to guide monetary policy. For example, if forecast inflation is above the target, the central bank will raise interest rates.[47]

Other elements, such as communication regarding the forecast and the monetary policy actions planned or undertaken, also play an important role in this framework.

Clearly, the success of this strategy depends crucially on the quality and reliability of the *inflation forecast*. 'Inflation targeting' is actually 'inflation forecast targeting'. Because of the uncertainty (over data and structure) analysed above, however, the ECB had every reason to exercise the greatest caution as regards forecasts of all kinds, quite apart from the fact that at the time models for the euro area were still in their infancy.[48]

We were aware of these difficulties from the beginning, and were confirmed in our assessment not least by major subsequent revisions to the data available in real time.[49] It also remained largely unclear which of the available models provided the closest approximation to reality. In other words, inflation targeting did not offer anywhere

[47] In the original inflation targeting model, both the inflation forecast horizon and the target horizon were fixed. Meanwhile, the forecast horizon has in many cases been extended to three years and a fixed horizon for meeting the inflation target replaced by 'in the medium term' or similar. I realise that I am simplifying here in order to focus on the essential arguments underlying our decision. Over the years, I have had many in-depth discussions, and also quarrels, on the subject, not least with Lars Svensson. I do not deny that the idea of inflation targeting has been handled flexibly in practice from the start, and that the theory has undergone refinement over time. But in fact, these developments in the concept of inflation targeting, and not least the increasing emphasis on 'judgement' (see footnote 50), represent elements that have been taken into account in the ECB's strategy from the beginning. My reservations and criticisms notwithstanding, I have learnt a great deal from the discussions on the subject.

[48] Significantly, in all the conversations I had with proponents of inflation targeting, I never received an answer to my question of how the data problem in the forecast could be satisfactorily overcome.

[49] Regarding the scale of the revisions to the output gap, see ECB, *Monthly Bulletin*, February 2005. See also ECB, 'Potential output growth and output gaps: concept, uses and estimates', *Monthly Bulletin*, October 2000, pp. 37–47.

near the kind of *robustness* required in light of the particular uncertainty facing the ECB.

Given these criticisms, the linkage between the forecast and the monetary policy response becomes less clear: inflation targeting becomes extremely complex, the 'charm' of its seeming simplicity is lost, and communication becomes correspondingly difficult. Nothing exemplifies this better than the fact that, over time, it has been conceded that inflation targeting requires 'judgement'.[50] These considerations argued against an inflation-targeting strategy for the ECB.

This certainly does not mean, however, that the ECB rejects inflation targeting lock, stock and barrel – quite the reverse.[51] As will be shown in the next chapter, the strategy adopted by the ECB shares important elements with inflation targeting. Chief among them are the priority accorded to price stability, underscored by quantification of the target, and the importance of transparency. The ECB also uses the same model types and analyses as those central banks that do follow this strategy. The ECB uses a whole series of inflation-forecasting models, but does not invest them with the same exclusive status. Thus the ECB does not regard inflation forecasts as providing *full* information on the economy and the future path of inflation. They are only one input – albeit an important one – in the assessment of the future evolution of prices.

Alongside these objections, one fundamental shortcoming of inflation targeting was a decisive factor in our decision, namely the fact that it completely ignores the relationship – borne out by overwhelming empirical evidence – between the growth of the money

---

[50] Compare, as but one example, the two papers by the eminent proponent L. E. O. Svensson: 'Inflation targeting as a monetary policy rule', *Journal of Monetary Economics*, 43 (1999); 'Monetary policy with judgement forecast targeting', UCB, *International Journal of Central Banking*, 1:1 (2005).

[51] If one restricts the definition of inflation targeting to the common elements, then one could also call the ECB an inflation targeter. See O. Issing, 'Inflation targeting: a view from the ECB', *Federal Reserve Bank of St Louis Review*, 86 (2004).

supply and inflation. The econometric models commonly used for inflation targeting are essentially models of the real economy, and thus do not assume any independent influence of monetary growth on price developments. This bears out the above-mentioned observation that inflation forecasts cannot provide a full picture of the economy, and of prices and their evolution in particular. The question that remains, therefore, is why central banks should rely for their assessment of current conditions and future inflation solely on models that completely disregard this important relationship between money and prices. In an inflation-targeting framework it is moreover almost impossible to take adequate account of developments in asset prices. It was for all these reasons that the ECB rejected the option of an inflation-targeting strategy.[52]

### Deciding against a monetary target

So, should the ECB not have opted for the second strategy considered by the EMI and adopted a *monetary target*? The relationship between money and prices argued in its favour, as did the consideration of thereby following on seamlessly from the successful policy of the Bundesbank, which had made this strategy virtually its hallmark since 1975.[53]

There were, however, serious reasons for not doing so. A monetary target presupposes a stable relationship between a chosen monetary aggregate and inflation. This is not a matter of 'belief' but of empirical evidence, which logically could not be satisfactorily adduced for a new currency. Although there were numerous studies that suggested such a stable relationship, these covered a smaller group of

---

[52] See also Issing *et al.*, *Monetary Policy in the Euro Area*, p. 103.

[53] There are, not surprisingly, a large number of publications on the monetary policy of the Bundesbank and its monetary strategy. For an excellent overview with extensive bibliography, see E. Baltensperger, 'Monetary policy under conditions of increasing integration', in Deutsche Bundesbank (ed.), *Fifty Years of the Deutsche Mark* (Oxford, 1999), p. 439.

countries and were based on synthetic time series (see the previous discussion of problems regarding data). The decisive factor, however, was that these studies necessarily related to a period *before* monetary union and hence it remained unclear whether the stable relationship identified between money and prices would continue to hold *after* the abolition of the national currencies and the introduction of the euro. Precisely in this case, the imminent *regime shift* might lead to a structural break that would have robbed a possible monetary target of its foundation.

Nor, finally, could one overlook the fact that the Bundesbank had itself been confronted at times with major problems in the pursuit of its monetary objective and the communication of its policy. Still relatively fresh in the memory were the problems encountered by the Bundesbank's policy in the years following reunification. How difficult it can be to explain a monetary policy decision when money supply growth is getting out of hand is vividly illustrated by the situation in April 1996. The target range for money supply growth for that year was 4–7 per cent (annual average). The annualised M3 growth rate for March, the latest number available for the meeting of the Central Bank Council on 18 April 1996, was no less than 12.3 per cent. Nonetheless, at my suggestion the Central Bank Council lowered the discount and Lombard rates by 50 basis points each, from 3 per cent to 2.5 per cent and from 5 per cent to 4.5 per cent respectively. In its statement, the Bundesbank pointed to the more favourable outlook for prices, as reflected in producer prices, rent and wage trends, etc. Concerning the growth of the money supply the Bundesbank stated:[54]

> Monetary conditions are unsatisfactory at present. The liquidity over-
> hangs from the past were dissolved last year, it is true, but the money
> stock M3 grew rapidly in the first quarter of 1996; in March it
> exceeded its level in the fourth quarter of 1995 by 3.9 per cent, or an

[54] See Deutsche Bundesbank, *Monthly Report*, May 1996, p. 19.

annualised rate of 12.3 per cent. The current money stock figures over-state underlying monetary trends, however. A true analysis of mone-tary conditions therefore shows that current monetary growth presents no obstacle to a lowering of the traditional key rates.

Subsequent events confirmed the correctness of the decision to lower policy rates, but also the grounds for the decision, namely that money supply growth was expected to weaken gradually over the course of the year. Despite all the – in some cases fierce – criticism, the pragmatic interpretation of the monetary objective proved its worth.

As is well known, the Bundesbank missed its annual money supply target to a greater or lesser extent roughly half of the time. This does not, however, alter the fact that even in such cases the growth of the money supply was a major factor in monetary policy decisions. In extreme situations like that of 1995, the Bundesbank's policy came under increasingly severe attack, and the strategy came in for fierce criticism even within the Central Bank Council. Under such cir-cumstances, it was no easy task to back the monetary targeting strat-egy with convincing arguments.

I was very mindful of these difficulties when it came to formulat-ing a strategy for the ECB. It was precisely because of my direct – per-sonal, so to say – experience of the problems with the Bundesbank's policy that I ruled out adopting the Bundesbank framework for the ECB. In the context of the start of EMU and the associated regime shift, the ECB had to assume there might be sizeable fluctuations in the growth of the money supply. Based on what information and on what arguments could the ECB have explained, for example, that this was a temporary development and not a structural break? With the new central bank being especially closely watched by the general public and the markets at the beginning, it would have had a great deal of explaining to do. Within the ECB's Governing Council, were it to have opted for a monetary target, there would inevitably have been violent disputes. The new institution would have suffered a serious loss of reputation. In an extreme case, it would have had to 'suspend' its strategy or abandon it altogether, possibly only months after the start. It would have taken the ECB quite some time to recover from such a shock.

Although there were certainly some who supported the choice of a monetary targeting strategy,[55] this option had to be discarded. After all the intensive discussions, therefore, it had become clear which path the ECB should *not* follow. What strategy it should choose, however, remained an unanswered question. Nevertheless, the process of 'negative selection' did provide important pointers as to where the solution was to be sought.

## The ECB's stability-oriented monetary policy strategy

### *Deciding on the strategy*

After the extensive groundwork had been carried out, it was first of all clear that the ECB needed a *strategy* for its future monetary policy. By strategy we mean a longer-term procedure for deciding how the instruments of monetary policy are to be deployed in order to achieve the objective.[56]

Beyond this general perspective, the ECB's strategy needed to meet a number of conditions: it had to take account of all relevant information within a consistent framework; it had to give due consideration to the empirically proven relationship between the money supply and prices; and, since after all 'monetary' policy has something to do with 'money', it was obvious that 'money' should play a prominent role.

The desired strategy had to meet the particular requirements of the launch of a new currency; that is, it had to take the high

---

[55] My presence was widely presumed to be a guarantee, as it were, that the ECB would opt to continue the Bundesbank tradition. One Council member expressed his disappointment at my dissenting view by saying 'I'm obviously more of an Otmar than he is himself.'

[56] See O. Issing, *Einführung in die Geldpolitik*, 6th edition (Munich, 1996), p. 254.

degree of uncertainty into account and hence, in economists' jargon, display a high degree of *robustness*. The ECB could not rely on a *single* model or particular data (e.g. the output gap). Thus the strategy had to be designed in such a way that it could integrate information from various models and did not need to have recourse to unreliable data.

At its meeting on 13 October 1998, the ECB Governing Council, upon my proposal,[57] resolved on its strategy. Concerned to ensure transparency vis-à-vis the public and to demonstrate accountability, the ECB published the content of the Governing Council's decision that very day:[58]

**A stability-oriented monetary policy strategy for the ESCB**
1. At its meeting on 13 October 1998 the Governing Council of the ECB agreed on the main elements of the stability-oriented monetary policy strategy of the ESCB. These elements concern:
- the quantitative definition of the primary objective of the single monetary policy, price stability;
- a prominent role for money with a reference value for the growth of a monetary aggregate; and
- a broadly-based assessment of the outlook for future price developments.

2. As mandated by the Treaty establishing the European Community, the maintenance of price stability will be the primary objective of the ESCB. Therefore, the ESCB's monetary policy strategy will focus strictly on this objective. In this context, the Governing Council of the ECB has adopted the following definition: 'Price stability shall be defined as a year-on-year increase in the Harmonised Index of Consumer Prices (HICP) for the euro area of below 2 per cent.'
Price stability is to be maintained over the medium term.
The current rate of HICP inflation in the euro area is in line with this objective.

---

[57] See Tietmeyer, *Herausforderung Euro*, p. 271.
[58] ECB press release of 13 October 1998, www.ecb.int/press/pr/date/1998/html/pr981013_1.en.html.

Three features of this definition should be highlighted:
- The HICP is the most appropriate price measure for the ESCB's definition of price stability. It is the only price index that will be sufficiently harmonised across the euro area at the start of Stage Three;
- by focusing on the HICP 'for the euro area', the Governing Council of the ECB makes it clear that it will base its decisions on monetary, economic and financial developments in the euro area as a whole. The single monetary policy will adopt a euro area-wide perspective; it will not react to specific regional or national developments;
- an 'increase (. . .) of below 2 per cent' is very much in line with most current definitions adopted by national central banks in the euro area.

Furthermore, the statement that 'price stability is to be maintained over the medium term' reflects the need for monetary policy to have a forward-looking, medium-term orientation. It also acknowledges the existence of short-term volatility in prices which cannot be controlled by monetary policy.

3. In order to maintain price stability, the Governing Council of the ECB agreed to adopt a monetary policy strategy which will consist of two key elements:
- money will be assigned a prominent role. This role will be signalled by the announcement of a quantitative reference value for the growth of a broad monetary aggregate. The reference value will be derived in a manner which is consistent with – and will serve to achieve – price stability. Deviations of current monetary growth from the reference value would, under normal circumstances, signal risks to price stability. The concept of a reference value does not imply a commitment to mechanistically correct deviations over the short term. The relationship between actual monetary growth and the pre-announced reference value will be regularly and thoroughly analysed by the Governing Council of the ECB; the result of this analysis and its impact on monetary policy decisions will be explained to the public. The precise definition of the reference aggregate and the specific value of the quantitative reference value for monetary growth will be announced by the Governing Council of the ECB in December 1998;

- in parallel with the analysis of monetary growth in relation to the reference value, a broadly based assessment of the outlook for price developments and the risks to price stability in the euro area will play a major role in the ESCB's strategy. This assessment will be made using a wide range of economic and financial variables as indicators for future price developments.

4. This strategy underlines the strong commitment of the Governing Council of the ECB to its primary objective and should facilitate the achievement of this overriding goal. It will also ensure the transparency of the ESCB's decision-making and its accountability. Based on its strategy, the Governing Council of the ECB will inform the public regularly and in detail about its assessment of the monetary, economic and financial situation in the euro area and the reasoning behind its specific policy decisions.

Thus, with two and a half months still to go before the start, the ECB had already announced the strategy on which it intended to base its monetary policy. In a special essay in the first *Monthly Bulletin*, the ECB set out its strategy in detail. Further articles in subsequent issues focused on various aspects of the strategy.[59] A book was published setting out the strategy and the thinking behind it for purposes of academic discussion.[60] At the press conference of 13 October 1998, when the President, Wim Duisenberg, presented the monetary policy strategy, a journalist asked about the 'dual pillars' for the strategy, namely the 'monetary element' and the 'inflation forecast or real economy element'. Duisenberg pointed out that money would play a prominent role in the strategy of the ECB. Taking up the reference to 'two pillars', he emphasised that he could not say which of the two was the 'stronger' or 'thicker' one.

In our internal discussions, we had already spoken about 'pillars',[61] but had not made any further use of the term. After the President's

---

[59] See the first articles in the *Monthly Bulletins* of January 1999, February 1999 and November 2000, and ECB, *The Monetary Policy of the ECB* (Frankfurt, 2001).

[60] Issing et al., *Monetary Policy in the Euro Area*.

[61] We had had 'three pillars' in mind, the two already mentioned plus the quantitative definition of price stability.

press conference, we debated whether to adopt this terminology. We were very much in two minds about it. On the one hand, we were aware that the concept of 'two pillars' could create the impression of separate analyses and thereby cause confusion. On the other hand, the term was a suitable way to help communicate the ECB's strategy and underline its special character. In the end, the latter consideration prevailed. The ECB soon began to use the expression and to speak of its 'two-pillar strategy'.[62] It quickly became clear that we had been right on both counts: the 'two pillars' became a trademark, but also drew repeated criticism.

### The quantitative definition of price stability

The EU Treaty states quite plainly that the ECB's primary objective is to ensure *price stability*. The wording leaves open the question of when price stability is achieved in concrete terms and by what measure this is to be judged. Since price stability cannot be achieved at any given moment, it remains unclear over what horizon the ECB seeks to reach price stability.

Particularly for a new currency, a crucial factor was what *expectations* economic agents would form concerning the stability of the future currency. If confidence in the new currency were low, investors would demand an 'inflation compensation' and long-term interest rates would rise accordingly. In order to anchor inflation expectations at a low level, the ECB's Governing Council decided to announce a *quantitative definition* of price stability. In so doing, the Governing Council entered into a commitment vis-à-vis the public

---

[62] See the article in the *Monthly Bulletin*, January 1999, p. 47. Originally, the ECB spoke about the first and second pillar. This was not meant to be a ranking. In the editorial of the *Monthly Bulletin* and in the President's introductory statement at the press conference, the core message of the two pillars was presented in that order. It soon became clear that it would be more expedient to begin with the (short-term) economic analysis and move on to the (longer-term) monetary analysis afterwards. In the review of the strategy in the spring of 2003, therefore, the sequence was changed. In order to avoid misunderstandings, the ECB has since then referred to the monetary and economic analyses, or pillars.

against which it would have to measure itself in future. Three questions had to be answered in this connection:

1. Which price index should be chosen?
2. How was price stability to be defined in terms of this index?
3. Over what time horizon was price stability to be achieved?

1. The question of a suitable price index was comparatively easy to answer. The evolution of the euro's purchasing power could only be measured in a single index relating to the average for the whole of the euro area. The Statistical Office of the European Communities (Eurostat) had developed the *Harmonised Index of Consumer Prices (HICP)* in collaboration with the national statistical offices. Data for this index extend back as far as 1995. It was the only harmonised index for the euro area, applied the latest statistical methodology and was available on a sufficiently timely basis. One shortcoming of the HICP is that – to date at any rate – it does not include the (imputed) prices of owner-occupied housing, owing to difficulties in compiling the statistics, although work is under way to overcome this problem.

Indices such as the HICP reflect current developments in consumer prices and hence are subject to wide fluctuations in the event of sizeable changes in major components such as energy prices. Monetary policy cannot prevent these fluctuations. The question was, therefore, whether it would not be better for the ECB to define its objective in terms of a rate of '*core inflation*' (or underlying inflation). Measurements of core inflation exclude volatile elements such as energy prices or seasonal food prices, and thus in general do not show such wide swings. However, core inflation is far from being an unambiguous concept, with relatively simple measures existing alongside theoretically much more sophisticated ones.[63] The principal objection to using a measure of core inflation, however, is that prices which are of great importance to consumers are left out of account.

---

[63] See, for example, D. E. Lebow and Jeremy B. Rudd, 'Inflation measurement', Finance and Economics Discussion Series, no. 43, Divisions of Research & Statistics and Monetary Affairs, Federal Reserve Board (Washington, DC, 2006).

Such measures are little understood by the public, and indeed might tend to suggest they are manipulated if the overall (headline) inflation rate is significantly higher. A central bank might create the wrong impression of attempting to explain away the actual level of inflation suffered by consumers. Such an impression would undermine confidence in the central bank. For these reasons, the ECB decided to define price stability in terms of the HICP. All the same, the ECB does utilise a whole range of other price indices to analyse developments in prices.

2. At first sight, defining price stability in terms of a suitable index looks straightforward: price stability is incompatible with either inflation or deflation and hence, given price stability, the rate of change in the index would be zero. Only then does money perfectly fulfil its role as unit of account and store of value.

Yet there are weighty arguments against choosing 'zero inflation' as the monetary policy objective. Complete stability of the index, that is, of average prices, cannot be achieved at every moment. Thus, over time, rises and falls in average prices would have to offset each other. This means there would inevitably be phases in which prices decline on average, i.e. in which inflation is negative. This could become problematic, and dangerous for the overall economy, if agents come to expect further declines in prices and therefore postpone spending. Such a 'wait-and-see' attitude could trigger a downward spiral of repeated price cuts and lead to a sharp fall in economic activity.

Another way in which the 'zero limit' of inflation works asymmetrically relates to the fact that while, in principle, there is no ceiling on increases in policy interest rates, the central bank cannot reduce interest rates below zero. At that point, the interest rate instrument is no longer available. Even if the central bank has other means at its disposal to supply the economy with extra liquidity (e.g. by purchasing securities), it loses an important policy tool.

Furthermore, measurement errors are unavoidable in compiling an index, not least owing to the difficulty of correctly accounting for quality changes in the goods comprising the index. Generally speaking, this 'measurement bias' can be assumed to lead to the rate of inflation being overstated, with 'actual' inflation therefore being lower. This, together with the macroeconomic considerations referred to above, argues in favour of expressing the price stability target as a (slightly) positive rate of inflation. Setting the target around the 2 per cent level seemed a reasonable approach insofar as some national central banks had already chosen this number. In order to demonstrate the seriousness of its intent, the ECB Governing Council chose to define price stability – HICP inflation incidentally stood at 1 per cent in October 1998 – as a rate of price increase of 'below 2 per cent'.

There were two further considerations behind the decision. An overshooting of the 2 per cent level was to be clearly understood as out of line with the objective, while a lower rate of inflation was regarded as being quite compatible with it. The fact that the magnitude of the presumed measurement error was unknown was also a factor in this. The Governing Council therefore rejected both a point target, which can never be hit exactly, and also a fixed target range. The objective was thus 'downwardly open', with the explicit qualification that the ECB was resolved to avoid deflation.

The chosen definition of price stability took account of both potential measurement errors and the (asymmetric) risk of deflation. It was also in line with the prevailing low levels of inflation and inflation expectations, and guaranteed continuity with the practice of the participating national central banks. Not specifying a floor took account of the uncertainty that existed and was intended to counter any impression that the ECB would more or less automatically switch to a more expansionary policy if inflation fell below a certain level.

3. Finally, there was the question of the time horizon. Monetary policy has no influence on current inflation, but produces its impact only with a long lag. Since the ECB – even more so than other

central banks – could not have any precise idea of the transmission mechanism of its monetary policy, indicating a concrete time span for achieving price stability was automatically ruled out. One option would have been to define the objective in terms of an average. Periods of undershooting (overshooting) of the target would then have had to be offset by periods of higher (lower) rates of inflation. The ECB decided against this option not least because the formulation of its objective ('below 2 per cent') would not have been compatible with a requirement to offset lower rates of inflation exclusively through higher ones.[64]

*How* – that is, when and in what steps – monetary policy should react to price increases or declines depends not least on the magnitude and type of the exogenous shocks that trigger such developments. The formulation 'over the medium term' takes account of this uncertainty and allows monetary policy to react flexibly.

In its first *Monthly Bulletin*, the ECB announced its policy in very clear terms:

> The statement that 'price stability is to be maintained over the medium term' reflects the need for monetary policy to have a forward-looking, medium-term orientation. It also acknowledges the existence of short-term volatility in prices, resulting from non-monetary shocks to the price level that cannot be controlled by monetary policy. The effects of indirect tax changes or variations in international commodity prices are good examples. The Eurosystem cannot be held responsible for these short-term shocks to the price level, over which it has little control. Rather, assessing the performance of the Eurosystem's

---

[64] By formulating the objective in terms of the annual rate of inflation, the central bank waives the possibility of compensating for past deviations – as it were, letting bygones be bygones. With an average objective, things are different. If this is defined as zero, for example, periods of inflation would have to be fully offset by periods of deflation, and the price level would remain constant over time. With an average target of, for example, 2 per cent inflation, the rise in the price level over time would be set at the same level. The pros and cons of price level stabilisation are analysed in depth in the literature. See, for example, V. Gaspar and F. Smets, 'Price level stability: some issues', *National Institute Economic Review*, 174 (October 2000), pp. 68–79.

single monetary policy over the medium term ensures genuine and meaningful accountability.[65]

## The monetary pillar

The reasons why the ECB rejected a monetary objective have already been set out in detail. This could not, however, mean that little or even no regard was to be paid to the importance of monetary factors in the evolution of prices.

The close relationship between the money supply and prices has been proven in countless studies all over the globe and all through history; it is one of the most certain facts in economics – insofar as anything is ever 'certain' in economics. Figure 6 shows the results of a study that identifies a relationship for 110 countries.[66]

Milton Friedman expressed this insight in a nutshell: inflation is always and everywhere a monetary phenomenon. In his analysis, there is no case where a significant change in the quantity of money per unit of output has not been associated with a significant change in the price level in the same direction; conversely, every significant change in the price level has been accompanied by a change in the quantity of money per unit of output.[67]

This relationship, it is true, holds only over the long run, but it can be regarded as robust across virtually all models of monetary economics.[68] Hence the ECB had every reason to treat this insight, and its own responsibility for monetary developments in the euro area,

---

[65] ECB, 'The stability-oriented monetary policy strategy of the Eurosystem', *Monthly Bulletin*, January 1999, p. 47.

[66] For additional literature, see Issing *et al.*, *Monetary Policy in the Euro Area*, p. 10.

[67] For further detail, see Issing, *Einführung in die Geldtheorie*, 14th edition, p. 155.

[68] See: R. E. Lucas, 'Two illustrations of the quantity theory of money', *American Economic Review*, 70 (1980). Lucas even goes so far as to say: 'I should think we would view any monetary model that did *not* have this neutrality property with the deepest suspicions, the way we would view a physical model that predicted different times for the earth to complete its orbit depending on whether the distance is measured in miles or kilometres' (R. E. Lucas, *Models of Business Cycles*, Oxford, 1987).

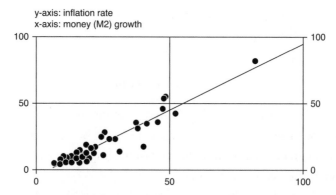

*Source:* G. McCandless and W. Weber, 'Some monetary facts', *Federal Reserve Bank of Minneapolis Quarterly Review*, 19:3 (1995).
**Figure 6** Money growth and inflation (per cent; long-term growth rates; 110 countries)

with due seriousness. How could the intention of 'assigning a prominent role to money' be put into practice? There were two aspects that were difficult to reconcile in this regard. On the one hand, the same reasons that led us to reject a money supply strategy argued against fixing on one monetary variable or relationship between money and prices. On the other hand, a concrete means had to be found to present any risks to price stability from the monetary side in operational form.

These considerations led to the concept of a *reference value* for monetary growth. The value so calculated was to serve as a guide to the rate of growth that is consistent with maintaining price stability.[69]

The first task was to determine which monetary aggregate demonstrated a close and stable relationship with prices. Again, we had to rely on synthetic time series for the period prior to monetary union. The final result was clear-cut. The narrower monetary aggregate M1 (currency in circulation and overnight deposits) showed a relatively good correlation with economic activity and was superior to broader aggregates as regards control by the central bank. For an indicator of

---

[69] In our internal investigations, we initially spoke of a 'benchmark' for monetary growth.

the future price trend, however, the choice had to fall on a broader aggregate. From among the various definitions, the 'best fit' method pointed to the *money supply* M3 defined as follows:

| | |
|---|---|
| Currency in circulation | |
| Overnight deposits | M1 |

| | |
|---|---|
| M1 plus | |
| Deposits with an agreed maturity of up to two years | |
| Deposits redeemable at notice of up to three months | M2 |

| | |
|---|---|
| M2 plus | |
| Repurchase agreements | |
| Money market fund shares/units | |
| Debt securities up to two years | M3 |

The reference value, that is the rate of M3 growth consistent with price stability over the medium to long term, was derived from the well-known quantity equation:

$$\Delta M = \Delta P + \Delta Y - \Delta V$$

whereby the change in the money supply ($\Delta M$) corresponds to the change in nominal GDP ($\Delta Y$ as real GDP and $\Delta P$ as the change in the price level) less the change in the velocity of money ($\Delta V$). The empirical calculation of the first reference value was based on the definition of price stability (annual inflation below 2 per cent), the medium-term trend growth of real GDP as estimated by ourselves and by international organisations (2–2.5 per cent) and an estimate of the trend (decline) in velocity of −0.5 to −1 per cent per year. Based on these assumptions, the Governing Council set the reference value at 4½ per cent in December 1998. The review of the reference value in the years that followed gave no grounds for changing this figure.

Money provides a natural anchor for a monetary policy committed to price stability. A reference value for monetary growth underlines the central bank's responsibility for 'monetary' impulses to inflation. As its rejection of a monetary objective showed, however, the ECB was aware of the difficulties that were to be expected in the practical implementation of monetary policy, as already reflected in the phrase 'under normal circumstances' in the press release. In the January 1999 article on its strategy, the ECB explicitly highlighted two aspects.

Firstly, the concept of a reference value does not entail 'a commitment on the part of the Eurosystem to correct deviations of monetary growth from the reference value over the short term. Interest rates will not be changed "mechanistically" in response to such deviations in an attempt to return monetary growth to the reference value'.[70]

Secondly, the monetary pillar does not consist solely and exclusively of the reference value and M3.[71] Other monetary aggregates, the various components of M3 and the counterparts to all these aggregates in the consolidated balance sheet of the monetary financial institutions would also play an important role in assessing the monetary risks to price stability on an ongoing basis.[72] After just a few years, the ECB was able to report that its monetary analysis had been considerably broadened and deepened.[73] In its quarterly Bank Lending Survey, developed in close collaboration with the national central banks, the ECB has an instrument that provides an important overview of current developments in lending, that is, in the 'counterpart' to M3.

### The economic pillar

Appropriate monetary policy decisions can only be taken on the basis of a comprehensive assessment of all relevant data. The strat-

---

[70] ECB, *Monthly Bulletin*, January 1999, p. 48.

[71] On the monetary pillar, see also L. Papademos, 'The role of money in the conduct of monetary policy', speech at the Fourth ECB Central Banking Conference, Frankfurt am Main, 9 November 2006 (available at www.ecb.int/press/key/date/2006/html/sp061110.en.html); A. Weber, paper in ECB (ed.), *Monetary Policy: A Journey from Theory to Practice. An ECB Colloquium in Honour of Otmar Issing* (Frankfurt, 2007).

[72] See ECB, *Monthly Bulletin*, January 1999, p. 49.

[73] See ECB, 'Monetary analysis in real time', *Monthly Bulletin*, October 2004; O. Issing, 'The monetary pillar of the ECB – broadened and reconfirmed', speech at the ECB Watchers Conference, 3 June 2005; J. Stark, 'Enhancing the monetary analysis', speech at the ECB Watchers Conference, 7 September 2007.

egy of the ECB is therefore founded on two pillars, the monetary together with the *economic* pillar in which all other information is analysed. In the short to medium term, prices are determined by non-monetary factors such as wages (unit labour costs), the exchange rate, energy and import prices, indirect taxes, etc. Indicators of developments in the real economy include data on employment and unemployment, data from surveys (such as the Ifo Business Climate Index), incoming orders, and so on. This economic analysis also encompasses financial sector data such as the yield curve, stock prices and real estate prices. Asset price trends can yield information, for example, on how the wealth effect is expected to influence the growth of demand of private households. As part of its economic analysis, the ECB takes a broad look at developments in macroeconomic demand and its structure, in costs and in the labour market. This includes taking account of the influence of fiscal policy (spending and revenue) and of external factors (the international economic environment, exports and imports). The analysis also addresses the problem of what shocks are already confronting the euro area, and what shocks are to be expected with what degree of probability.

The ECB's economic analysis, therefore, spans a wide range of indicators that are, moreover, to a greater or lesser degree interdependent. For example, if the exchange rate declines, the price competitiveness of the domestic economy will tend to improve, with potential positive effects on the economy. At the same time, however, import prices rise; the resultant cost increases put upward pressure on prices, which in turn may lead to higher wage demands, and so on. In its *Monthly Bulletins*, the ECB provides detailed information on the evolution of the individual indicators and on the macroeconomic situation.

A special position in the economic pillar is occupied by the *macroeconomic projections*. The ECB uses the term projections (and not forecasts) to make it clear that these are in the nature of scenarios. Essentially, they involve estimating the future trend of prices and of

GDP and its components based on certain assumptions. For example, the exchange rate is assumed to remain unchanged over the projection horizon. Initially, the ECB also assumed a constant short-term interest rate, but in 2006 it switched to basing the projection on market rates.

In their projection exercises, the Eurosystem experts use various methodologies and models, including a (euro) area-wide model and a multi-country model.[74] How the projections are produced is described in detail in an ECB publication.[75]

Four times a year, the staff elaborate projections with a two-year horizon. In June and December of each year, this is done by the ECB experts jointly with their counterparts at the national central banks; in the quarters in between, the ECB experts produce the projections on their own.

The ECB first needed to gain experience with its projections. Organising the cooperation between the experts at the ECB and at the national central banks was far from easy. Before long, however, the resources available and the possibility of discussion between the experts were coming together to yield a good overall result. Once the procedure had been set up and the results had been tested over a certain period of time, the ECB Governing Council decided in December 2000 to publish the projections. Initially, only the Eurosystem staff's projection was published, but later that of the ECB staff was published as well. To illustrate the uncertainty associated with such projections, the results are published in the form of projection ranges. The ranges are determined based on the difference between previous projections and actual outcomes. The ECB decided not to use the 'fan chart' method in order to avoid giving the impression that it had specific knowledge of the profile and distribution of forecast uncertainty.

---

[74] See G. Fagan et al., 'An area-wide model (AWM) for the euro area', ECB Working Paper, no. 42 (2001); G. Fagan and J. Morgan (eds.), Econometric Models of the Euro-area Central Banks (Cheltenham, 2005).

[75] ECB, A Guide to Eurosystem Staff Macroeconomic Projection Exercises (Frankfurt, 2001).

The ECB's projections are produced by a staff of experts in time for the Governing Council's last monetary policy meeting in each quarter. The Governing Council receives the projection results together with a detailed report that sets out the underlying technical assumptions, describes the risks to the projections and discusses alternative scenarios. The Governing Council itself, however, does not exert any influence on the elaboration of the projections. Its very size means that the Governing Council would not be suited to producing projections. It is, however, the task of the Governing Council to discuss its assessments – which may well diverge between individual members – and their significance for the monetary policy decision to be taken.[76]

The strategy adopted by the ECB takes appropriate account of the projections: they represent an important input into analysis and decision-making, but are not the central basis, still less the only one. Their results are uncertain, and are subject to rapid and large changes if the assumptions, for example about the oil price or exchange rates, do not (or no longer) reflect reality. Quite apart from that, the projection results depend in large measure on the chosen methodologies. Finally, the already limited reliability of the projections decreases as the projection horizon lengthens.

Projections cannot incorporate all relevant data, and thus are only ever a partial reflection of a comprehensive analysis. They therefore form only one element, albeit an important one, in the economic pillar of the ECB's strategy. They are not suited at all to take full account of monetary factors.

### The role of cross-checking and communication

There are important arguments in favour of organising the analytical work for the assessment of economic conditions and of risks to

---

[76] See O. Issing, 'The role of macroeconomic projections within the monetary policy strategy of the ECB', *Economic Modelling*, 21 (2004), pp. 723–34.

price developments in *two pillars*, two departments, or whatever. Each area has its own special position. Neither one is more important than the other, and their message differs chiefly because each provides information on risks to price stability over a different time horizon.

The *economic* analysis considers factors that have an immediate impact on the HICP, such as changes in the oil price. The time horizon extends over the short to medium term, for example as regards the influence of unit labour costs or the assessment of how economic activity will affect prices. In terms of the time horizon, the *monetary* analysis begins where the economic analysis leaves off, and thus adopts a medium- to long-term perspective. Here the relationship between money (as well as other factors taken into account in the monetary analysis) and prices comes into play. In the light of current knowledge, it is difficult to imagine how these assessments could be carried out in a logically sound and methodologically correct manner 'under one roof', as it were. The strategy of the ECB reflects the state of the art in economics: to date, nobody has come up with a way of unifying the economic and monetary factors in a consistent model. Nonetheless, the ECB's strategy is open to progress in economic research: the more closely monetary and non-monetary factors can be combined in a single model, the more that linking the two analyses would make sense. Eventually, we might be left with one pillar – always providing that it offered a solid foundation for the ECB's stability-oriented monetary policy.

Naturally, the ECB's Governing Council ultimately makes its decisions based on a consistent overall judgement of the economic situation and the risks to price stability.

Under the ECB's strategy, the huge amount of incoming data is split, so to speak, into two channels (see figure 7) and analysed using the methods that are appropriate in each case. The two-pillar strategy provides a framework within which the two sets of information are first of all checked and evaluated in the separate pillars before

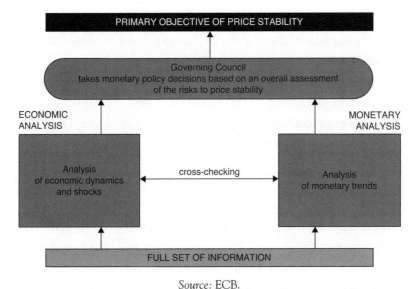

Source: ECB.

**Figure 7** The stability-oriented monetary policy strategy of the ECB

being finally compared and if necessary weighed against each other. This *cross-checking* culminates in an assessment that takes all relevant information into account and at the same time properly evaluates it in terms of its relative significance and the different time dimensions.

This procedure meets two conditions for a stability-oriented monetary policy. On the one hand, it enables the origin, size and nature of shocks to be taken into account. This is an extremely demanding and difficult task. But on the other hand, it is hugely important for the central bank, in a world of uncertainty, ongoing change and the high volatility of many data, not to lose the orientation towards its objective. Here, the monetary analysis is the suitable anchor for a long-term orientation towards price stability.[77]

In choosing its strategy, the ECB placed great importance on the requirements in terms of transparency and accountability. As already

---

[77] O. Issing, 'Monetary policy in a changing economic environment', in Federal Reserve Bank of Kansas City, *Rethinking Stabilization Policy* (Kansas City, 2003).

mentioned, the ECB announced its strategy in advance of the start of policy implementation, spelt out the reasons for its choice of strategy, and reported regularly on the progress made in its analysis.

The two pillars of the strategy also determine the structure of the introductory statement to the President's press conferences, while the argumentation leads to the outcome of the cross-checking.

## The 2003 evaluation of the strategy

With any policy, it is wise to check regularly whether its actions continue to fulfil the institution's mandate and the related expectations. Criticism from the outside plays an important role, and is a constant incentive to review one's own work. Critical observations from the inside should come as a matter of course. From time to time, policymakers should carry out a fundamental review of their thinking and/or their strategy.

This principle was all the more applicable to the ECB as a new institution. Thus we began at a very early stage to evaluate internally our experience with the new strategy. A whole series of in-house studies was devoted to questions such as the stability of the demand for money or the development of inflation expectations. There was also no shortage of 'ideas' from outside. Even before the start of monetary union, various groups had been formed with the objective of casting a critical spotlight on the new central bank's monetary policy. From the outset, the focus of the debate was on the issue of strategy. Thus the three groups represented at the first conference on 'The ECB and its Watchers' on 17 and 18 June 1999 all criticised the ECB's strategy.[78]

At my suggestion, the ECB's Governing Council decided in December 2002 on a thorough review of the strategy. Following

[78] The arguments, however, were in part completely contradictory. See O. Issing, 'The ECB and its Watchers', speech, 17 June 1999. See also Center for Financial Studies conference, 'The ECB and its Watchers 1999–2006', Frankfurt, 5 May 2006.

intensive discussions, which also involved experts from the national central banks, and based on extensive documentation, the Governing Council announced the results of its reflections in the following press release:[79]

### The ECB's monetary policy strategy

After more than four years of conducting monetary policy for the euro area, the Governing Council of the ECB has undertaken a thorough evaluation of the ECB's monetary policy strategy.

This strategy, which was announced on 13 October 1998, consists of three main elements: a quantitative definition of price stability, a prominent role for money in the assessment of risks to price stability, and a broadly based assessment of the outlook for price developments.

More than four years of implementation have worked satisfactorily. Nevertheless, the Governing Council deemed it useful to evaluate the strategy in the light of this experience, taking into account the public debate and a series of studies undertaken by staff of the Eurosystem.

'Price stability is defined as a year-on-year increase in the Harmonised Index of Consumer Prices (HICP) for the euro area of below 2 per cent. Price stability is to be maintained over the medium term.' Today, the Governing Council confirmed this definition (which it announced in 1998). At the same time, the Governing Council agreed that in the pursuit of price stability it will aim to maintain inflation rates close to 2 per cent over the medium term. This clarification underlines the ECB's commitment to provide a sufficient safety margin to guard against the risks of deflation. It also addresses the issue of the possible presence of a measurement bias in the HICP and the implications of inflation differentials within the euro area.

The Governing Council confirmed that its monetary policy decisions will continue to be based on a comprehensive analysis of the risks to price stability. Over time, analysis under both pillars of the monetary policy strategy has been deepened and extended. This practice will be continued. However, the Governing Council wishes to clarify communication on the cross-checking of information in coming to its unified overall judgement on the risks to price stability.

---

[79] ECB press release of 8 May 2003, www.ecb.int/press/pr/date/2003/html/pr030508_2.en.html.

To this end, the introductory statement of the President will henceforth follow a new structure. It will start with the economic analysis to identify short- to medium-term risks to price stability. As in the past, this will include an analysis of shocks hitting the euro area economy and projections of key macroeconomic variables.

The monetary analysis will then follow to assess medium- to long-term trends in inflation in view of the close relationship between money and prices over extended horizons. As in the past, monetary analysis will take into account developments in a wide range of monetary indicators including M3, its components and counterparts, notably credit, and various measures of excess liquidity.

This new structure of the introductory statement will better illustrate that these two perspectives offer complementary analytical frameworks to support the Governing Council's overall assessment of risks to price stability. In this respect, the monetary analysis mainly serves as a means of cross-checking, from a medium- to long-term perspective, the short- to medium-term indications coming from economic analysis.

To underscore the longer-term nature of the reference value for monetary growth as a benchmark for the assessment of monetary developments, the Governing Council also decided to no longer conduct a review of the reference value on an annual basis. However, it will continue to assess the underlying conditions and assumptions.

The ECB will today publish on its website a number of background studies prepared by its staff which, together with papers published earlier, served as input into the Governing Council's reflections on the ECB's monetary policy strategy.

Thus the Governing Council largely reaffirmed the strategy decided on five years earlier. This by no means came as a surprise. In the more than four years since the start, the Council's experience had been positive in every respect. The strategy had created the framework for purposeful discussions and a basis for consensual decision-making by the Governing Council. Nevertheless, one could not overlook certain difficulties in communication, which were the main focus of critical commentary. Hence the two changes to the strategy were predominantly aimed at improving communication.

The unanimous confirmation of the strategy was underpinned by numerous in-house studies, the most important of which were published at the time, and were released later that year, after slight editing, as a single volume.[80]

The modifications related to the following elements: the definition of price stability as a year-on-year increase in the HICP of below 2 per cent had proved its worth, not least as an anchor for inflation expectations. The often repeated criticism that this definition was asymmetrical, without a clear ceiling and with no floor at all, and was thus unsuitable to firmly anchor inflation expectations, was refuted at both the theoretical and empirical level.[81] Various studies testified to the fact that maintaining a sufficient distance from 'zero inflation' is an effective means of avoiding the problem of a deflationary process. The definition of price stability was left unchanged. But in an environment marked by concerns about the possibility of deflation, the ECB emphasised that in the pursuit of its policy it would aim to maintain inflation at 'close to' 2 per cent over the medium term.

A series of studies evidenced the stability of the demand for money, and overall they provided confirmation for the prominent role assigned to 'money'. All the corresponding studies also lent support to the Governing Council in its arguments in favour of the two-pillar strategy. The only change was to the order in which the economic and monetary analyses appeared in the President's introductory statement (and in the editorial of the *Monthly Bulletin*). A comparison of the 'old' and 'new' formats reveals two points. There was no change in terms of content. Beginning with the information on current economic developments, and turning to the more medium- to long-term monetary analysis afterwards, enabled the

---

[80] O. Issing (ed.), *Background Studies for the ECB's Evaluation of its Monetary Policy Strategy* (Frankfurt, November 2003).

[81] See: 'Definition of price stability, range and point inflation targets: the anchoring of long-term inflation expectations', in the above-mentioned volume. One of the disappointments from discussion with critics is that such studies in some cases are quite obviously not even read, while the criticism is simply levelled again.

information to be better structured and made the arguments easier to follow.

Finally, the annual review of the reference value was discontinued. This had in fact occasionally led people mistakenly to conclude that the reference value was an annual concept, whereas it is basically without any definite temporal dimension. In any case, major changes in the data from which this value is derived are only expected to occur at lengthy intervals.

The evaluation served to confirm the strategy with which the ECB had taken over monetary policy responsibility for the euro area in January 1999. Choosing a suitable strategy before the start of monetary union was the biggest challenge facing the new central bank. I was the one who had developed this strategy in close collaboration with my colleagues. Inevitably, it meant a great personal responsibility. Had it failed, had it misled the ECB's Governing Council and – based on my proposals – resulted in monetary policy decisions that clearly failed to meet the objective of maintaining price stability, I would naturally have had only one option. In light of the success of the strategy, the reader will doubtless understand my personal sense of relief.

In the field of economics in general, and of monetary policy in particular, nothing is ever completely reliable or absolutely certain. It was all the more important, therefore, that, based on this strategy, the ECB's Governing Council should have been able to pursue a monetary policy that even its greatest critics do not deny has been a success.

## The instruments of monetary policy

### The Treaty

The powers of a central bank, including its monetary policy instruments, are normally laid down quite clearly. The Deutsche Bundesbank Act, for example, contains detailed provisions regarding the individual instruments of monetary policy and their configuration.

This is not so, however, in the case of the ECB. The Treaty contains relatively few provisions, which are, moreover, couched in very general terms. Thus the Eurosystem 'shall act in accordance with the principle of an open market economy with free competition, favouring an efficient allocation of resources' (Article 105 (1) of the Treaty and Article 2 of the Protocol). The Protocol on the Statute of the ESCB and of the ECB goes into more detail. In accordance with Article 18, the ECB and the national central banks may conduct open-market operations as well as credit operations with credit institutions and other market participants against adequate collateral. The ECB establishes general principles for this purpose. In accordance with Article 19, the ECB may require credit institutions to hold minimum reserves and is entitled to levy penalty interest or impose other sanctions with comparable effect in the event of non-compliance. Under Article 20, the Governing Council of the ECB, acting by a two-thirds majority, may decide to use other instruments.[82]

### Prior experience and preliminary considerations

While for a long time many central banks had relied on administrative monetary policy measures, instruments such as credit ceilings proved increasingly ineffective and incompatible with free-market conditions.[83] As a result, by the early 1990s there had been a large degree of convergence in the monetary policy instruments used by the national central banks in Europe. This made the preparatory work undertaken by the EMI easier. In some respects, however, policy instruments still

[82] Subject, as in Article 19, to the provisions of Article 2.

[83] See, for example, *Bankhistorisches Archiv*, supplement 27: 'Monetary Policy Instruments: National Experiences and European Perspectives' (Frankfurt, 1994), with papers by A. Icard, A. Wellink, O. Issing and M. King. For a discerning theoretical overview of the problems of monetary policy implementation and its development, see U. Bindseil, *Monetary Policy Implementation* (Oxford, 2004).

diverged considerably, owing to the differing interests pursued by the national central banks. And finally, adjusting to the common set of instruments for the implementation of the single monetary policy was in some cases associated with substantial costs. In the interests of monetary policy efficiency, conformity with free-market principles and neutrality, the centrepiece of the ECB's monetary policy was to be the control of bank liquidity via *open-market operations*. Owing to the differences in national practices, there were some differences of opinion as to how the banks' credit facilities should be organised.

One issue on which views parted company was *minimum reserves*. In particular, for as long as representatives of the Bank of England continued to be involved in the preparatory work, agreement on the use of this instrument appeared beyond reach.

The Bundesbank's experience with this instrument proved extremely instructive. Minimum reserves had played a central role in Germany's monetary policy for many years. The Bundesbank periodically attempted to 'sterilise' the central bank money liquidity created by purchases of foreign exchange by substantially raising minimum reserve ratios. Changes in the minimum reserve ratios were a regular occurrence. In addition, the ratios were differentiated according to various criteria – maturity of deposits, size of credit institution, domestic and foreign liabilities. After 1973, the Bundesbank gradually shifted away from its policy of frequent adjustments to the minimum reserve ratios. The minimum reserve instrument was to serve principally as a way of 'forcing the banks into the central bank', i.e. to take credit from the central bank thus ensuring a predictable and stable demand for central bank money.[84] In one respect, however, the Bundesbank's policy did not change. Minimum reserves were unremunerated, and thus in effect acted as a special tax on certain banking activities. This created an incentive to avoid reserve requirements. This effect increased in line with the respective minimum reserve ratio

---

[84] Deutsche Bundesbank, *Monthly Report*, March 1990, p. 22.

and the opportunity cost of maintaining non-interest-bearing reserves. Such reserve avoidance tactics fostered the emergence of a DM market outside Germany that was not affected by the reserve requirements. This 'Euro–DM market' was largely the result of the Bundesbank's minimum reserve policy.[85] It meant that a tight monetary policy became increasingly ineffective on account of the rising opportunity costs of unremunerated reserves.[86] This, incidentally, was the major point on which I dissented from the Bundesbank's policy.[87]

Since February 1987, the minimum reserve ratios for overnight deposits in the highest category, for time deposits and for savings deposits had stood at 12.1 per cent, 4.95 per cent and 4.15 per cent respectively. In order to make this instrument 'fit for Europe', the Bundesbank would have to abandon the 'old' policy to the greatest extent possible. This could only mean setting the reserve ratio at the lowest possible level and on a uniform basis, i.e. without differentiation (between categories of liabilities, etc.). This was indeed done in a series of rapid steps. Finally, as from 1 August 1995, there was only a uniform ratio of 2 per cent for overnight deposits (with no distinction between sizes of credit institution) and time deposits, and of 1.5 per cent for savings deposits.

The Bundesbank's discount policy had, fundamentally, long become outmoded.[88] The much vaunted 'real bills doctrine' was

---

[85] The term 'Euro' has nothing to do with the later single currency. It chiefly denotes the external market for DM deposits and loans.

[86] The Bundesbank conceded as much itself: 'the minimum reserve weapon, one of the Bundesbank's most important instruments of monetary policy, is blunted if it can be evaded relatively easily by shifting domestic business to offices abroad' (Deutsche Bundesbank, *Monthly Report*, May 1985, p. 33).

[87] Since there was no question of 'harmonising' minimum reserve requirements in Europe, and remunerating reserve balances also seemed to be a non-starter, I accordingly argued in favour of abolishing the minimum reserve requirement: O. Issing, 'Der Euro-DM-Markt und die deutsche Geldpolitik', in A. Gutowski, *Geldpolitische Regelbindung: Theoretische Entwicklungen and empirische Befunde*, Schriften des Vereins für Socialpolitik, vol. 161 (Berlin, 1987).

[88] The Land Central Banks set great store by a continuation of the discount policy on the same basis as before, as its practical implementation accounted for a not inconsiderable portion of their business.

supposed to ensure the 'real underpinning' of monetary policy. But, quite apart from the fact that the theoretical foundation of the real bills doctrine had long since been refuted, the fact that this source of refinancing acted as a kind of subsidy meant that trade bills had long been produced, as it were, according to need.[89]

With its other instruments and the manner in which it deployed them, however, the Bundesbank did not need to fear comparison with any other central bank in the implementation of monetary policy. Thus in the preparations for the monetary policy of the ECB, the opinion of the Bundesbank's representatives carried a lot of weight, backed as it was by the Bundesbank's success in policy implementation.[90]

### The operational framework of the Eurosystem

In selecting and subsequently in deploying its instruments, the ECB had to take account not just of the aforementioned Treaty provisions, but also of the requirements that arose out of its special status as supranational institution:[91] while the ECB's monetary policy decision-making is centralised (in the Governing Council), policy is implemented on a decentralised basis. The ECB coordinates the operations, and the national central banks carry them out.

The same rules and procedures apply throughout the euro area. In particular, all financial institutions are to receive equal treatment. Simplicity and transparency ensure that monetary policy actions are widely understood. On the principle of continuity, abrupt changes in

---

[89] For a critical view, see O. Issing and B. Rudolph, *Der Rediskontkredit* (Frankfurt, 1988).

[90] For an assessment of the Bundesbank's policy instruments, see O. Issing, 'Das geld-politische Instrumentarium unter dem Aspekt der Wettbewerbsneutralität', in W. Ehrlicher and D. B. Simmert, *Wandlungen des geldpolitischen Instrumentariums der Deutschen Bundesbank, Kredit und Kapital*, supplement 10 (Berlin, 1988).

[91] On this, see ECB, *The Monetary Policy of the ECB*, 2nd edition (Frankfurt, 2004). For a detailed textbook illustration of its instruments and the ECB in general, see E. Görgens, K. Ruckriegel and F. Seitz, *Europäische Geldpolitik*, 4th edition (Stuttgart, 2004).

instruments and procedures are to be avoided. Finally, the principles of security and cost-effectiveness serve to minimise the financial and operational risks in the Eurosystem and to keep the costs of implementation as low as possible both for the Eurosystem itself and for its counterparties.

In principle, all euro area credit institutions are potential counterparties for the Eurosystem. To be eligible for particular transactions, however, they have to fulfil certain criteria, namely: they must be integrated into the minimum reserve system, be financially sound and meet the relevant operational requirements. Of the 7,521 euro area credit institutions (end-2000 figures), only 2,542 qualified for participation in open-market operations, 3,059 for the marginal lending facility and 3,599 for the deposit facility. (The actual number of participants in, for example, open-market operations, however, was much lower – generally between 200 and 300.)

As required not just by the Treaty but also by the principles of sound monetary policy, the Eurosystem grants credit only against suitable collateral. The ECB sets out the requirements for the posting of collateral in an extensive catalogue.[92] In a reflection of both the uniformity and the decentralised nature of the euro area, this catalogue indicates, for example, that collateral can be utilised on a cross-border basis, i.e. between national central banks.

The individual countries are becoming increasingly similar in their financial structure, although in some respects the differences remain considerable. Hence, in order to ensure that counterparties receive equal treatment, the Eurosystem accepts a broad range of both public and private sector securities. These were grouped into two categories. The first category ('tier one assets') consists of marketable debt instruments fulfilling uniform, euro area-wide

---

[92] ECB, *The Implementation of Monetary Policy in the Euro Area: General Documentation on Eurosystem Monetary Policy Instruments and Procedures* (Frankfurt, September 2006); ECB, 'The single list in the collateral framework of the Eurosystem', *Monthly Bulletin*, May 2006.

eligibility criteria laid down by the ECB. 'Tier two assets', in contrast, comprise assets of particular importance for national financial markets and banking systems which fulfil eligibility criteria laid down by the national central banks based on ECB minimum standards.[93]

As the ECB subsequently also stated publicly, it accepts only collateral with a rating from one of the three leading agencies of at least A– (or equivalent).[94]

## The instruments

Working within the scope permitted under the Treaty, the ECB Governing Council decided on a set of instruments comprising open-market operations, standing facilities and minimum reserves.

### Open-market operations

In principle, the ECB may utilise the whole range of relevant open-market operations, from short- to long-term transactions and from outright purchases or sales of securities to reverse transactions ('repos', whereby, for example, securities are sold with an agreement to repurchase).[95]

The most important open-market operation is the weekly *main refinancing operation*. This is the principal means whereby the ECB

[93] The ECB is in the process of combining the two tiers into a single list; see the publications referred to in the preceding footnote.

[94] The Eurosystem's collateral arrangements have occasionally been criticised for hindering the emergence in the market of an appropriate interest rate differential between good and less good quality public sector issuers. For a refutation of such arguments, see F. Papadia, 'The ECB's collateral framework', *Central Banking*, 16:3 (February 2006), pp. 33–40.

[95] There have repeatedly been misunderstandings in this regard. For example, sceptics feared that the ECB would be unable to combat a highly deflationary development because it lacked the requisite 'ammunition'. But, just like other central banks, the ECB could if necessary inject virtually unlimited amounts of central bank money through the purchase of all kinds of debt securities. The ban on 'monetary financing' of government prohibits the ECB merely from purchasing government securities in the primary market.

supplies the banking system with central bank money. All eligible euro area credit institutions can take part in these operations, which are executed through tenders, against collateral. They submit their bids (normally on Monday, or Tuesday morning at the latest) to their respective national central banks, which transmit the bids electronically to the ECB; the Executive Board then decides how much will be allotted overall, and its decision is communicated to the national central banks; settlement of the money transactions and transfer of collateral are then effected the following day via the counterparties' accounts with the national central banks. This procedure is a clear example of how the ECB's single monetary policy is decided centrally and implemented in a decentralised manner.

In conducting open-market operations, the ECB can choose between *fixed rate* and *variable rate* tenders and between different methods of allotment.[96] Initially, the ECB carried out its main refinancing operations via a fixed rate tender, that is, the ECB Governing Council fixed the single interest rate at which it was prepared to accept the credit institutions' bids and provide liquidity. The total allotment determined by the ECB was then distributed among the credit institutions pro rata. When in early 2000 expectations firmed that the ECB would raise rates further, the banks' bids (at the given rate of interest) came to exceed the amount of liquidity finally allotted by ever greater margins. When this overbidding took on extreme dimensions (with the allotment being only a small percentage of the bids), the ECB switched to variable rate tenders. In these, the Governing Council sets a minimum interest rate at which it is prepared to accept bids. The allotment follows an 'American auction' procedure, whereby amounts are allotted to the bids with the highest interest rate first; at the marginal interest rate, i.e. the lowest rate offered and accepted, bids are scaled down, that is satisfied in part, based on the total allotment decided by the ECB.

[96] For details, see the publications referred to in footnote 92.

Finally, the ECB subsequently reduced the maturity of main refinancing operations from two weeks to one.

In addition to the weekly main refinancing operations, the Eurosystem conducts monthly *longer-term refinancing operations*. The ECB Governing Council announces in advance the total volume to be allotted (via variable rate tender); in other respects, the procedure is the same as for the main refinancing operations. This instrument is used to supply longer-term liquidity (with a maturity of three months) to the banking system.

With a view to steering the money market at very short notice, the ECB carries out *fine-tuning operations* (quick tenders). These operations are not standardised, but are conducted on a case-by-case basis and serve either to provide central bank money to, or absorb it from, the market.

Finally, in the framework of its open-market operations the ECB can conduct so-called *structural operations*. These operations, for which there is also no standardised procedure, serve the purpose of adjusting the structural, i.e. longer-term, liquidity position of the banking system. To date, this instrument has not been utilised.

### Standing facilities

With the standing facilities the ECB enables credit institutions to obtain overnight liquidity (under the *marginal lending facility*) or to place interest-bearing overnight deposits with the central bank (under the *deposit facility*). The Governing Council fixes the interest rates on each facility. Since banks can in effect obtain or invest central bank money at these rates at any time, the two rates provide a ceiling and a floor, respectively, for movements in market interest rates.

In order to prevent potential major swings in interest rates at the start of the single monetary policy and to counter any related uncertainty, the ECB initially set a narrow interest rate corridor (50 basis points), which was subsequently widened. Since April 1999 the rate

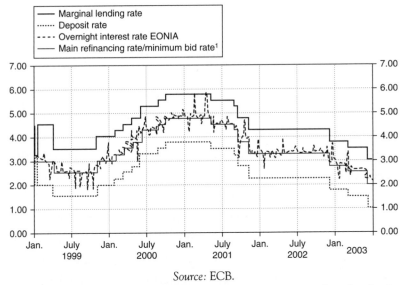

*Source:* ECB.

[1] Before 28 June 2000 the main refinancing operations were conducted as fixed rate tenders. Starting from the operation settled on 28 June 2000, the main refinancing operations were conducted as variable rate tenders with a pre-announced minimum bid rate. The minimum bid rate refers to the minimum interest rate at which counterparties may place their bids.

**Figure 8** Conduct of money market rate (percentages per annum; daily data)

for the marginal lending facility has stood 200 basis points above that for the deposit facility. And since the switch to variable rate tenders, the minimum bid rate for the main refinancing operations has been exactly at the midpoint between the two rates for standing facilities (see figure 8).

## Minimum reserves

As described above, the problems with the minimum reserve policy in the past stemmed from its having acted as a special tax on certain banking activities and from its discrimination at an administrative level between different categories. If these shortcomings are eliminated, minimum reserves are an extremely useful tool, in particular for supporting the effectiveness of the other instruments of monetary policy.

For this reason, the ECB Governing Council made use of the minimum reserve requirement provided for under the Treaty and designed it in such a way as to avoid the problems. The uniform reserve ratio of 2 per cent – unchanged since the start – is applied to all deposits with credit institutions up to an agreed maturity of two years and redeemable at notice of up to two years, to debt securities issued by credit institutions with an original maturity of up to two years, and to money-market paper.

Credit institutions' reserve holdings are remunerated at market rates,[97] and hence there is no incentive to try and evade reserve requirements. The reserve requirement has to be complied with on an average basis over a maintenance period.[98] This enables credit institutions to smooth the effects of fluctuations in their liquidity requirements in the first instance by adjusting their minimum reserve holdings. Under normal circumstances, this makes a major contribution to stabilising money-market conditions.

The reserve requirement, moreover, creates a structural demand for central bank money by the credit institutions, with banks being 'forced to come to the central bank'; this effect might prove important in particular if the use of electronic money makes further advances.

### The implementation of monetary policy

The operational target in the implementation of the ECB's monetary policy is the *money-market rate*. The ECB steers this rate using its policy instruments, with the aim of influencing via the level of, and

---

[97] My proposal to that effect evidently came as a surprise, and initially met with resistance.

[98] Originally, the maintenance period ran from the 24th of one month to the 23rd of the following month. Since the changeover to weekly tenders, the maintenance period begins in each case on the Wednesday following the first Governing Council meeting of the month.

changes in the short-term rate, the relevant macroeconomic variables (long-term rates, lending, economic activity, and so on) so as to achieve the (final) objective of price stability. The overall framework for the implementation of monetary policy is given by the monetary policy strategy.

In the *implementation* of monetary policy, that is, in steering the money market rate, the ECB has been extremely successful from the very beginning. With the corridor determined by the two standing facility rates, movements in short-term interest rates have been limited even in extreme situations. Owing to the flexibility in complying with the reserve requirement (the averaging provision), day-to-day fluctuations have remained within narrow limits in normal circumstances, with somewhat larger swings only for very brief periods at the end of the maintenance period.

The principles referred to above under the heading of the 'operational framework' (equal treatment of credit institutions, etc.) have all been fulfilled. Both individually and in combination, the instruments have worked in an efficient and highly flexible way, as evidenced both in 'routine' operation and in exceptional circumstances. For example, the ECB was able to master the 'Y2K' problem (the year 2000 software problem), which gave rise to widespread concerns at the time, without major difficulties through (moderate) recourse to fine-tuning measures, while other central banks had to add special instruments to their armoury. The strains on bank liquidity in the wake of the terrorist acts of 11 September 2001 were overcome without any problems by means of fine-tuning operations.[99]

Through various adjustments, such as the switch from fixed to variable rate tenders or the shortening of the maturity from two weeks to one, the ECB has adapted the specific features of the main refinancing operations in the light of changing conditions.

---

[99] A swap agreement concluded with the US central bank enabled a short-term gap in dollar liquidity to be overcome.

The ECB meets the bulk of credit institutions' demand for central bank money through its main refinancing operations, supplemented by the longer-term refinancing. In contrast, only limited recourse is had to the marginal lending facility. In using its monetary policy instruments, the ECB relies entirely on market mechanisms. Its actions in the market are essentially confined to the weekly rhythm of the main refinancing operations. Its philosophy of adopting a 'hands-off approach' can also be seen in the cautious use of fine-tuning operations. In normal circumstances, the flexibility permitted in complying with the reserve requirement keeps fluctuations in money-market rates within narrow limits.

The Treaty left the ECB a good deal of latitude in developing an appropriate set of instruments with which to implement its monetary policy. It is no exaggeration to say that the ECB has made optimal use of this possibility. Fears that serious technical difficulties would arise, in particular at the beginning, proved unfounded. Both in this phase and notably also in subsequent exceptional situations, the policy instruments performed impeccably. Through the underlying adherence to market principles and the efficient, simple and flexible design of its set of policy instruments, the ECB is optimally equipped to face the challenges the future may bring.

# FOUR

# The ECB – monetary policy for a stable euro

## Orientations in the ECB Governing Council

When the Governing Council of the ECB convened for its first meeting in Frankfurt on 9 June 1998, the assumption of monetary policy responsibility for the euro still seemed such a distant prospect, and yet the calendar showed it to be so close at hand. As was to be expected, and out of sheer necessity, the first few meetings were dominated by organisational and technical matters such as procedural rules, budget issues or the conditions of employment for the ECB's staff.

In developing the policy instruments as part of the monetary policy preparations, consideration also had to be given to their organisational and legal framework. For the difficult task of producing macroeconomic projections for the future euro area, the groundwork had to be laid for efficient cooperation between the ECB and the national central banks.

Inevitably, little time remained to discuss the economic situation. Moreover, a lot of what the national central bank governors had to say was, understandably, still focused on the specific situation in the individual countries. The national institutions, after all, continued to bear responsibility for the national currencies. However, the Governing Council could not possibly wait for the start of monetary union to direct its attention towards the euro area as a whole. Switching abruptly from the national orientation of the member central banks, which up until 31 December 1998 would retain their national monetary policy competencies, to a focus on supranational responsibility as from 1 January 1999 would have been much too risky. Before then, the Council needed to 'practise' concentrating on the euro area and the responsibility for the euro.

The ECB was absolutely bound to play a leading role in this. The Executive Board, with the President at its head, was destined for the task, not least because of the very fact that its members – in contrast to the national central bank governors – are appointed by the EU Council, meeting in the composition of the heads of state or government, and are charged exclusively with 'European' functions. On the other hand, success also depended in large measure on this role of the ECB and its Executive Board being accepted by the national central banks (and their organisational structures). The indispensable prerequisite for this was that the 'head office' be acknowledged to have the requisite professional competence. To the surprise of many sceptics, the ECB achieved this within a very short space of time. A decisive factor was the way in which the meetings of the ECB Governing Council were prepared and, above all, organised. This I shall dwell on in more detail later. At any rate, in gaining acceptance for the ECB's leadership role, it was crucial that the report on the economic situation, on the assessment of risks to price stability in the euro area, and the conclusions to be drawn for the monetary policy decisions to be taken, was presented by a member of the Executive Board and not by representatives of the staff. It was this approach, unusual if not unique in the world of central banking, that made it possible to focus all monetary policy deliberations in the Governing Council on the euro area from the very beginning.

Heading the Directorates General for both Economics and Research was a huge responsibility for me, not least owing to the role I had to play in the Governing Council. Had it not been for the outstanding quality of the economists working in the two Directorates General, their high motivation, unflagging commitment and absolute loyalty, I would not have been able to do it. In the regular post-meeting debriefing sessions with the senior staff, we already started preparing for the Governing Council's next monetary policy meeting. Beyond these management teams, it was only through the permanent contact with virtually all the economists that continuity of analysis and consistency in the publications, first and foremost the *Monthly Bulletin*, could be ensured.

Even if this excellent collaboration took time to fully evolve, the structures were put in place at a very early stage. This was also true of the meetings of the Governing Council. How successful we were in concentrating minds on the start of the single monetary policy was already in evidence in the run-up to monetary union.

At only its seventh meeting, on 1 December 1998, the Governing Council provided remarkable proof of its early focus on the task to come. In the preceding years, the national central banks, acting on their own responsibility, had significantly reduced their policy interest rates. For example, in April 1996, as inflationary pressures abated, the Bundesbank had lowered the discount rate to 2.5 per cent and the Lombard rate to 4.5 per cent. The interest rate on fixed-rate securities repurchase tenders stood at 3.3 per cent.

Against the backdrop of a continuous decline in inflation and a further weakening of the economic situation, the Governing Council was unanimous in considering that a further downward adjustment of policy rates was called for. Essentially, it was only a question of timing, that is, of deciding whether to cut rates *before* or only *after* the start of monetary union. Ultimately the arguments in favour of a rate cut by the national central banks – at that time still with authority over monetary policy – prevailed. Accordingly, all the national central banks lowered their main interest rate to 3 per cent in a coordinated action on 3 December.[1]

Two considerations were paramount. Firstly, these decisions presented an opportunity to complete the process of convergence of national policy rates that had begun some considerable time before. Secondly, a policy rate cut by the ECB shortly after the start might have created the impression that the new central bank inclined more towards an 'expansionary' stance than the national central banks. In order also to demonstrate to the outside world their consensus on the assessment of the situation and the appropriate monetary policy response, the national central banks agreed on the following procedure:

1. All the central banks would announce their decision on the same day (3 December) at the same time (2.00 p.m. ECB time).
2. The President of the ECB would provide a collective orientation in his press conference.
3. The ECB would prepare a statement which all national central banks would issue as far as possible with identical wording.
4. The ECB would follow up the decision with its own press statement pointing out that the decision was taken in anticipation of the start of monetary union and that the ECB intended to maintain this level of interest rates for the foreseeable future.

At its subsequent meeting on 22 December 1998, the Governing Council decided to conduct the first main refinancing operation at a fixed rate of 3 per cent on 4 January 1999. At the same time, the Council set the interest rate for the marginal lending facility at 4.5 per cent and for the deposit facility at 2 per cent. Thus, in view of market expectations of further interest rate reductions, the Governing Council set an asymmetric corridor. The Council also decided, as a transitory measure, to restrict the range between the rates on the standing facilities to 50 basis points (3.25 per cent and 2.75 per cent). This very narrow corridor was designed to limit

[1] Except for the Banca d'Italia, which lowered its discount rate to 3.5 per cent.

the possible volatility of money-market interest rates and thereby to facilitate the transition to monetary union.

Before the start of monetary union, therefore, the initial conditions for the single monetary policy had been fixed, and the foundations had been laid for a smooth transition.

## Assuming responsibility for monetary policy

When the Governing Council of the ECB came together on 7 January 1999 for its first meeting as the supreme decision-making body for the new currency, the euro, the sense of entering into a new era was all-pervading. (Those with a tendency to dramatise thought they glimpsed the *zeitgeist*, not exactly like a knight on horseback, but in the shape of the euro symbol. In fact, euro notes and coins would not appear for another three years.) The monetary policy decisions necessary for the start had already been taken the month before. At that particular moment, therefore, the dominant feeling was one of relief that the transition from the national currencies to the euro, and from the operations of the national central banks to those of the Eurosystem, had passed off so smoothly – more so than virtually anybody had dared hope.

Yet the sceptics had predicted that so much was bound go wrong, their doomsaying willingly transmitted and even amplified by sections of the media, not least outside the euro area. And the Governing Council itself, based on studies by the Eurosystem experts, had identified so many risks and run through all conceivable permutations in a crisis scenario. After all, just a few weeks previously, the national central banks were still providing the banks with central bank money in their national currency following procedures they had honed for years, if not decades. And now – overnight, as it were – they were to work together with the seemingly inexperienced ECB at the centre to supply liquidity without a hitch to a heterogeneous banking community stretching all the way from

Finland to Portugal and from Ireland to Austria. Little wonder, under these circumstances, that the members of the Governing Council needed to be on call day and night.

Against this backdrop, the report on the 'changeover', i.e. the introduction of the euro, at the Governing Council's meeting on 7 January 1999 was extremely brief. The system had been working practically perfectly from the word go. Although adjustments needed to be made as time went by, the single market for central bank money had been established from the outset. Not that this success was accidental. For months, there had been increasingly intensive collaboration not only between the ECB and the national central banks, but also with the banking industry. In the final phase of the changeover, an estimated 50,000 experts were involved in preparations for the introduction of the new currency.

A successful outcome does, however, usually require a little luck, and luck was indeed necessary insofar as not all the factors in the success of the changeover were under the control of the Eurosystem's experts. Had communications broken down owing to a power failure in one region, for example, any resultant problems in the provision of liquidity would doubtless have been blamed on the 'system'.

This scenario of huge efforts by the experts accompanied by a chorus of sceptics[2] was, incidentally, destined to be repeated with the introduction of euro banknotes and coins at the beginning of 2002.[3] It would be interesting to look back again to see which of the media had stooped to reporting about desperate citizens and mile-long queues at banks, airports or railway stations. In fact, as we all know, what was probably the largest peacetime logistical exercise ever was carried out in a manner that earned 'Europe' the greatest respect, even on the other side of the Atlantic.

---

[2] See chapter 2, section on 'The euro area economy'.
[3] A uniform design for the new banknotes had been agreed on a number of years before they were first issued. Reaching agreement had been anything but easy, as a choice had had to be made between fundamentally different alternative designs. It had quickly

In January 1999, at any rate, it was first of all satisfaction at the successful introduction of the euro that predominated. But we very soon had to look ahead, in particular to the most important task of the ECB, that of making the euro a stable currency and of building and maintaining confidence in the ECB's resolve and ability to pursue a successful monetary policy.

In this regard, too, there was no lack of scepticism. Would the large and seemingly heterogeneous ECB Governing Council be able to fulfil its responsibilities? Would it be able to withstand political pressure, which soon came to personified in (to name but one) the new chair of the Ecofin Council (of Finance Ministers), the then German Finance Minister Oskar Lafontaine, who seized every opportunity that presented itself to call for an 'employment-oriented' monetary policy (or some such formulation), which simply boiled down to a demand that the ECB reduce interest rates?

Some advocated that a sure way for the ECB to quickly gain credibility would be to deliberately adopt a hard, restrictive monetary policy stance from the outset, in order to rule out any suspicion that it might be less focused on stability than the Bundesbank. I had previously objected most strongly to any such ideas. To follow them would have meant initial ECB monetary policy decisions that would have gone beyond what was necessary to maintain price stability. Sooner or later (and most likely sooner), the ECB would have had to correct such an overly restrictive stance, revealing itself to be a weak central bank rather than a 'strong' one. In doing so, the ECB would not have built trust in its policy and its competence, but rather would have forfeited it for the foreseeable future. For the new institution, the only maxim to follow was: from the beginning, act as necessary to fulfil the mandate in accordance with the previously announced

become clear, however, that in view of Europe's troubled history, differences of opinion on persons or locations as motifs were virtually inevitable. Thus the choice of neutral motifs reflects on the one hand the burden of the past, but on the other hand also the resolve to proceed along the path of a common future.

strategy, and pay no heed to any sniping from political quarters in particular.

At the same time, the circumstances that faced the ECB when it began implementing monetary policy were anything but favourable. The rise in the Harmonised Index of Consumer Prices (HICP) in January and February 1999 stood at a historically low level of 0.8 per cent. On the one hand, this testified to the stability-oriented policy of the national central banks, supported by wage and fiscal policy in the individual countries, in the run-up to monetary union. In this respect, therefore, the ECB enjoyed a positive legacy. On the other hand, this low rate of inflation was also the result of exogenous factors, not least a decline in the oil price to an unusually low level (of around 10 US dollars a barrel).

It would have been completely unrealistic to assume that this extremely low rate of inflation would be sustainable over time. For the new central bank, the prospect of higher inflation in the future was not very promising. For the immediate future, however, the economic situation pointed in the opposite direction. Major foreign markets were still suffering the effects of the Asian crisis in late 1997, and the repercussions of the Russian crisis of summer 1998 were also still being felt.

Economic growth in the euro area was weakening. On balance, the inflation risks were on the downside. In its communication with the public, the ECB avoided using the term 'deflationary tendency', for two main reasons. In a situation of high uncertainty and spreading pessimism over the economic outlook, the ECB wished to avoid anything that might have exacerbated the negative sentiment. Moreover, comparisons were repeatedly drawn between the situation in the euro area and the persistent weakness in Japan. Any reference to 'deflation' might have lent extra weight to this – inappropriate – comparison. The assessment of risks to price developments as being on the downside underlay the ECB Governing Council's decision to reduce the interest rate on the main refinancing facility by 50

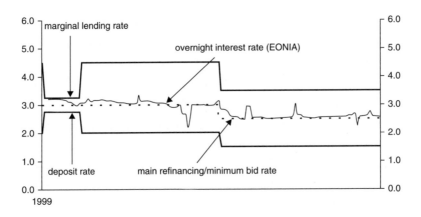

*Source:* ECB.

**Figure 9** ECB interest rates and money market rates at the beginning of the monetary union (percentages per annum; daily data)

basis points to 2.5 per cent at its meeting on 8 April 1999. At the same time, the Council lowered the rates on the marginal refinancing facility and deposit facility respectively to 3.5 per cent and 1.5 per cent. This created a symmetrical interest rate corridor of 200 basis points, with the main refinancing rate exactly in between (see figure 9). This corridor arrangement subsequently proved to work well and was therefore retained.

Over the months that followed, the economic prospects improved, and the risks to price developments, from being on the downside, increasingly tended to move in the opposite direction, not least as a result of a depreciating exchange rate and rising oil prices. The signals from the two pillars of the monetary policy strategy, for their part, clearly pointed to increasing upside inflation risks. Against this background, the Governing Council decided at its meeting on 4 November to raise the three central bank rates by 50 basis points each. As a result, the interest rate corridor for the two standing facilities lay between 4 and 2 per cent, with the main refinancing rate in the middle at 3 per cent.

As (upside) risks to price developments continued to increase, the Governing Council raised policy rates in the months that followed in three steps of 25 basis points each to 3.75 per cent (for the main refinancing rate). On 9 June 2000 the Governing Council raised rates by 50 basis points, while the next two 25 basis point steps ultimately brought the main refinancing rate to 4.75 per cent on 6 October 2000. Since 28 June 2000, the interest rate on fixed-rate tenders had been superseded as the main refinancing rate by the minimum bid rate for variable-rate tenders.

With its decision on 11 May 2001 to cut the central bank rates by 25 basis points each, the Governing Council ushered in a lengthy phase of reductions in policy rates. The 50 basis point cut implemented on 6 June 2003 brought the rates on the deposit facility, main refinancing facility and marginal refinancing facility to lows of 1, 2 and 3 per cent respectively. Over a period of two and a half years, the Governing Council reaffirmed this level of interest rates in its policy decisions, before initiating the phase of interest rate increases when it decided at its meeting on 6 December 2005 to raise the ECB's policy rates by 25 basis points each (see figure 10).

It was not least the lengthy phase of unchanged central bank rates that exposed the ECB to criticism that – unlike other central banks, in particular the US Federal Reserve – it was doing too little to counter a weakening of growth and to support economic activity. First of all, reaffirming a given level of policy rates should not be confused with 'doing nothing' or a 'non-decision'. In each individual instance, the ECB's Governing Council decided not to change interest rates based on a thorough discussion. Measuring a central bank's monetary policy in terms of the number of times it adjusts interest rates, which sometimes happens, does not in any case deserve to be taken seriously.

Whether monetary policy has reacted appropriately or not can only be meaningfully assessed on the basis of an analysis of exogenous shocks and the ability of the macroeconomy to adjust. Through its strategy, which takes all relevant information into account, adopts a forward-looking approach and factors in the lags with which monetary policy operates, the ECB has striven to fulfil precisely these

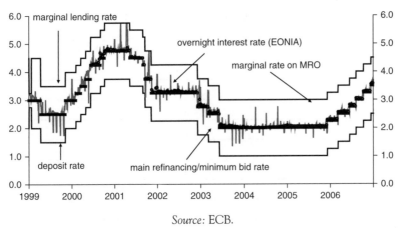

Source: ECB.

**Figure 10** ECB interest rates and money market rates 1999–2006 (percentages per annum; daily data)

requirements. The best gauge of its success is the anchoring of inflation expectations, which is moreover a reflection of the degree to which monetary policy actions are understood by the markets and the general public. 'Monetary policy activism' carries a large risk of the central bank soon having to reverse over-hasty decisions. It is also likely to create the false impression that the central bank is able to influence economic activity in the short run and produce results that are fundamentally beyond its power to achieve. Over time, such an approach to monetary policy is not supportive of the credibility of the central bank.[4]

### Monetary policy success: a stable euro

Nine years on, the ECB can lay claim – virtually undisputed – to the success of its monetary policy. Those observers that remain sceptics at heart might at most add the qualification 'so far'. Over this period, the average annual increase in the HICP has been 2.06 per cent (see table 4 for the annual figures).

[4] On this, see ECB, 'Monetary policy "activism"', *Monthly Bulletin*, November 2006.

TABLE 4: *Annual change in the Harmonised Index of Consumer Prices (in %)*

| Year | Annual change (in %) |
|------|----------------------|
| 1999 | 1.1 |
| 2000 | 2.1 |
| 2001 | 2.3 |
| 2002 | 2.3 |
| 2003 | 2.1 |
| 2004 | 2.1 |
| 2005 | 2.2 |
| 2006 | 2.2 |
| 2007 | 2.1* |

\* preliminary figure
*Source:* ECB.

This figure of 2.06 per cent is significantly below the average annual rate of inflation in most countries before monetary union. Even the D-Mark performed considerably less well over the period from 1950 to 1998, with a rate of 2.8 per cent. Admittedly, nine years is only a short episode compared to the performance of currencies such as the D-Mark over many decades. Nevertheless, it should be recalled, not least in Germany, that in the first few years of its existence the euro has not needed to fear comparison with the stable D-Mark.

It may be objected that, at 2.06 per cent, the outcome for the euro has been slightly, but since 2000 persistently, above the level that the ECB itself has declared to be compatible with price stability. Moreover, the ECB can scarcely attribute the low figure of 1.1 per cent to its own policy success since, as is well known, monetary policy operates with long lags. After all, moderate inflation has been a global phenomenon since the mid 1990s.

These objections must be taken seriously, but can at least be qualified by the following arguments. For one thing, as a new currency, the euro had to assert itself as a stable currency among others. As already mentioned, in early 1999 the rate of inflation, at 0.8 per cent, was at a level that had been reached only in exceptional instances in the past. After the start of momentary union, the euro area was confronted with a series of sizeable increases in the prices of major goods. These exogenous price shocks included in particular the more or less continuous rise in the oil price (from around US$ 10 per barrel to over US$ 90). In addition, epidemics (BSE, foot and mouth disease) temporarily put significant upward pressure on food prices. Finally, most countries increased indirect tax rates and major administered prices almost on a regular basis.

These price increases, admittedly, were in each case fundamentally *one-off* shocks. While the central bank cannot – and should not even attempt to – hinder the direct effects on individual prices and the consumer price index, the challenge for monetary policy is to prevent such one-off price impulses from becoming a persistent inflation process.

This danger is all the greater, the less that economic agents, and not least the financial markets, are persuaded that if necessary the central bank will do everything in its power to counter the threat of an inflationary development. A lack of trust in the orientation of monetary policy towards stability reveals itself first of all in higher inflation expectations. These can very soon lead to rising longer-term interest rates. If price rises persist, there is an increasing risk that workers will factor higher inflation expectations into their wage demands. Over time, the current rise in prices and increased inflation expectations can then be reflected in nominal contracts (debt securities, wages) with higher prices. For the term of such contracts, the rise in prices thus becomes embedded in the macroeconomy, with the danger of further rises starting from the higher level. Once such second-round effects have occurred, a tightening of monetary policy is required to prevent them from persisting and spreading. Temporary losses in output and employment are then virtually inevitable.

Such a constellation might have been expected to arise in particular with a new institution like the ECB and a new currency like the euro. But in fact it turned out differently. Inflation expectations have always

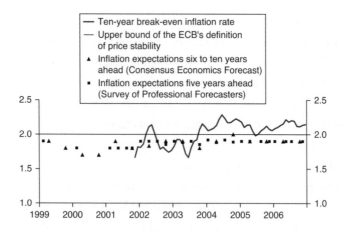

Sources: ECB, Consensus Economics, Reuters.

**Figure 11** Long-term inflation expectations in the euro area

remained under control, both during the transition from the national currencies to the euro and even in situations where prices rose especially sharply in the wake of an exogenous shock (see figure 11).[5] This is where the monetary policy of the ECB has been most successful.

The ECB has succeeded, therefore, in anchoring inflation expectations at a level corresponding to its own quantitative target and compatible with price stability. This credibility of the ECB's monetary policy has brought sizeable wealth gains both to the euro area overall and to the individual countries' economies.

Long-term interest rates remained low because of the low uncertainty over the evolution of euro inflation. Both private and public sector borrowers benefited from low long-term rates. As evidenced by the persistent moderation in wage growth, the trade unions trusted the ECB to deliver on its promise of a stable euro. This is not to deny that wage restraint should also be viewed against the background of high unemployment and the competitive pressures arising from globalisation.

---

[5] For example, in the early part of 2001 the rate of increase in the HICP rose to 3.4 per cent (the figure was only revised downwards much later).

From the outset, the ECB has fulfilled what must be regarded as the most important task of a central bank, namely the anchoring of inflation expectations at the level of stability.

The ECB Governing Council directed its monetary policy mission towards that goal from the very beginning. Reaching the objective was aided by announcing a quantitative definition of price stability and an appropriate strategy in the run-up to monetary union. The general public and the markets alike have acknowledged the credibility of the ECB in its resolve and also its ability to fulfil its mandate. The ECB's consistent monetary policy approach and the resultant credibility have spared the euro area economy the volatility that many observers had expected, particularly in light of the high degree of uncertainty at the start of monetary union. Monetary policy has thus made the contribution that is in its power to make towards price stability, growth and employment. The reasons why growth has been unsatisfactory are structural in nature, and therefore lie beyond the control of monetary policy.

There is meanwhile a consensus also among academic economists on the central importance of controlling – or rather, to put it more cautiously, 'guiding' or 'anchoring' – inflation expectations.[6] How the central bank conveys its monetary policy intentions plays an important role in this.[7] Some even go so far as to suggest that, in the final analysis, stability-oriented announcements by the central bank are sufficient to control inflation expectations, which is to say that 'words' can (largely) take the place of 'actions'. I consider this to be a dangerous illusion. Inflation expectations, whether they are ascertained through surveys or derived from financial market prices, always also incorporate expectations about future monetary policy

---

[6] 'Not only do expectations about policy matter, but, at least under current conditions, very little else matters.' M. Woodford, *Interest and Prices* (Princeton, 2003), p. 15.

[7] I shall return to the ECB's communication in more detail later.

actions by the central bank.[8] Inflation expectations will only remain durably anchored at the level of the central bank's target if there is absolute confidence that monetary policy will take whatever action is needed to avoid missing the target. Consequently, in the timing of its decisions, the central bank also has to take account of the constant challenge to its credibility. If, for example, it waits too long before implementing an interest-rate increase that it deems to be fundamentally necessary, it may suffer a loss of confidence. Hesitancy in monetary policy can then only be compensated for by larger interest-rate increases later on, and may therefore be detrimental to the overall economy. Such macroeconomic costs represent the longer-term consequences of a monetary policy that is not sufficiently strongly oriented towards stability, and which could have been avoided by taking timely action.

On numerous occasions, the ECB has been faced with situations where inflation expectations derived from financial market prices rose significantly. However, with the chosen combination of communication and monetary policy decisions, it has always been possible to keep inflation expectations contained. Nonetheless, one cannot overlook the fact that these numbers have for some time been persistently higher than in the early days. It goes without saying that the ECB is keeping this development under close scrutiny and taking it into account in its decision-making.

### Monetary policy-making in the ECB Governing Council

The Maastricht Treaty endowed the Governing Council of the ECB with responsibility for monetary policy and determined its

---

[8] Over the years, the ECB has developed a whole series of instruments to calculate inflation expectations from financial market prices. The most commonly used indicator is still the so-called break-even rate, which is (roughly speaking) the yield differential between nominal and index-linked bonds of the same maturity. For a further discussion, see ECB, 'Measures of inflation expectations in the euro area', *Monthly Bulletin*, July 2006.

composition. At that time, the supreme monetary policy decision-making body in some countries was a committee, as for example in Germany (the Central Bank Council of the Bundesbank) and in the USA (Federal Open Market Committee, FOMC), while other countries' regimes vested full competence in one individual, either the central bank governor (as in the Banca d'Italia) or the finance minister (in the UK, the Chancellor of the Exchequer).

In the beginning, academic economists devoted little attention to this matter. Their models, whether in published papers or in textbooks, assumed more or less implicitly that monetary policy decisions are made by *one* person. Since around the mid 1990s, the picture has changed radically.[9] It would seem appropriate to begin with a brief review of the major relevant conclusions from the academic debate, before going on to examine the actual working of the ECB Governing Council.

### Monetary policy-making by committee

To anticipate the principal finding in much of the literature, there is a broad consensus that in monetary policy-making a *committee structure* is clearly superior to a one-person arrangement.

The main reason for this conclusion is that the wide-ranging opinions and discussion in a group in the end yield better results than does an individual decision-maker.[10] How far these advantages of a committee set-up are realised in practice obviously depends very much on the way in which the committee is structured and its work is organised. It is only in the context of an open discussion that

---

[9] There is now an extensive literature on this topic. See, for example, the bibliographical references in H. Fujiki, 'The monetary policy committee and the incentive problem: a selective survey', Institute for Monetary and Economic Studies, Bank of Japan, *Monetary and Economic Studies*, special edition, 23: S-1 (October 2005).

[10] See, for example, I. Mihov and A. Sibert, 'Credibility and flexibility with independent monetary policy committees', *Journal of Money, Credit and Banking*, 38:1 (February 2006).

differing views can carry weight, and that the better arguments have a chance of gaining acceptance.[11] The substantive quality of the discussion also depends on how well meetings are prepared and organised; here the role of the chairperson is especially important. The group should moreover not be too small to encompass a broad spectrum of opinions, nor should it be too big, as otherwise the discussion process can no longer take place effectively.[12] Finally, numerous papers draw a connection between the discussion and decision-making in the group and transparency vis-à-vis the public.

The disadvantage of a committee structure is often perceived to lie in the 'inertia' in decision-making due to the discussion process. At first sight, this seems obvious – in principle an individual would seem likely to reach a decision more quickly than a group. But on closer examination the conclusion is at best ambiguous. Firstly, it is by no means certain that, especially in difficult situations, an individual – not least on account of the weighty responsibility – does not take even longer to reach a decision. Secondly, the criticism of committees' 'hesitancy' in decision-making frequently relates precisely to complex circumstances where assessing the situation and reaching the necessary decision is anything but straightforward. If it means the careful weighing-up of all arguments, 'hesitancy' may well be of benefit, while 'speediness' will rather increase the risk of making a wrong decision.

One important aspect tends to be neglected in the 'individual vs. group' debate. Central bankers do not just appear from nowhere, but are generally appointed in a political process (see also the discussion in chapter 2, pp. 26–7). Appointments that are purely politically motivated, and which are therefore problematic from the perspective

---

[11] Two 'laboratory experiments' that largely confirm the theory are reported on in A. S. Blinder and J. Morgan, 'Are two heads better than one? An experimental analysis of group vs. individual decisionmaking', NBER Working Paper, no. 7909, September 2000. See also M. King, 'The monetary policy committee: five years on', speech, London, 22 May 2002.

[12] See, for example, A. Sibert, 'Central banking by committee', CEPR Discussion Paper Series, no. 5626, April 2006; Fujiki, 'The monetary policy committee', p. 52.

of society as a whole and of a sound monetary policy, logically have more far-reaching consequences in the case of an individual than in the appointment of one among several committee members.[13] A member of a committee, moreover, is exposed to peer pressure, team spirit, or however one wishes to describe the group's sense of identity. Generally, this self-conception can be presumed to coincide with the central bank's mandate. Newly appointed committee members may even find that, under the influence of the discussion, they shift their initially diverging position and come round to the central bank's 'way of thinking'.[14]

### The ECB Governing Council as monetary policy committee

The first few years' experience of the decision-making process in the ECB Governing Council largely confirms these theoretical considerations, but also helps fill in some more detail in the overall picture.

Again, to begin with the major conclusion: notwithstanding all the scepticism, the ECB Governing Council took the right monetary policy decisions at the right time. This success cannot be put down to luck or coincidence, but is the outcome of shared convictions and efforts directed towards the intended goal.

That does not, and is not intended to, imply that the Governing Council from time to time did not experience strong controversy

---

[13] To some extent, governments have addressed this problem at an early stage, i.e. starting with the process for selecting and appointing senior central bankers. An example is the complex procedure for appointing members of the Bundesbank's Central Bank Council, with responsibilities split between the two chambers of the Federal Government and also the *Länder* governments. In the Statute of the ECB, the stipulation that members of the Executive Board be appointed by common accord is aimed in the same direction.

[14] I have called this shift the 'Becket effect', in reference to the experience of King Henry II of England, who appointed his confidant Thomas à Becket as Archbishop of Canterbury after violent quarrels with the Church. However, in his new function Becket came to regard himself as the upholder of the Church's interests and thus acted contrary to his sovereign's intent. (In the end, Henry ordered the assassination of the man he considered a renegade.)

and persistent differences of opinion. These, however, related not to monetary policy but to areas that impinged on the respective interests of the national central banks. At the start of monetary union, virtually all the national central banks faced as yet unresolved organisational problems. These can be briefly summarised under the simple heading of 'overcapacity'. In most cases, staff numbers far exceeded what was needed to perform the tasks that remained. This owed not so much – if at all – to the loss of monetary policy responsibility; rather, it was above all technical developments in payments and changes in the national banking system (mergers, branch closures, etc.) that had considerably reduced the scale of previous activities. It was very unfortunate that those in charge of the national central banks were confronted with the need for huge structural reforms, not least staff cuts, at the same time as they had in any event forfeited a significant amount of prestige among the general public owing to the loss of monetary policy sovereignty. Where the 'allocation of tasks' had to be decided at the level of the Eurosystem, as in payments or in banknote printing, tensions were inevitable.

It is remarkable how the Governing Council also succeeded in solving problems such as these over time. In particular, the Council deserves huge respect for having reached consensual solutions to two difficult, sensitive issues with a high potential for causing conflict. One was the decision on how the central bank's profits were to be divided up, and the other was the agreement on a model for voting in the Council following an expansion of the monetary union. The second point will be returned to later.

In the area of *monetary policy*, the decision-making process in the ECB Governing Council worked splendidly right from the beginning, much more so than the vast majority of observers, and even insiders, had dared hope. How did it come about that there was in fact no collision of differing 'national' views and interests, and that in reaching its decisions the Governing Council instead always focused on the euro area and on maintaining price stability across the currency area as a whole?

A major element in this success was the way in which the meetings were prepared and organised. In the course of just a few meetings, a model emerged that, while undergoing continuous improvements over time, soon evolved a stable basic structure. From the start of monetary union, the item 'Economic, monetary and financial situation and monetary policy decisions' was on the agenda of every Governing Council meeting. This reflected not least the need for better knowledge of the euro area economy and to gain experience in the orientation of monetary policy for the new currency. Once this had been achieved, the Governing Council switched from a fortnightly to a monthly frequency for the meetings with monetary policy on the agenda. One of the main reasons was that, generally speaking, the data that are of relevance for monetary policy are unlikely to change within a fortnight. If necessary, the Governing Council can alter the agenda, and if need be it can take decisions at any time via telephone conference. One occasion when this famously happened was on 17 September 2001, the Monday following the terrorist attacks of 11 September. The other reason was that the short space of time between 'monetary policy meetings' created uncertainty in the markets, which factored in the possibility of monetary policy decisions being taken. By meeting instead for monetary policy decisions on a monthly basis, the Governing Council satisfactorily addressed both issues.

The item 'Economic, monetary and financial situation and monetary policy decisions' follows immediately after the procedural formalities. For the purposes of *preparation*, the Governing Council members were given extensive documentation sufficiently well in advance. The most important data are contained in the 'Orange Book', so called on account of its original colour. This provides a manageable overview of all the available data. It is updated once a fortnight and is also circulated among the experts at the national central banks. As the data situation improved, the Orange Book was continually expanded. In addition, Governing Council members were sent a so-called 'Briefing Note' on economic developments in the euro area and the rest of the world. This information was regularly supplemented by 'Annexes' containing detailed analyses on a wide range of important topics by the ECB's experts. The discussions in the Governing Council often elicit suggestions for follow-up research in still greater depth. This work plays a major role in picking up on new developments and providing the theoretical underpinnings for the exchanges of opinion in the Governing Council. This documentation was supplemented by detailed overviews on recent monetary policy operations in the market and on financial market developments.

In addition to this material provided on a monthly basis, the members of the Governing Council received substantial documents at less frequent intervals. Chief among these are the reports on the quarterly projections produced twice a year by the Eurosystem experts working together, and twice a year by the ECB's experts. Alongside the baseline scenario, these regularly also contain simulations based on other assumptions, such as higher oil prices or a different exchange rate. On a quarterly basis, the Council members also receive detailed analyses on monetary growth and evaluations based on the Bank Lending Survey and on the survey of experts in the euro area member countries regarding their assessment of the outlook (the Survey of Professional Forecasters).

The meetings of the ECB Governing Council themselves were organised as follows. First of all, the member of the Executive Board responsible for market operations reported on the most recent developments in the financial markets and on the market operations that had been carried out since the preceding meeting.

As the Executive Board member with responsibility for economics and research, I had the task of presenting a detailed report on developments in the euro area economy and the rest of the world, together with an analysis of monetary developments. Once a quarter, this presentation also covered the major results of the projections and relevant aspects from the documentation circulated in advance. The structure of this report followed that of the monetary policy strategy, which proved to be an extremely useful aid to discussion in the Governing Council and the monetary policy-making process. After the cross-checking of all the information, I ended my presentation with an assessment of the risks to price stability and the conclusion to be drawn with a view to the decision to be taken that day. This task I carried out until the end of my term of appointment in May 2006.

With these reports, and based on the comprehensive documentation provided, the ground was prepared for a discussion in the Governing Council focused on the euro area and the risks to price stability. As was to be expected, participation in this exchange of opinions, which also allowed for spontaneous interjections, depended very much on how difficult it proved to assess the situation and the risks to price stability in the euro area, and to reach the necessary decision. After the monetary policy decision had been taken, the Governing Council discussed and approved the introductory statement with which the President would begin the press conference scheduled for 2.30 p.m. This document is translated into all euro area languages and is meanwhile practically identical with the editorial of the *Monthly Bulletin* to be published in the following week.

In the matter of policy decisions, the ECB Governing Council, as is well known, decided against voting amongst its members and instead followed the *consensus principle*. Strange misconceptions still abound today as to what this method involves. This may be partly related to the fact that the term 'consensus' has largely negative connotations. Drawing parallels with the kind of 'consensus democracy' that is supposed to prevail in Germany in particular creates the impression of a method that, after virtually endless discussions, leads nowhere, or at best to unsatisfactory compromises. Moreover, equating 'consensus' with 'unanimity', as is frequently done, is purely and simply a misinterpretation.

The fundamental misunderstanding regarding the consensus principle was revealed, for example, in the following (contradictory) commentaries. When the Governing Council lowered the central bank policy rates by 50 basis points in April 1999 and then raised them by 50 basis points again half a year later, these actions were first of all seen as the expression of a tortuous discussion process in a heterogeneous group that was ultimately forced to make substantial changes to interest rates. When at a later stage 25 basis point changes were decided on, this was deemed to be the expression of a timid policy, again typical of such a group that finds it hard to decide on large interest rate changes.

The ECB may perhaps have failed to make it clear that consensus-based decision-making by no means implies waiting until the very last member of the Governing Council is in full agreement with the decision. Consensus as practised by the Governing Council means, formally speaking, no more and no less than that at the end of the discussion, in which each member has been able to express his or her opinion and thus the preferences for the policy decision to be taken are all clearly on the table, the chair person formulates the group will as a decision by the Governing Council. Consensus is established at the end of a Governing Council meeting that, firstly, takes its place in the unbroken line of previous meetings and, secondly, has been very thoroughly prepared and organised with a view to reaching a consensus.

But consensus also means that one or more members who at the time would have preferred a different decision – rather to act later, or less or more strongly (e.g. a 25 instead of a 50 basis point move, or vice versa) – are able to live with the 'consensus', that is, they acknowledge the weight of the arguments in favour of the decision. For the rest, there logically needs to be a general agreement on this way of decision-making – a consensus on the application of the consensus principle.

Accordingly, the consensus principle becomes the foundation of a core element of the ECB's policy. In such a complex currency area – consider only all the different languages – *all* members of the Governing Council need to show active support for the monetary policy vis-à-vis the public. This aspect is – to some degree understandably – overlooked by critics who see the number of Governing Council members (twenty-one as from 2008) as far beyond any conception of an optimal size. Each Governing Council member bears a shared responsibility for a collective decision, and the long-run success of the ECB's monetary policy depends critically on the fact that all the members of the Governing Council uphold and explain monetary policy decisions in public, which also means doing so 'at home', in their respective languages and national environments. The consensus principle plays a hugely important role in this.

Reference has already been made to the preparation of the meetings by means of relevant documentation. In this material, as in the meetings themselves, the monetary policy strategy plays a decisive role. It provides the framework not only for the presentation by the Executive Board member responsible, but also for the ensuing discussion. Without a clearly structured strategy, it would be next to impossible to organise the discussion in such a large group efficiently. Not least because of the two pillars and the cross-checking, individual interjections can be kept relatively brief without giving rise to misunderstandings. Each argument, so to speak, finds its place in the framework of the strategy – whatever its nature and its 'weight'.

At any rate, judging by the way in which the ECB Governing Council has run its meetings under the guidance of the respective chairperson, monetary policy success can on no account be regarded as a happy coincidence but must rather be seen as the goal-oriented response to an unquestionably difficult challenge. An important factor is that the discussions were confidential. This meant that it was also possible to test objections of a rather heuristic nature that do not necessarily expect to gain approval. It is precisely such frank and open debate that is needed in order to take the best possible decision under the given circumstances. In this connection, it was very important with a view to reaching a consensus that, in the report and conclusions presented by the Executive Board member responsible, a basis had already been established that could then be tested by discussion in the Governing Council. This procedure ensured that consensus was not reached too quickly but – depending on how difficult it was to assess the situation and the risks to price stability – was first of all tested in critical debate. This method of organising the meetings of the ECB Governing Council worked very well right from the beginning.

Naturally, it also involved a process of learning in order to evolve a common approach from among the differing behaviours and traditions of the individual national central banks. For example, the Governing Council had to decide whether the ECB should publish the experts' macroeconomic projections. Here the very different experiences and practices of the national central banks came into collision. Some, such as the Dutch central bank, had been publishing their forecasts for decades, while others, such as the Bundesbank or the Banque de France, had never done so. Both camps had very respectable reasons for their respective approaches. Here, too, in opting for publication, the Governing Council reached a consensual solution that has undoubtedly stood the test of time.

### Transparency, communication, accountability

Even an independent central bank does not stand apart from, and still less above, the state and society. It must justify its policy vis-à-vis the responsible authorities and the public, and to do that it needs to explain it. The central bank's communication to that end is not just a duty, however, but also offers an opportunity to influence expectations and thereby increase the probability of implementing policy successfully. And in communicating the central bank's monetary policy and its assessment of the economic situation and the outlook, the media also have a key role to play.

For a *new* institution, the related challenges are all the weightier. From the very beginning, we were aware that:

- The success of the ECB overall and its monetary policy in particular would hinge very critically on how it handled its *communication*. In such a heterogeneous currency area, with so many languages and such different media structures, this is an enormous challenge.
- *Transparency* in monetary policy-making was the most important requirement.
- Especially in view of its independent status, the ECB needed to be held *accountable*, *de jure* chiefly to the European Parliament, and *de facto* to those it ultimately served, namely the citizens of the euro area.

### The ECB's communication

How did the ECB meet this challenge? As I have already emphasised, the ECB Governing Council had prepared the ground in important ways in the run-up to monetary union. The information provided to the public on the monetary policy strategy in October 1998 had been a major step in this direction: even before taking over responsibility, the Governing Council had been fully transparent in communicating how it intended to pursue monetary policy. By quantifying the price stability objective, it had given a commitment to the public that established a duty of accountability for the future.

This announcement was soon followed by concrete measures that set new standards for central bank communication. The central element in communicating monetary policy decisions is the (normally) monthly *press conference* held by the President and

Vice-President. This is preceded by the immediate announcement of the Governing Council's policy decision – which is nowadays taken for granted.[15] The President's *introductory statement* explains the assessment of the situation and of the risks to price stability, and the reasons underlying the policy decision just taken. The monetary policy strategy provides the logical framework for the structure of the press release, thereby making the arguments easier to follow.

The procedure and the content of the introductory statement do not differ in any substantial way from the announcements made by other major central banks.[16] The ECB need not fear comparison in matters of transparency. The practice of the ECB Governing Council does, however, have one marked advantage that cannot be too highly rated: the information provided by the ECB is extremely timely, which means that the ECB is able to explain the reasons underlying its decisions virtually in 'real time'. This communication strategy enables the ECB to avoid a problem that increases as the publication lag lengthens. If there is a significant delay in providing information on the assessment of the situation and the reasons for the policy decision, a tricky information problem can arise. Announcing the decision in 'real time' produces an immediate market impact. By contrast, an *ex post* explanation no longer necessarily coincides with the public's assessment of the situation at the time the decision itself was announced. Hence a delay in providing information can trigger volatility in the financial markets that does not arise if communication is timely. This inherent advantage in the ECB's approach is further strengthened by the fact that the President is prepared to take questions from the media so soon after the end of the Governing Council's meeting.

---

[15] The ECB thus followed from the outset a practice that other major, long-established central banks had in some cases introduced only a few years earlier.

[16] From among the wealth of literature on this topic, see, for example, A. Blinder, Ch. Goodhart, Ph. Hildebrand, D. Lipton and Ch. Wyplosz, *How Do Central Banks Talk?* (Geneva, 2001).

It is difficult to comprehend why the ECB's communication policy should nonetheless have met with at times harsh criticism, especially in the early stages.[17] Part of the reason may be that the ECB entitled its explanatory document 'Introductory statement' (to the press conference) and not 'Minutes'. As already mentioned, there is little recognisable difference in terms of content between the ECB document and what is published by other central banks as 'Minutes'. The difference would seem to be primarily one of semantics. 'Introductory statement' sounds less enticing than 'Minutes', which suggests a kind of verbatim account of what went on at the meeting. Reading the minutes is, it would appear, as informative as actually being there, and thus minutes seemingly make for full transparency.

Not that any central bank claims that this is so. Minutes are carefully drafted documents that undergo what may be a difficult and protracted internal review process.[18]

The fact that the ECB is able to publish its explanations with such little delay is moreover also a reflection of the high degree of consensus within the Governing Council. If there were major disagreement on fundamental monetary policy issues, it would scarcely be

---

[17] See for example W. H. Buiter, 'Alice in Euroland', CEPR Policy Paper, no. 1 (April 1999), p. 4: 'The lack of openness, transparency and accountability written into the statutes of the ECB and reinforced by the ECB's own operating procedures could yet undermine the viability of the whole enterprise' (with further references). (On p. 13 he continues: 'Dr Issing, in his emerging role as enforcer for the ECB Opaqueness Squad . . .'.)

See also my riposte: O. Issing, 'The Eurosystem: transparent and accountable, or Willem in Euroland', CEPR Policy Paper, no. 2 (April 1999). Both articles subsequently appeared in the *Journal of Common Market Studies*, 37:2 and 37:3 (1999).

[18] At the FOMC meeting of 27 and 28 January 2004, the discussion on whether the time lag before publication of the minutes should be reduced from six weeks to three (which was in fact done) elicited the following objections: 'Some members expressed concern, however, that accelerated release of the minutes might have the potential to feed back adversely on the deliberations of the Committee and on the minutes themselves. The members also emphasized the importance of allowing sufficient time for them to review and comment on the minutes and for reconciling differences of opinion among the members of a large and geographically dispersed committee' (published in the minutes (!) of that meeting). Available at: www.federalreserve.gov/FOMC/minutes/20040128.htm.

possible to present the 'Introductory statement' so soon after the end of the meeting.

The ECB follows up these explanations just one week or so later with the extensive analysis in its *Monthly Bulletin*. Taken together, the prompt statement and the detailed report present a comprehensive picture. The monetary policy strategy provides the framework for consistency in communication both between the two publications and over time. With articles published in the *Monthly Bulletin* covering a broad range of topics – well beyond the sphere of monetary policy[19] – the ECB helps to foster a deeper understanding of the euro area economy and also contributes to the academic debate on important topics.

### Disclosure of voting records?

In actual fact, what excites critics of the ECB's communication policy most is that it does not disclose the *voting records* behind its policy decisions. This line of criticism was espoused not least by a group of MEPs. As explained earlier, in reaching its monetary policy decisions the ECB works on the consensus principle. Thus there is no voting at all. This method has stood the test of time, and one can see no good reason why the Governing Council should be obliged to abandon what is held to be a correct and advantageous approach to policy-making.

Disclosing who voted which way casts the spotlight on the personal decision of individual committee members. There may be sound reasons for this, chiefly relating to the question of individual responsibility. But this is precisely where such an approach is dangerous. Personalising decisions, which the media in particular are understandably inclined to do, risks focusing the public's attention more on the process of decision-making and on individual opinions

---

[19] As can be seen from a glance at the list of titles (at the back of every *Monthly Bulletin*).

than on the actual outcome of the meeting and the relevant economic arguments. Individual members would find it hard to avoid
the public discussing why they voted the way they did and not with
the majority (or the minority, as the case may be), why they 'changed
sides' (or not) compared with the previous meeting, and so on.
Debates of this kind might well prove counterproductive and
increase uncertainty over the future course of monetary policy.

In the case of the ECB there is a particular, and particularly important, additional reason. In a European monetary union that meanwhile comprises fifteen member countries, and with fifteen national
central bank governors in the supreme decision-making body, any
identification of persons in connection with monetary policy decisions would be absolutely bound to take on a 'national' tint.
Whatever considerations might have conditioned a national central
bank governor's vote, they would inevitably be open to interpretation as being an expression of national preferences or, conversely, as
being, for example, out of line with the national government's position.[20] Efforts by the Governing Council member concerned to set
the record straight, even if successful, would lead to long-drawn-out
public debate, triggering further explanations by other committee
members, and would tend to confuse rather than clarify the situation.
How, under such conditions, could the ECB Governing Council ever
hope to be acknowledged as a body consciously obligated under its
sovereign mandate always and exclusively to safeguard price stability
in the euro area as a whole? How, in such an environment, could *all*
members of the ECB Governing Council hope convincingly to
uphold the monetary policy decisions taken vis-à-vis the public?
Ultimately, there would be a high risk of one or other of the national
central bank governors voicing criticism of the ECB's monetary
policy 'at home'.

---

[20] On this question, see S. C. W. Eijffinger and M. Hoeberichts, 'Central bank accountability and transparency: theory and some evidence', *International Finance*, 5:1 (2002).

In such a situation, the conduct of individual governors in the Governing Council and the monetary policy of the ECB in general would almost inevitably be drawn into the political – and ultimately party-political – debate. Political pressure on individual governors would be bound to ensue. It would then be far from easy to maintain a 'neutral' stance – that is, neither to yield to the pressure nor to counter it by steering policy 'in the opposite direction' – and also to demonstrate this convincingly vis-à-vis the public. Such controversies make it much harder to pursue an appropriate monetary policy oriented solely towards fulfilment of the mandate. Public slanging matches are highly unlikely to foster confidence in the central bank and the credibility of its monetary policy.[21]

Such reasons make the ECB's reservations regarding the disclosure of voting records only too understandable. Nor does the suggested 'compromise', whereby the ECB should 'dispense with naming names and just publish the bare numbers', constitute a solution – rather, it would be a trap. Media interest in finding out who was on which side of the published voting records would be overwhelming. There would be various ways of achieving this. Were a Governing Council member to be suspected (rightly or wrongly) of being in one camp or the other in the vote, a public justification would almost inevitably surface sooner or later, whether deliberately or by mistake. Repeated probing of this kind would, however, rob the practice of disclosing anonymous voting numbers of its *raison d'être*. In my opinion, therefore, this would not be a sustainable solution but only

---

[21] It is obviously in the interest of the media not only to uncover differences of opinion but also to exaggerate them. To take just one example: under the headline 'Euro fall blamed on confusing remarks', an article in the *Financial Times* of 29 February 2000 reported on remarks made in public by the then Vice-President of the ECB, Christian Noyer, and by Klaus-Dieter Kühlbacher, 'senior member of Germany's Bundesbank'. As a member of the Central Bank Council of the Bundesbank, the latter was in no way involved in the monetary policy of the ECB, as was generally known. Therefore, there could not have been any 'confusing remarks' from the body with sole responsibility in the matter.

an unsteady and highly disadvantageous interim stage on the way to full, that is to say named, disclosure of voting records.

### Transparency and communication[22]

One aspect of general relevance that is usually entirely overlooked relates to the *feedback* from the mode of communication to the process of monetary policy discussion and decision-making: one should, in fact, not just bear in mind the public impact of the central bank's communication but also examine whether there are not also effects that run in the opposite direction.

Can one simply assume that a person's voting behaviour is completely unaffected by the knowledge of the subsequent disclosure? Might it not even be the case that a person will vote one way and not the other precisely because they know that it will be made public afterwards? A wide variety of motivations may be in play here – after all, central bankers too are only human: an urge to raise one's profile, in order to stand out from the 'herd'; or a tendency towards conformity, because one does not wish to be an outsider? Particular combinations of factors may further increase the complexity of such potential feedback effects. To take just one example: might not the chairperson counter the risk of being outvoted by siding (against their own personal conviction) with the likely majority? But if the chair is outvoted, subsequent meetings will be coloured not least by the public's waiting to see whether or not the scenario occurs again. Against this backdrop, a committee member may possibly not wish to weaken the chair's position by voting a certain way. But in an extreme case, might there not even be motives for weakening the position of a disagreeable chairperson by this means?

---

[22] On the various aspects (and for further bibliographical references), see O. Issing, 'Communication, transparency, accountability: monetary policy in the twenty-first century', *Federal Reserve Bank of St Louis Review*, 87:2, part 1 (March/April 2005), pp. 65–84.

These may all be hypothetical instances. They are intended only to illustrate that the feedback effect of communication on the central bank itself should not be neglected. This can be clearly seen from another, perfectly realistic case.

If the discussions by the decision-making body are recorded and subsequently published, this has a serious impact on the way in which the meeting is conducted. The members of the committee can scarcely fail to have the later publication in their minds. As a result, they may desist from making provocative statements – not that these need in any way reflect the opinion of the speaker, but they may at times be invaluable for a fruitful debate. Individual committee members will almost exclusively read from well-formulated prepared statements that in the later release will stand out agreeably from spontaneous interjections.[23] Such conditions are not exactly conducive to frank, high-quality discussion.

Naturally, such considerations do not alter the fact that in a democracy a central bank has to justify and substantiate its decisions vis-à-vis the public. It has a duty of transparency. But what exactly does that mean?

*Transparency* is sometimes understood as a duty to disclose all available information immediately, fully and unrestrictedly. Not for nothing are rankings established where a central bank is placed higher in the table, the more information it makes available on its analyses, decision-making processes, etc.[24] On this view, therefore, any selection of information or retention of knowledge – or of an admission of ignorance – would violate the principle of transparency.

This call for 'see-through' central banks needs only to be taken to its logical conclusion to show that it is illusory. Unless every meeting,

---

[23] Former Fed Governor Laurence H. Meyer describes his disappointment at experiencing exactly this in FOMC meetings: L. H. Meyer, *A Term at the Fed: An Insider's View* (New York, 2004), p. 39.

[24] See, for example, S. C. W. Eijffinger and P. M. Geraats, 'How transparent are central banks?', *European Journal of Political Economy*, 22:1 (2005).

and every preparatory meeting, and so on, is made *completely* transparent – maybe by televising them? – what is possible in terms of information is always going to be less than what unlimited transparency implies. This approach will, at any rate, not yield any useful answer to what is a difficult question.

Upholding the principle of transparency can only mean making available all the information that is relevant and hence suited to help the central bank fulfil its mandate, and is consequently in the public interest.[25] The central bank has an obligation to provide such information, and the public has an entitlement to it.

A discussion of monetary policy communication and transparency that starts in the abstract, without reference to the actual task of the central bank, is bound to lead one astray. *Transparency is not an end in itself.* A central bank is not established with the primary aim of communicating with the public. Its mandate derives either directly from the monetary system, as for example under the gold standard, or is laid down by legislation, as has become necessary in times of the paper standard. Nowadays, the mandate is, either solely or in combination with other objectives, to keep the value of money stable, or inflation low. The central bank is in this sense the agent and society its principal, and to facilitate the fulfilment of its mandate the central bank is today mostly endowed with independent status. The central bank is essentially accountable first and foremost for the fulfilment of its mandate. Consequently, transparency is subordinate to the actual task.

Communication has an important role to play in this. Monetary policy can only set the central bank interest rates, and hence can

---

[25] The question of the optimal degree of transparency is increasingly being addressed in the academic literature. See, for example, the special issue 'Transparency, communication and commitment' (March 2007) of the *International Journal of Central Banking* with the contributions by C. E. Walsh, P. M. Geraats, A. H. Kara, M. Ehrmann and M. Fratzscher (available at www.ijcb.org/journal/ijcb07q1.htm). For an early treatment, see A. Cukierman and A. H. Meltzer, 'A theory of ambiguity, credibility, and inflation under discretion and asymmetric information', *Econometrica*, 54:5 (1986).

only control the (very) short end of the interest rate spectrum. The influence of monetary policy on the long end depends very largely on the markets' *expectations* of the central bank's policy actions in the future and of future inflation. If the mandate is price stability or low inflation, the evolution of interest rates all along the yield curve, and in addition the decisions of agents in virtually all markets, will hinge on how far the latter expect the central bank to fulfil its mandate.

Efficient and effective communication can play a major part in influencing expectations in line with the central bank's policy. In guiding expectations in the financial markets, two dimensions need to be distinguished. On the one hand, short-term indications can be given in advance of policy decisions. In the simplest case, certain keywords suffice *de facto* to signal the intended future decision to market participants. Such 'code words' are easy to identify and can be quickly factored into market activity; they can reduce or eliminate uncertainty in the period before meetings of the policy-making body; and they can help to avoid short-run mistakes and hence reduce interest rate volatility. On the other hand, in giving such signals the central bank puts itself under pressure to actually deliver on a 'quasi-promise'. If, however, the assessment of the situation has changed owing to new developments, the central bank is faced with a dilemma: by disappointing expectations it could trigger market disturbances even if it can adduce convincing reasons for its reassessment. Thus indications of future decisions can only ever be provided by way of a *conditional* promise. Even so, in practice it is extremely difficult to communicate such a reservation with sufficient clarity. The simpler the announcement, the plainer the code, the more difficult it is to make this conditionality clear *ex ante*. Regular recourse to code words also carries the risk that observers will base their assessment of the central bank's policy intentions solely on them. Such shorthand, however, can never be a substitute for thorough study of the central bank's detailed communication.

If the communication is regarded as an unconditional (largely, at any rate) announcement of future decisions, the markets (financial markets, foreign exchange market) will reflect ('price in') such expectations.[26] Obviously, the risks of a strategy whereby announcements take the place of concrete action become all the greater as the time horizon over which it is aimed to influence expectations lengthens.

On no account should a central bank set out to unsettle the markets or even to mislead them as to its true intentions. The world is uncertain enough, and it cannot be the intention of a central bank to create additional uncertainty. This would cost the economy dear in terms of higher volatility and higher risk premia, and ultimately lower growth and employment.

If monetary policy is pulled one way or the other by the markets, it runs the risk of losing sight of its objective. Monetary policy operates through its impact on the financial markets, and the participants in these markets are directly affected by monetary policy decisions. They may pay a heavy price if they misjudge monetary policy actions. Quite understandably, therefore, market praise and censure are a constant accompaniment to monetary policy. Central banks may consequently be tempted to accord market responses a greater weight than is warranted by their 'transmission channel' role.

In its communication, the ECB has endeavoured to find a suitable answer to these challenges. The President's 'Introductory Statement' and press conference are an efficient and effective instrument for guiding short-term expectations. At the same time, this communication is integrated into the monetary policy strategy, which looks further ahead, towards the risks to price stability over the medium to long term. The *Monthly Bulletin* is the communication tool that ensures consistency between the short-term guidance of

[26] See also D. L. Kohn and B. P. Sack, 'Central bank talk: does it matter and why?', Federal Reserve Board Finance and Economics Discussion Series, no. 55 (Washington, DC, 2003).

expectations for upcoming decisions and the longer-term orientations of monetary policy that arise out of the strategy.

Finally, in its communication the central bank has to bear in mind that the information it 'transmits' is picked up by a wide variety of 'receivers'. Clearly, the content of the central bank's 'message' should not differ according to who receives it; but on the other hand, if it is to be successful, communication needs to vary the instruments it uses.[27] The ECB recognised this problem at an early stage and has developed various means of communication.[28] At the start, the press conference and *Monthly Bulletin* were the instruments to hand, aimed at the media, market participants, bank experts, etc. The ECB has put a great deal of effort into fostering dialogue with academic economists (see pp. 186ff). After lengthy and – not least on account of the complexity of the single currency area – extensive preparatory work, the Eurosystem has developed an 'information kit' as an educational tool for the younger generation.[29]

Transparency and accountability are the essential counterpart to the independence of the central bank, but at the same time they are, given appropriate communication, instrumental in the successful implementation of monetary policy. These principles are inter-dependent and more or less universal, although their application always needs to be seen against the background of the actual environment.

The ECB has put its communication policy entirely at the service of its price stability mandate. In so doing, it had to take account of the particular conditions of its start as a new institution and the complexity of the euro area. Its approach to communication was a very conscious decision, rejecting demands (above all for the publication

---

[27] Information theory has developed numerous different approaches to this. See D. Kahneman, 'Maps of bounded rationality: psychology for behavioral economics', *American Economic Review*, 93 (2003).

[28] For an overview of the various instruments, channels and target groups and the practice at major central banks, see Issing, 'Communication, transparency, accountability?.

[29] www.ecb.int/ecb/educational/html/index.en.html.

of voting records) that it considered wrong. The ECB's communication continues to face the challenge, and the obligation, of convincing the public that its chosen approach is fit and proper. Initial empirical studies do indeed confirm that the ECB need not fear comparison with other, established central banks.[30] Not a bad outcome for such a young institution, one which moreover has to formulate monetary policy under inordinately more difficult conditions.

## Monetary policy and the exchange rate

### Fundamental significance of the exchange rate regime

One of the most important economic policy decisions at the macro level concerns the choice of *exchange rate regime*. This can best be illustrated by looking at the two extremes of a fixed and a floating exchange rate respectively. If a country fixes, or pegs, the exchange rate of its currency to that of another country, this has serious consequences for monetary policy in particular. Given full convertibility, such a *fixed exchange rate system* can only mean that the institution responsible, generally the central bank, must intervene in the foreign exchange market whenever the market rate threatens to diverge from the fixed rate, or parity.[31] Essentially, this obligation to intervene implies that monetary policy must be geared to stabilising the exchange rate. The consequence for the orientation of monetary policy is as obvious as it is serious: monetary policy-making cannot be directed, or at least not primarily, towards the achievement of a domestic objective such as price stability.

---

[30] M. Ehrmann and M. Fratzscher, 'Communication and decision-making by central bank committees: different strategies, same effectiveness?', ECB Working Paper, no. 488 (May 2005), ECB, *Monthly Bulletin*, April 2007.

[31] In reality, the market rate is in most cases allowed to fluctuate within certain bounds. This does not alter the principle of the central bank's obligation to intervene. The same considerations apply if the currency is linked to a metal (such as under the gold standard) or the price of a basket of commodities (commodity-reserve currency).

If, in contrast, the market is left to determine the exchange rate, and the central bank therefore has no obligation to intervene, it can in principle direct its policy measures towards fulfilling a domestic mandate. Only with a *flexible (floating) exchange rate* is the central bank able to achieve a domestic objective (generally speaking, the objective of price stability).[32]

The choice of exchange rate regime is of central importance for monetary policy and also for the place of the central bank in the macroeconomic policy framework. If a fixed exchange rate system is chosen, this ultimately means no less than that, even if it may continue to exist *de jure*, the independence of the central bank exists *de facto* only on paper, in that its obligation to intervene in the foreign exchange market fundamentally robs the central bank of its sovereignty over monetary policy-making.[33]

The same considerations as for an individual country also apply to the currency and the central bank of a monetary union. Hence, as regards the position of the ECB and its monetary policy, a pivotal role is played by the arrangements governing exchange rate policy responsibility, and in particular by the exchange rate regime.

According to Article 111 (1) of the Treaty, 'the Council may, acting unanimously on a recommendation from the ECB or from the Commission, and after consulting the ECB in an endeavour to reach a consensus consistent with the objective of price stability, after consulting the European Parliament . . . conclude formal agreements on an exchange-rate system for the ecu in relation to non-Community currencies'.[34]

---

[32] In the real world mixed forms of these two basic types of exchange rate regime dominate. Depending on how far the fixed or floating element dominates, the room for manoeuvre of monetary policy is restricted to a greater or lesser extent.

[33] Thus, in the years before the changeover to a floating rate regime in March 1973, the Bundesbank at times became a kind of conversion agent for US dollar inflows. Central bank money in D-Marks was created almost exclusively via the purchase of foreign currency.

[34] At the time the Treaty was passed, the (potential) name for the European currency was still 'ecu'.

Chief among the provisos mentioned is undoubtedly that of *unanimity* in the Council; it is of the utmost importance in ensuring that the conditions for a (price) stability-oriented monetary policy are maintained. In the context of the Intergovernmental Conference in late 2000 an initiative was launched with the aim of radically reducing the number of cases in which a unanimous decision was required under the Treaty, to be replaced by majority voting. When I heard that this possible list also included Article 111, all my alarm bells started ringing. For a central bank with independent status and a mandate to ensure price stability, approving such an initiative would have been tantamount to institutional self-denial.

The crucial reason for insisting on unanimity, as I see it, is as follows. If a country's accession to monetary union is justified not least by arguing that the independence of the ECB and its mandate can be regarded as an institutional guarantee of the stability of the euro, a switch to majority voting in the choice of exchange rate regime would imply a lasting, fundamental change to the 'contractual basis' for accession – and its justification vis-à-vis parliament and citizens.[35]

As it turned out, the requirement of unanimity in the quoted passage of Article 111 remained in place. Even if for the present – and presumably for quite some time to come – the question of a formal exchange rate regime is purely hypothetical, it remains central to the monetary policy system of the euro area, and we should continue to bear this in mind in the future.

### Monetary policy under a floating regime

The euro area is the world's second largest currency area, and the euro the world's second most important currency. There has therefore never been any serious discussion of pegging the euro to another currency.

---

[35] Such a change might even be challenged in the courts as being unconstitutional.

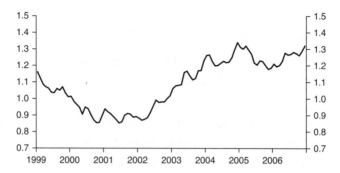

Sources: BIS and ECB. Latest observation: December 2006.
**Figure 12** Nominal exchange rate US dollar/euro 1999–2006

Accordingly, the euro started out as a currency with a flexible exchange rate, and remains so to this day. At its introduction, the exchange rate against the US dollar was 1.1789 dollars per euro. Subsequently, the euro's exchange rate fell sharply and substantially (see figure 12).

This exchange rate weakness posed a difficult challenge for the ECB in two respects. First and foremost, the considerable depreciation might have shaken confidence in the still very new currency. In such circumstances, investors might have demanded a risk premium on securities denominated in euros; as a consequence there would have been a large increase in long-term interest rates. In the event, this did not happen, one important reason being that the ECB never left any room for doubt as to its monetary policy orientation. The communication was consistently clear: in accordance with its mandate, the ECB's Governing Council would do everything to maintain price stability in the euro area. Despite all urging, the ECB also resisted the temptation to indicate a 'critical' level of exchange rate depreciation.[36]

---

[36] As a kind of 'mantra' I always repeated: in the history of money, there is no instance of a major currency with domestic price stability (given stable political conditions) having experienced a lasting depreciation of its exchange rate; it could therefore only be a matter of time before the exchange rate trend reversed. Sooner or later the ECB would be faced with the opposite situation and come under attack for an excessively strong exchange rate.

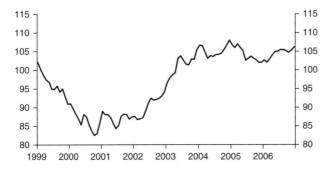

Real effective exchange rates are nominal effective exchange rates deflated by a
weighted average of foreign, relative to domestic, prices or costs. As such they
serve as measures of price and cost competitiveness.

*Sources:* BIS and ECB. Latest observation: December 2006.

**Figure 13** Euro real effective exchange rate 1999–2006 (1999 Q1=100)

Secondly, the exchange rate depreciation made euro area imports
more expensive and thus complicated the maintenance of price stability. What was important in this context was not just the euro's
movement against the US dollar, on which most attention was
focused, but against all currencies of importance for the euro area.
This so-called effective exchange rate showed a similar, albeit less
pronounced, movement (see figure 13).[37]

Once again, the monetary policy strategy (and its early announcement) helped explain the ECB's behaviour and bolster confidence in
its orientation towards price stability. The ECB at no time left any
doubt that the mandate to give priority to maintaining price stability refers to the domestic purchasing power of the euro and excludes
any exchange rate orientation of monetary policy. The development
of the exchange rate is given appropriate consideration within
the economic analysis; its respective level is included among the

Without committing ourselves to an exchange rate forecast, we attempted to
provide guidance through an overview of numerous estimates of the 'equilibrium
exchange rate'. See the article on this topic in the ECB *Monthly Bulletin*, January 2002.

[37] Strictly speaking, one should look at changes in the *real* exchange rate, that is, the
exchange rate adjusted for differences in domestic and foreign inflation. However, during
this period the changes in real and nominal exchange rates were largely identical.

exogenous factors in the projections and hence affects their outcome in terms of prices and growth according to its 'weighting'.

It did not take long for the exchange rate of the euro to rebound towards its initial value. The ECB continued to follow the line it had adopted from the beginning. After the difficult episode of exchange rate depreciation and its monetary policy consistency, the ECB subsequently had no major difficulties in gaining acceptance for its stance.

Given the high importance of the exchange rate and the role of exports in the euro area economy, it was clear from the outset that politicians would use a substantial rise in the exchange rate as a reason to criticise the ECB. One cannot but be concerned if this happens even in times when the economy is strong. In these circumstances, calling for an 'exchange rate orientation' of monetary policy means asking domestic price stability to take a back seat. Apart from the fact that it is unlawful to seek to exert political influence on the ECB, such calls are incompatible with its mandate. The ECB cannot pay them any heed.

It remains to be seen whether policy-makers will avail themselves of the possibility provided for in Article 111 (2) of the Treaty and 'formulate general orientations for exchange-rate policy'. In such an event, the ECB should have no difficulty in defending its standpoint by referring to the last sentence of Article 111 (2): 'These general orientations shall be without prejudice to the primary objective of the ESCB to maintain price stability.'

### Foreign exchange market intervention

By *intervening* in the foreign exchange market, that is, by buying or selling foreign currency, the central bank can try to influence the exchange rate. Purchases of foreign currency per se increase the quantity of central bank money, and sales reduce it. Fundamentally, therefore, such interventions represent monetary policy measures executed via the foreign exchange market. If the exchange rate is basically floating, the central bank will only have recourse to such measures if they serve the purpose of ensuring price stability.

However, the central bank may offset the effect of its exchange market transactions on the quantity of central bank money, in which case one speaks of *sterilised* interventions. To a certain extent, such interventions therefore represent a 'pure' exchange rate policy instrument that in principle has no monetary policy impact. In the economic literature, there is a vast amount of theoretical and empirical research into whether such sterilised interventions – leaving aside very short-term effects – have any lasting influence on the exchange rate.

Without attempting to summarise the findings of so many studies, it can be said that, under certain conditions, some impact cannot be ruled out. There is, however, also the risk that the aimed-for effect does not materialise and that confidence in policy is weakened. The ECB very soon faced the question of whether it should intervene to strengthen the euro exchange rate. As the euro fell ever lower, in September 2000 – with the exchange rate standing at only around 0.84 US dollars – the ECB decided to intervene, that is, to sell foreign exchange (from its reserves) against euros in the market. A crucial factor in this decision was the willingness of the USA to participate in this concerted intervention (together with Japan, the UK and Canada). Accordingly, the press release highlighted the shared concern of the USA (and Japan) about the potential implications of the decline in the euro exchange rate for the world economy. In November 2000 the ECB intervened again, this time acting alone, citing concern about the repercussions of exchange rate weakness on price developments in the euro area as well as on the global economy.

Over and above the question of whether, and under what conditions, interventions in the foreign exchange market (may) produce the desired effect, the complex structure of the euro area makes competency a very important issue. While in the USA and Japan the government (finance ministry) has responsibility for such measures, in the case of the euro the task clearly falls to the ECB.[38] At the same time, the Eurogroup is involved in the opinion-forming process.

## The euro as an international currency

Even before the euro saw the light of day, there was speculation about its role as an *international currency*. It seemed as though a rival to the US dollar was emerging, and, over and above the purely economic aspects, many saw the euro as a kind of European weapon against the superpower USA, whose hegemony was not seldom linked precisely to the dominant position of the American currency.

Viewed objectively and in purely economic terms, there were weighty reasons for expecting that the euro would play an important role in the international monetary system[39] – the same factors that had made individual national currencies into international ones in the past. In normal circumstances, the function of a currency is largely confined to the area of issue, that is, to the state (or group of states) in which it is the legal tender. An *international currency*, in contrast, is one which also has an appreciable monetary role outside this jurisdiction, that is, it is used by foreigners.

In practice, such international currencies have existed throughout history.[40] For example, in the nineteenth century it was the pound sterling that dominated, with London as the financial centre, while later, in particular after the Second World War, the US dollar came to prominence. Occasionally several currencies played a leading role simultaneously. The history of money also teaches us that in most cases currencies changed positions only very slowly, in a long-drawn-out process.

---

[38] See Articles 105 (2) and 111 of the Treaty and Article 3 (1) of the ECB Statute.
[39] On this topic, see O. Issing, *Von der D-Mark zum Euro* (Tübingen: Walter Eucken Institut, 1998); C. F. Bergsten, 'The dollar and the euro', *Foreign Affairs*, 76:4 (1997).
[40] See O. Issing, *Leitwährung und internationale Währungsordnung* (Berlin, 1965).

The position of international currency does not come about by chance, but follows more or less inevitably from a combination of different factors. Leaving aside purely political contexts, such as the relationship between a colonial power and its dependencies, the factors in question are economic ones. These have remained the same throughout history, but their relative weight has varied.

The chief factors are:[41]

1. the depth, breadth and openness of domestic financial markets (in this case, the euro area financial markets)
2. the stability of the currency and confidence in its future stability
3. the size and strength of the domestic economy and its international integration.

Factors (1) and (3) are an expression of the liquidity of the financial instruments denominated in a given currency. They determine the extent to which securities can be bought and sold readily, without incurring particular costs. As the size of an economic area and its international integration (3) increase, so does the scale of commercial relations and hence the desire and also the need to hold assets denominated in the relevant currency and/or to borrow in that currency. Finally, it is obvious that only a currency whose stability is beyond doubt can play an international role in the longer run (2).

Let us begin with the last condition, the need for stability. From the outset, the euro enjoyed the confidence of investors, worldwide. At the same time, the euro area became the world's second-largest single currency area after the USA. Although the integration of individual market segments still has some way to go, the abolition of the national currencies and introduction of the euro created a large international financial market, also in global terms.[42]

---

[41] See, for example, B. P. Hartmann and O. Issing, 'The international role of the euro', *Journal of Policy Modeling*, 24:4, July 2002.

[42] The ECB regularly publishes reports on the position of the euro and its evolution as an international currency. See, for example, ECB, *Review of the International Role of the Euro*, June 2007.

Thus the preconditions were fulfilled for one of the functions of an international currency, namely one in which investors and borrowers from all over the world place assets and take up credit respectively. Generally, one speaks of an *investment currency*.

Within only a short space of time, the euro gained a sizeable market share in certain segments. Table 5 provides the principal figures for the euro as an international currency. The high share of the euro in international loan and deposit markets has meanwhile declined slightly. Its share in daily foreign exchange market trading averaged 39.3 per cent between July 2005 and December 2006. In comparison, the dollar's share of 93 per cent reflects its continued dominance of international payments. Just under half of euro area goods exports and imports are settled in euros. The euro's share in global foreign exchange reserves has risen steadily to stand at 25.8 per cent at the end of 2006. The cumulative net shipments of euro banknotes to destinations outside the euro area, totalling 60 billion euros at December 2006, illustrate the growing volume of euro cash in circulation outside the single currency area.

Notably on account of its stability, but also because of favourable market conditions, the euro was also attractive for investments by monetary authorities – generally speaking, central banks. In this *reserve currency* role, the euro in practical terms initially superseded the D-Mark, which over time had become the second most important reserve currency after the US dollar. The D-Mark had come to play this role when the US dollar exchange rate weakened appreciably in the 1970s and a growing number of central banks sought an alternative to dollar investments. Meanwhile, the euro is playing an increasing part in the diversification of foreign exchange reserves by many central banks. The euro is – albeit a long way behind the US dollar – the world's second most important reserve currency. Table 6 shows the euro's share in the official foreign exchange reserves of various groups of countries. In the 'All countries' group, the share of the euro has increased somewhat since

TABLE 5: *The euro as an international currency*

| Share of the euro in: | Date | Date |
|---|---|---|
| Narrowly defined stock of international debt securities | 2006 Q4: 31.4% | 2005 Q2: 33.7% |
| All cross-border loans | 2006 Q4: 19.8% | 2005 Q1: 21.2% |
| Cross-border loans from euro area banks to non-bank borrowers outside the euro area[a] | 2006 Q4: 16.7% | 2005 Q1: 20.2% |
| All cross-border deposits | 2006 Q4: 21.6% | 2005 Q1: 24.5% |
| Cross-border deposits of non-euro area non-banks in banks outside their country of residence excluding the euro area[a] | 2006 Q4: 18.0% | 2005 Q1: 18.0% |
| Daily foreign exchange turnover (settled with CLS (Continuous Linked Settlement))[b] | 07/2005–12/2006 (average) 39.3% | 07/2004–06/2005 (average) 40.7% |
| Settlement/invoicing of goods exports from selected euro area countries to non-euro area countries | 2005: 39%/62% | 2004: 44%/63% |
| Settlement/invoicing of goods imports of selected euro area countries from non-euro area countries | 2005: 34%/56% | 2004: 41%/61% |
| Global foreign exchange reserves (at current exchange rates) | End 2006: 25.8% | End 2004: 24.9% |
| Cumulative net shipments of euro banknotes to destinations outside the euro area | Dec. 2006: €60 billion | Jun. 2005: €55 billion |

[a] At constant fourth-quarter 2006 exchange rates. [b] Given the convention of counting both sides of an exchange market trade, percentages sum to 200%. Thus the share of the euro in total turnover is half the percentage reported in the table.
*Source:* ECB, *Review of the International Role of the Euro,* June 2007.

December 2004 (from 24.9 to 25.8 per cent) as that of the US dollar has fallen.

Naturally, in central banks' decisions on how to invest their exchange reserves, just as in private investors' investment decisions,

TABLE 6: *Official foreign exchange reserves: currency shares*[a]

|  | Dec. 04 | Dec. 05 | Mar. 06 | Jun. 06 | Sep. 06 | Dec. 06 |
|---|---|---|---|---|---|---|
| **All countries** | | | | | | |
| US dollar | 65.8 | 66.7 | 66.5 | 65.5 | 65.8 | 64.7 |
| Euro | 24.9 | 24.2 | 24.6 | 25.4 | 25.1 | 25.8 |
| Japanese yen | 3.9 | 3.6 | 3.3 | 3.2 | 3.1 | 3.2 |
| Pound sterling | 3.4 | 3.6 | 4.0 | 4.2 | 4.3 | 4.4 |
| Other currencies | 2.0 | 1.8 | 1.6 | 1.7 | 1.7 | 1.8 |
| **Industrialised countries** | | | | | | |
| US dollar | 71.5 | 73.6 | 74.0 | 72.9 | 73.1 | 71.9 |
| Euro | 20.8 | 19.0 | 19.1 | 19.8 | 19.6 | 20.4 |
| Japanese yen | 3.6 | 3.4 | 3.5 | 3.6 | 3.5 | 3.5 |
| Pound sterling | 1.9 | 2.1 | 2.1 | 2.3 | 2.3 | 2.5 |
| Other currencies | 2.3 | 1.8 | 1.4 | 1.4 | 1.4 | 1.6 |
| **Developing countries** | | | | | | |
| US dollar | 60.2 | 61.0 | 60.6 | 59.9 | 60.4 | 59.7 |
| Euro | 29.0 | 28.5 | 29.0 | 29.5 | 29.2 | 29.6 |
| Japanese yen | 4.1 | 3.7 | 3.1 | 2.9 | 2.8 | 2.9 |
| Pound sterling | 4.9 | 4.9 | 5.5 | 5.6 | 5.7 | 5.8 |
| Other currencies | 1.8 | 1.9 | 1.9 | 1.9 | 2.0 | 2.0 |

[a] Percentage share of total disclosed holdings.
Source: ECB, *Review of the International Role of the Euro*, June 2007.

a central role is played not just by confidence in the stability of the currency, but also in political and economic conditions. Worries that the particular complexity of the euro area and its progressive expansion might have a negative impact on investor behaviour were not borne out.

The euro also acts as an *anchor currency*. More than fifty countries, admittedly including a large number of small states, use the euro as a stability anchor for their own monetary policy. At the limit, some of them, such as San Marino or the Vatican State, do not have a currency of their own. Kosovo and Montenegro have decided not to issue their own currency and to use the euro instead. Such cases are referred to as 'euroisation', whereby the adoption of the currency rests on a unilateral decision by the country concerned. As with the

US dollar ('dollarisation'), such decisions lie outside the control of the central bank issuing the currency.

The forms taken by currency pegs range from currency boards through participation in the European exchange rate mechanism (ERM) to arrangements in which the euro has a significant weight in the respective currency basket (as for example in Russia). Table 7 illustrates the regional character of the euro's role as anchor currency. Half of the EU countries that have not yet joined the euro area participate in ERM II, while the other EU countries, like the heterogeneous group of other countries listed in the table, have adopted a wide spectrum of exchange rate regimes.

Pegging the exchange rate to another currency inevitably entails a commitment to intervene in the foreign exchange market if the market rate threatens to move outside the agreed band. Hence the central banks concerned will hold a substantial portion of their exchange reserves in the relevant currency, in this case the euro.

Alongside this quasi-official role of the euro, the amount of euro *cash in circulation* outside the euro area has become quite considerable. Estimates suggest that it accounts for some 10–20 per cent of the total.[43]

A further role is that of *transaction currency*, that is to say, the currency's use in foreign exchange market transactions. Not least because many currencies cannot be exchanged directly, or not at an acceptable cost, such transactions are generally carried out using a third ('transaction') currency. Here, too, the euro takes second place to the US dollar.

Finally, foreign trade transactions are frequently invoiced not in the domestic currency but in an international currency. As an *invoicing currency* the euro has to date played a largely regional role. The US dollar remains the predominant currency of denomination in, for example, the international commodity markets.

[43] On the evolution of the use of euro cash outside the single currency area, see ECB, *Review of the International Role of the Euro*, June 2007. At the end of 2006 the figures for the euro were comparable with those for the US dollar.

TABLE 7: *Countries with exchange rate regimes linked to the euro*[a]

| Region | Exchange rate regimes | Countries |
|---|---|---|
| European Union (non-euro area) | ERM II | Cyprus, Denmark, Estonia, Latvia, Lithuania, Malta, Slovakia |
| | Euro-based currency boards | Bulgaria |
| | Peg arrangements with fluctuation band based on the euro | Hungary |
| | Managed floating with the euro as reference currency | Czech Republic, Romania |
| | *Pro memoria*: Independent floating | Poland, Sweden, United Kingdom |
| Candidate and potential candidate countries | Unilateral euroisation | Montenegro |
| | Euro-based currency boards | Bosnia and Herzegovina |
| | Peg arrangements or managed floating with the euro as reference currency | Croatia, FYR Macedonia, Serbia |
| | *Pro memoria*: Independent floating | Albania, Turkey |
| Others | Euroisation | Kosovo, European microstates, French territorial communities |
| | Peg arrangements based on the euro | CFA Franc Zone, French overseas territories, Cape Verde, Comoros |
| | Peg arrangements and managed floats based on the SDR and other currency baskets involving the euro (share of the euro) | Seychelles (37.7%), Russian Federation (40%), Libya, Botswana, Morocco, Tunisia, Vanuatu |

[a] As at 1 January 2007. As of 1 January 2008, the monetary union also includes Malta and Cyprus.

*Source:* ECB, *Review of the International Role of the Euro*, June 2007.

The various functions of an international currency are mutually complementary. Where those of anchor currency and reserve currency are combined, the connection is obvious. But it also makes sense for exporters and importers to hold transaction balances in a currency in which their foreign business is denominated. Similar considerations apply to borrowing and to investment in financial assets. The functions of an international currency thus clearly display properties of a so-called 'network good', that is, the individual functions promote each other. This also explains why large changes in the position of international currencies occur only gradually (in other words, the 'incumbent' has advantages over the 'challenger').

From the beginning, the ECB left no doubt as to its *neutral* position with regard to the role of the euro as an international currency: it would neither seek to promote this role, nor do anything to counteract it. The process whereby the euro establishes itself as an international currency is therefore market-determined. The preference of market participants, be they official (central banks) or private, determines the extent to which they will use the euro as an international currency.

Nor has the ECB become involved in speculation about the future of the euro in the international monetary system. At present, the US dollar continues to play the dominant role in the global monetary and financial system. Nonetheless, it has long since been impossible to overlook the increased importance of the euro, whereas the Japanese yen, globally speaking, continues to occupy only a minor position. There is little indication that the Japanese currency will gain significantly in importance. To that extent, one may say that the international monetary system is bipolar rather than tripolar.

In monetary history, situations with more than one leading currency proved unstable when a marked loss of confidence occurred in one of them, leading to a major restructuring of international portfolios as investors reassessed the position. Herein lies a potential weakness of a 'multi-currency system'. On the other hand, the existence of a second (or third) currency opens up possibilities for diversification that can make the system less vulnerable to crisis.

Being ultimately responsible for the currency, the central bank also has a special responsibility as regards the role its currency plays internationally. It can best fulfil this by maintaining confidence in the stability of its currency. In the final analysis, therefore, national (domestic) and international responsibility are aligned with each other.

## Economic theory and monetary policy practice

I shall never forget that evening in the summer of 1998. Once again, I was discussing the outlines of a possible strategy for the (future) monetary policy of the ECB with a chosen group of economists from the Directorates General for Economics and Research. Looking around, I saw nothing but young faces. Together, we were seeking an answer to open questions. The setting made me blurt out: 'It's like being in a university seminar. But there are two things that make this radically different from an academic exercise. Firstly, time is short, and we need to reach a conclusion soon. Secondly, we need to realise that the success – and, even more so, any failure – of the ECB's monetary policy will have very real repercussions for a huge number of people.' Not for a second will a central banker lose sight of the responsibility entrusted to him or her on being appointed. But there, in that special situation, the linkage between academic theory and monetary policy practice was palpable.

During the last ten to twenty years, economic research has become increasingly important for monetary policy all over the world; more and more, senior positions at central banks are being filled by economists. Beyond the day-to-day business of monetary policy, the ECB was faced with a unique situation. The (future) euro area for which it was mandated to maintain price stability was largely *terra incognita*. There was no blueprint for the introduction of a new currency under these special circumstances. The obvious first step was to take stock of current economic thinking. Zero hour for the ECB as a new central bank was the hour of economics. What insights were relevant, and had they been put to the test in central bank experience? In spite of all our diligence and all our efforts – including in-depth discussions with experts from other central banks and academia – we realised that, while being indispensable in designing a successful monetary policy, economics could not provide a clear, conclusive answer that would relieve the central bank of the need to decide for itself. So we had to discuss all the possible options and weigh up their respective advantages and drawbacks (see in particular chapter 3, section on 'Monetary policy options').

It has become customary to refer to central banking as an 'art'.[44] One reason is that, in making policy, the central bank inevitably has to go beyond what is backed by solid knowledge. The counterpart to this degree of latitude, however, is that central bankers have to take responsibility for the decisions they make.

Economists are generally convinced the results of their research are correct. There is nothing fundamentally wrong with this; on the contrary, it is the major stimulus in the search for knowledge. Economists are interested in the world's problems and are motivated by the idea

---

[44] See the title of the book by R. G. Hawtrey, *The Art of Central Banking*, 2nd edition (London, 1962).

Writing on monetary theory, a well-known economist comes to the following conclusion: 'However, economists should be under no illusion that central banking will ever become a science. Academic critics love to chide central bankers for their lack of a fully articulated doctrine of monetary policy, based on testable – and perhaps even tested – hypotheses. These critics mistake central bankers for what they are themselves, namely teachers and intellectuals. In fact, a good central banker is a doer and a politician, for whom even ambiguity and inconsistency may sometimes serve his purposes . . . This treatise may thus end on a note of humility: However far monetary theory may progress, central banking is likely to remain an art.' J. Niehans, *The Theory of Money* (Baltimore, 1978), p. 294.

On the current state of the debate on the relationship between 'theory and practice' in monetary policy, see C. E. Walsh, 'The contribution of theory to practice in monetary policy: recent developments', in ECB (ed.), *Monetary Policy: A Journey from Theory to Practice. An ECB Colloquium Held in Honour of Otmar Issing* (Frankfurt, 2007).

of finding better solutions. What could be more natural – in the case in point – than to urge the central bank to use models deemed correct by the experts in the field and to criticise practices that deviate from them? Indeed, ongoing critical discussion with academic economists in encounters of every conceivable kind is still indispensable in order constantly to improve monetary policy and to correct mistakes. The fundamental difference between academic and practitioner in monetary policy, however, lies precisely in the *practical application*, in putting the knowledge to use in monetary policy-making. Ultimately, the economist bears no responsibility for the consequences of policy decisions founded on his or her thinking, but the central banker most certainly does. The closer economists get to actual policy with their thinking and their models, the more they should also address questions of practical applicability – especially if they publicly advocate adoption of their approach. One can scarcely say that this is done adequately all of the time, or even most of the time. There have even been cases of economists arguing for practical implementation of a very vague approach – whether laid out in minute detail as a theoretical model or simply outlined verbally – but these need not detain us any further. It is a different matter, however, if, based on theoretical-empirical study, economists set out in concrete terms how they think a central bank should act. In such cases, they cannot duck the question of whether their approach is also practicable, for example insofar as the necessary data are available on a sufficiently timely and reliable basis. Viewed in this light, it is surprising how economists doggedly assign a major role to, for example, the output gap and its changes in numerous models, even though this complex indicator is known to be susceptible to substantial revision.[45]

The ECB has sought contact with academia from the beginning, and large numbers of eminent economists have taken up our invitation. We

[45] A. Orphanides and S. van Norden, 'The unreliability of output gap estimates in real time', CIRANO Working Papers, no. 2001s-57 (Québec, 2001).

have kept up an intensive dialogue in the framework of in-house seminars, discussions in smaller groups and countless one-on-one conversations. It was a personal concern of mine that the ECB as an institution should be open to dialogue in particular with those who criticised our policy. Scarcely a week passed without my staff and myself having an opportunity to engage in such discussions. Nor was the flow of ideas by any means one-way. All of us, myself included, undoubtedly learned a great deal from these contacts; but on numerous occasions economists also told us how fruitful such discussions were for them and how they gave them new ideas for further research.[46]

Even before the start of monetary union, groups of economists had come together with the aim of keeping a critical eye on the ECB's monetary policy. As early as the spring of 1999, the first reports by individual *ECB Watchers Groups* emerged. The ECB was thus faced with the question of how to respond to this 'surveillance'. Maybe just ignore it, at least in public? When one of these groups invited me to take part in a discussion, we had to bear in mind that, on the one hand, the ECB could not discriminate between the individual groups; on the other hand, taking part in a series of events, scattered as they were across the whole euro area, would have severely over-stretched our resources. But nor did we want to create the impression of being unwilling to answer criticism. Moreover, a public event also presented an opportunity to explain our thinking and to publicise it more widely, a key task for a new institution. In collaboration with the *Center for Financial Studies* at Frankfurt University, we found a solution that was unique in the world of central banking. On 17 and 18 June 1999, the first conference on 'The ECB and its Watchers' was held, with discussions centred on the ECB's monetary policy strategy. No fewer than four 'Watchers Groups' were represented at this

---

[46] The large number of renowned economists – not just those contributing papers or acting as panellists – who took part in the colloquium on 16 and 17 March 2007 marking my departure from the ECB was an impressive illustration of the closeness of these contacts.

event.[47] At the end of a long (first) day, I had the opportunity to respond to critical remarks and to set forth our own arguments.

Since then, the conference has been held every year.[48] The list of participants reads like a roll-call of eminent names from academia, the media and banking, and the themes extend across monetary policy and related topics. These conferences have made a major contribution to promoting an understanding of the ECB's monetary policy. They have given the central bank a unique opportunity to discuss its monetary policy with a changing group of representatives from academia and the banking industry.

This direct contact, occasionally – albeit rarely – confrontational, has been very fruitful. By way of a side-effect, these events have also served to spur the intellectual competition between the different groups of researchers. The media representatives, included in the conference programme where relevant topics – such as the central bank's communication – are being discussed, have always reported on the events in detail. For our part, we have repeatedly taken away new ideas which we have then explored further within the ECB.

The Directorate General for Research and its staff not only play a major role in the ECB's in-house research, but also organise the contact with the 'outside world' via a wide range of initiatives such

---

[47] David Begg (Birkbeck College) et al., Centre for Economic Policy Research (CEPR); Jürgen von Hagen (Bonn University) et al., Centre for European Integration Studies (ZEI); Daniel Gros et al., Centre for European Policy Studies (CEPS); Harald Benink (University of Maastricht), Reinhard Schmidt (Frankfurt University) et al., European Shadow Financial Regulatory Committee (ESFRC). Other speakers included Lars E. O. Svensson (Institute for International Economic Studies) on 'Inflation Targeting', John Taylor (Stanford University) on 'Interest Rate Rules', Stefan Gerlach (Bank for International Settlements, BIS), Ignazio Visco (OECD) and Thomas Mayer (Goldman Sachs). The 'Watchers Groups' kept the ECB's monetary policy under surveillance with a series of critical reports. The first to appear were: CEPR, D. Begg et al., 'The ECB: safe at any speed?' (London, 1998); CEPS Macroeconomic Policy Group, 'Macroeconomic policy in the first year of Euroland' (Brussels, 1999).

[48] In 2002 the fourth conference was held in Milan (Bocconi University). The experiment with a different venue was not pursued further, for logistical reasons. The international experts from the media are all stationed in Frankfurt, and it also involved a lot of extra time and money for the representatives of the ECB. The conference held on 7 September 2007, meanwhile, was no less than the ninth such event.

as visitor programmes, seminars and so on. Numerous publications, above all in the Working Paper series, testify to the high productivity of ECB researchers – including those working in other Directorates General, notably Economics.[49]

It took only a few years for the ECB to acquire an outstanding position in the world of economics.[50] Today, scarcely a conference takes place on topics of relevance without representatives of the ECB being invited to attend and contributing important papers.

From the beginning, we were anxious to tap the huge research potential in the *Eurosystem* and to exploit the obvious synergies. Where this was most urgently called for was in a core area of monetary policy, the *transmission mechanism*. No central bank fully knows how its policy actions ultimately affect prices, real activity and employment via the various transmission channels – banks and financial markets, firms and households. For a new central bank and a new currency, there was a lot we did not know, and the uncertainty was correspondingly high. In a network encompassing research staff of the ECB and the national central banks, and with the support of external economists (the Monetary Transmission Network), an extensive amount of work has been carried out over time that has considerably advanced our knowledge of the transmission mechanism of the ECB's monetary policy.[51]

Subsequently, and following the same model, the Eurosystem Inflation Persistence Network was set up. The work of this research group has brought to light a wealth of data on price setting behaviour in the euro area. For example, the analysis of the degree of price

[49] By the end of 2007, over 800 ECB Working Papers had been published, including papers by numerous 'guest' authors who worked on their projects as research fellows at the ECB and/or in cooperation with ECB economists.
[50] The well-known economist Peter Kenen rates the two Directorates General, Economics and Research, among the best in the world of central banking – a notable accolade for such a young institution. See International Monetary Fund, 'Navigating uncharted waters', *Finance and Development* (December 2006).
[51] See I. Angeloni, A. K. Kashyap and B. Mojon, *Monetary Policy Transmission in the Euro Area* (Cambridge, 2003).

rigidity, or flexibility, in the euro area relative to the USA has yielded insights that are of great importance for monetary policy.[52]

There is arguably no other area of policy where academic research plays such a large role as in monetary policy, not least because their independent status means central banks are better positioned to take account of research findings they consider correct and important in their policy-making. This constitutes a great opportunity for the central bank, but at the same time places it under a special responsibility in the way it handles the output of economic research. This is a challenge that the ECB has successfully mastered.

[52] Numerous studies on this subject have been published in the ECB's Working Paper series. See, for example, I. Angeloni, L. Aucremanne and M. Ciccarelli, 'Price setting and inflation persistence – did EMU matter?', ECB Working Paper, no. 597 (March 2006).

FIVE

# The central bank and monetary policy in the EMU framework

Without monetary stability, a stable society of free citizens cannot endure. Not for nothing did Lenin hold that the way to destroy bourgeois society is to debauch the currency.[1] Within European economic and monetary union (EMU), this may apply with even greater justification than within the boundaries of a nation state. After all, the single currency embodies in a special way a commonality of interest among the participants. Only if the euro is stable can it foster a sense of identification; a lack of confidence in the stability of the common currency would also undermine confidence in a 'European community'.

Consequently, the central bank that is responsible for the currency occupies an important position in the structure of the nation state, and all the more so in a monetary union of largely sovereign states. Naturally, the central bank is not alone. It does not operate in a policy vacuum; the effects of its monetary policy depend very much on policy in other areas. Chief among these is fiscal policy. The state

---

[1] As reported, among others, by J. M. Keynes: 'Lenin is said to have declared that the best way to destroy the capitalist system was to debauch the currency . . . Lenin was certainly right. There is no subtler, no surer means of overturning the existing basis of society . . .' (*The Economic Consequences of the Peace*, 1919, chapter 6).

of labour markets, the behaviour of employers and labour, and the intensity of competition in the markets also play an important role. Finally, an overarching question needs to be answered: that of the relationship between monetary union and political union. Is EMU ultimately viable without political union?

## Fiscal and monetary policy in EMU

### The relationship between monetary policy and fiscal policy

The relationship between monetary policy and *fiscal policy* is fundamentally determined by the statutory framework of the public finances. In an extreme case, the central bank is a department of the finance ministry, or is obligated, for example, to finance government deficits as decreed by policy. Such cases are considered irrelevant for present purposes and are therefore left out of account. The Maastricht Treaty expressly prohibits monetary financing and privileged access by the government or public bodies to financial institutions. It grants the ECB independence from political influence.

In the EMU context, the primary question relates to the stabilisation of economic activity. There has been a great deal of controversy among economists over the respective roles or tasks of monetary policy and fiscal policy in this regard. This is not the appropriate place to go any further into this general debate.[2] In what follows, I shall focus exclusively on the specific aspects of EMU.

### Fiscal policy rules in EMU

In the heyday of Keynesianism, fiscal policy was regarded as playing the decisive role in stabilising the economy. Thus, in economic

---

[2] For a brief overview, see O. Issing, 'The role of fiscal and monetary policies in the stabilisation of the economic cycle', in Banco de México, *Stability and Economic Growth: The Role of the Central Bank* (Mexico, 2006).

downturns, the state should increase expenditure, and lower taxes and other contributions, in order to stabilise the economy. This policy of deficit spending was to be offset by corresponding restrictive measures during upswings. In the long run, cyclically induced government deficits and surpluses would largely cancel each other out.

This model has proved to be more or less illusory. Quite apart from the purely technical difficulty of deploying fiscal policy instruments in a timely manner, the mechanisms of the political process stand in the way of such discretionary fiscal policy action. The periodicity of elections restricts the time horizon for fiscal policy action, and the long-term objective of sound fiscal policy is easily lost sight of. The consequence is a tendency towards rising budget deficits and increasing public debt, as was indeed observed in Europe in the 1970s. But if the government deficit rises during an upswing or even at the top of the cycle – if, that is, fiscal policy acts procyclically – major tensions are bound to arise in the interaction with a stability-oriented monetary policy.

In a monetary union, however, the risk of such conflicts between monetary and fiscal policy, with very serious macroeconomic consequences, is even greater than in a nation state. It is easy to see why. In a single currency area, the political benefit from deficit spending (gaining votes) is enjoyed by *national* players, while the potential negative effects in the form of higher interest rates (due to increased government borrowing) are felt by *all* member states. Thus the resistance to deficit spending is reduced, and the propensity to pursue an (inappropriate) expansionary fiscal policy increases – a typical case of what is known as *moral hazard*.

In the consultations on the constitution for the future monetary union, this problem could not be disregarded. On the one hand, a 'European government' with corresponding powers was not an option. The national governments (and parliaments) would basically retain their fiscal policy sovereignty. On the other hand, moral hazard and the danger of individual member states acting in a way that was detrimental to stability had to be avoided if the success of monetary union was not to be put at risk from the outset.

These considerations had informed the Maastricht Treaty. In the first place, Article 103 (1) stipulates that: 'The Community shall not be liable for or assume the commitments of central governments, regional, local or other public authorities, other bodies governed by public law, or public undertakings of any Member State.' This *exclusion of liability* ('*no-bail-out*') is couched in comprehensive terms.[3] Moreover, the Treaty prohibits not only the monetary financing of public institutions (Article 101) but also their privileged access to financial institutions (Article 102).

But were more far-reaching statutory rules needed, or could and should the further disciplining of member states' fiscal policy not be left to the market, that is, the financial markets? There were not a few who wanted to place their trust in such a mechanism. If doubts emerged about the creditworthiness of a sovereign borrower, the interest rates on its debt would increase sharply. With the awareness of this sanctioning mechanism, there would not even be any attempt to pursue an unsound fiscal policy, or, if there were, it would be abandoned at the first sign of rising interest rates.

Two considerations argue against such expectations. Firstly, in a monetary union the *exchange rate risk* associated with denominating sovereign debt in the national currency disappears. All debt is in the common currency, the euro. This removes the decisive sanctioning mechanism that operates via worldwide investors' risk assessment and translates into rising risk premia due to the higher currency risk. Secondly, any risk premia on interest rates in the event of an unsound fiscal policy – as compensation for doubts about a country's solvency – generally remain very limited over an extended period

---

[3] The ongoing debate in the federal state of Germany about the *Finanzausgleich*, the system for revenue equalisation across different levels of government, is an instructive illustration of how important this clause and its absolute credibility are.

of time.[4] But a small rise in interest rates is unlikely to have any significant disciplinary impact on the fiscal policy of the deficit country. Ultimately, were a real crisis to arise where the country's solvency was actually at stake, the extent of the damage would be incalculable and the probability of political compromises correspondingly high. The possibility could then not be ruled out that the no-bail-out clause would be circumvented. Lastly, even an effective market mechanism would not solve the problem of ensuring that fiscal policy is cyclically appropriate.

The consultations on the EMU constitution were accordingly bound to reach the conclusion that a regulatory framework to discipline member states' fiscal policy was necessary.

Once the principle has been agreed on, the question is how the *rules* are to be formulated. Simply put, they have to fulfil the following conditions:

1. Budget balances in the member states and in the monetary union as a whole should behave in a cyclically appropriate manner. Scope needs to be created for the budget to 'breathe' over the cycle so that the automatic stabilisers can work.

   Because the single monetary policy can only be geared to the whole euro area, national budgets need sufficient room for manoeuvre to be able to respond to the cyclical position of the economy. This takes place via the so-called automatic stabilisers if revenue and spending are free to fluctuate over the cycle and deficits and surpluses offset each other over time. A fiscal policy designed in this way contributes both to the sustainability of the public finances and to their stabilising effect. If these conditions are met at the national level, they will automatically be met in the euro area aggregate as well. This in turn supports expectations of macroeconomic stability and makes the task of the single monetary policy oriented towards maintaining price stability easier.

---

[4] See ECB, 'Fiscal policies and financial markets', *Monthly Bulletin*, February 2006.

2. The rules must lead to sustainable budget policies in the member states and offer protection against moral hazard. As the sanction imposed by the market (interest rates) is insufficient, precautions must be taken so that the case of sovereign insolvency due to over-indebtedness never arises and the no-bail-out principle is never put to the test.

3. While committing governments to a sound budget policy, the rules must also strengthen the incentives for structural reforms to promote employment and growth.

4. The rules must be simple and enforceable.

5. National autonomy should be infringed as little as possible, that is, the rules should be in line with the currently limited (and likely to remain so for the foreseeable future) degree of political integration and democratic legitimacy.

Taken together, this means limits on the overall EU budget deficit are necessary. There being no higher political authority for this, the limits must be applied by the Community-level institutions, i.e. the Council, and 'broken down' at national level.

### The Stability and Growth Pact

In Article 104, the Maastricht Treaty already lays down the basic rules for member states' conduct of fiscal policy.[5] Paragraph 1 states succinctly: 'Member States shall avoid excessive government deficits.' Compliance with budgetary discipline is assessed on the basis of two criteria: whether, firstly, a country's *level of indebtedness* and, secondly, its *budget deficit* exceed a certain threshold.

In the protocol on the excessive deficit procedure, the two reference values are defined as 60 per cent and 3 per cent of GDP at market prices respectively. The Treaty also contains provisions on

---

[5] Note that these provisions – just like Article 103 on the no-bail-out – apply to *all* EU member states, not just members of the monetary union.

the procedure for monitoring compliance. This was laid down in more detail in the 1997 *Stability and Growth Pact*. Briefly, the objective is to avoid the 3 per cent fiscal deficit ceiling being exceeded at all. Alongside this 'preventive arm' of the Pact, the 'corrective' or 'deterrent arm' is aimed at committing a country's fiscal policy to bringing any excessive deficit back within the 3 per cent ceiling. Only for members of the monetary union can the procedure lead to the imposition of *sanctions*.

The fiscal policy rules of the Pact attracted – and continue to attract – in some cases fierce criticism, mostly centred on the two numerical reference values.

The figures of 3 per cent and 60 per cent cannot be justified in precise 'scientific' terms. There are, however, important arguments for setting numerical reference values in the first place. In the absence of quantitative limits, any surveillance procedure lacks a fixed point of reference. A ceiling for *government debt* (in relation to GDP) is necessary in order to ensure that public debt does not 'get out of hand' and that government borrowing does not impede the access of private investors to financing (the so-called 'crowding-out' effect). Should the 60 per cent limit be felt to be too low, moreover, it needs to be borne in mind that it concerns only the *explicit* government debt. The *implicit* government debt, that is, future spending resulting from statutory commitments, is left out of account. This relates in particular to future pension payments, which in the ageing societies of Europe represent a kind of 'demographic time-bomb' for the public finances.[6]

Not that the figures of 3 per cent for the fiscal deficit and 60 per cent for government debt were chosen arbitrarily. The underlying

---

[6] Based on demographic trends, (explicit) government debt in the euro area is projected to rise from approximately 70 per cent today to almost 200 per cent in 2050. See European Commission, *Quarterly Report*, 5:4 (2006). See also A. Maddaloni *et al.*, 'Macroeconomic implications of demographic developments in the euro area', ECB Occasional Paper, no. 51 (August 2006).

calculation was as follows. Assuming a growth rate of nominal GDP of 5 per cent (3 per cent real growth plus 2 per cent inflation), a fiscal deficit of 3 per cent would stabilise government debt at 60 per cent of GDP (roughly equal to the country average at that time). With a higher level of debt, compliance with the 3 per cent ceiling would bring it back down towards the reference value. If growth were lower, a lower fiscal deficit ceiling would have to be maintained in order to keep debt constant.[7]

The 3 per cent ceiling for budget deficits is often criticised as being too low to be able to counteract a sharp economic downturn effectively by means of a sufficiently expansionary fiscal policy. Against this it may be argued that:

1. The Pact itself provides for exceptions to the limit in the event of very severe slowdowns in economic activity.

2. Focusing on the 3 per cent limit means assessing the stabilising function of the rules contained in the Pact in purely negative terms. This overlooks the fact that the principal fiscal policy message of the Pact is something very different, namely that in normal economic conditions a country's budgetary position should be in (or close to) balance – or even in surplus if, in particular, the level of government debt is high.

This perfectly positive rule under the Pact enjoins the member states to pursue a sound budget policy in good times so as to create sufficient scope for the automatic stabilisers to operate in a downturn. Indeed, a reserve of 3 percentage points of GDP (or even more if starting from a surplus) gives fiscal policy huge leeway that has only very seldom been fully utilised in the past.

In the hard test of practical politics, the Pact only partly held up in its first major challenge. It is true that deficits are lower overall than they had been in the early 1990s, and that all the countries

---

[7] See, for example, ECB, 'Challenges to fiscal sustainability in the euro area', *Monthly Bulletin*, February 2007, p. 62.

which exceeded the 3 per cent limit subsequently introduced measures to consolidate the public finances. Nonetheless, as a member of the Economic and Financial Committee I found it particularly dispiriting that Germany too should have infringed the Pact over a period of several years. Admittedly, I myself was under no illusion as to the likely effectiveness of the rules. I had voiced my scepticism long before the start of monetary union by pointing out that decisions under the procedure are taken at the European level by the governments, which may yet violate the rules at home themselves. How can one expect potential transgressors to pass judgement on actual transgressors?

All the same, it was depressing to see how the German and French governments in particular flouted the Pact. First of all, Germany got its way and prevented the Commission from issuing the warning it had recommended in January 2002 (on account of a deficit expected to be 'dangerously close' to the 3 per cent limit). Then, in November 2003, the finance ministers yielded to German (and French) requests – or pressure – and rejected the Commission's proposed stepping-up of the procedure and had the procedure halted. What is more, the then German Chancellor even stated unashamedly, in an article appearing under his name in the *Financial Times*, that Germany would not have its fiscal policy course dictated by 'Brussels'. Following in the slipstream of German and French fiscal policy, as it were, Italy too broke the rules. Greece was not long in joining them.

In so doing, the three largest EMU countries, including the country that originally pushed the Stability and Growth Pact through against stiff resistance, took an axe to one of the pillars of monetary union. This behaviour, not least, also created the impression that the 'little' countries would have to adhere strictly to the rules, while in borderline cases exceptions would be made for the 'big' ones. For such a complex entity as EMU, this development is anything but conducive to the necessary policy cohesion. In the meantime the Pact has been reformed. It remains to be seen whether the application of the revised rules will allow the Pact to fulfil its purpose in its new form.[8]

The decision is in the hands of the politicians. In the final part of this chapter, I shall return to this in more detail from the 'monetary union – political union' perspective.

## Policy coordination in EMU

### Pros and cons of ex ante coordination

The start of monetary union in Europe created a situation without historical precedent. On the one side, there are the ECB as a supra-national institution, the euro as a single currency, and the single monetary policy with a clearly defined mandate. On the other side, the other instruments of macroeconomic policy remain in national hands. This is true of fiscal policy – with the restrictions under the Stability and Growth Pact – and wage policy, which is set exclusively at national level. (The other policy areas regulated at Community level, such as trade policy, competition policy and transport policy, are basically not relevant to the present discussion.)

Even before the start of monetary union, there were calls for this asymmetry in macroeconomic policy to be corrected. These demands have not died down since, but are continually trotted out by members of national governments, European and national parliamentarians, trade union representatives and industrialists. Contrary to what is normal in the national context, it is claimed, the ECB lacks a 'political counterpart'. In a strange juxtaposition, this is viewed on the one hand as a weakness, as a shortcoming of the monetary constitution, and on the other hand as a politically worrying strengthening of the

---

[8] In this connection, see R. Morris, H. Ongena and L. Schuknecht, 'The reform and implementation of the Stability and Growth Pact', ECB Occasional Paper, no. 47 (June 2006).

position of the central bank which, on account of its independence, is already seen to be (too) powerful. In any case, it is considered to be in the interests of the euro area economy that monetary policy measures be coordinated with those in other policy areas *ex ante*.

There would appear to be obvious arguments in support of such calls. *Monetary policy, fiscal policy* and employers and labour exert an influence on macroeconomic development. If each area acts in isolation and denies the interdependencies with the actions of the other stakeholders, the outcome for the overall economy is bound to be unsatisfactory, or at any rate suboptimal. If, in contrast, the actions of policy-makers were coordinated in advance, in order to arrive at the right 'policy mix', such inefficiencies could be avoided.

The call for such *ex ante* policy coordination would seem to have both political and economic logic on its side. Indeed, theoretical models confirm the expected result: measures coordinated in advance yield superior results compared to the individual stakeholders acting in isolation.

However, the following considerations make this view much less attractive and lead to very different conclusions.[9] For one thing, any attempt at *ex ante* coordination requires a huge amount of information. To begin with, there needs to be an accurate evaluation of the macroeconomic situation and outlook, leading to a common assessment. Since this analysis is likely to be conditioned by very different sets of priorities, the whole venture may fail even at this stage. Conceivably, and not improbably, a 'compromise' will be reached. But this by no means implies an improvement over a situation where the analyses diverge, as will become clear when we look at the differing objectives of the parties involved.

In addition, ideas and theoretical models of *ex ante* coordination generally neglect the political economy background, or even ignore

---

[9] O. Issing, 'On macroeconomic policy coordination in EMU', *Journal of Common Market Studies*, 40:2 (June 2002).

it completely, by simply assuming that the different parties always act in the interests of some vague conception of 'welfare'. But do they not (also) follow their own interests, which may conflict with the model world?

One fundamental difference compared with the world of nation states is the starting situation, the 'European dimension'. For obvious reasons, trade union representatives cannot deliver a binding vote on a wage growth path coordinated with monetary and fiscal policy. This is generally already true at the national level, and requires no further explanation at the level of EMU.

Similar restrictions apply to fiscal policy. There is no such thing as a 'European fiscal policy', nor can the finance ministers of the member states deliver binding commitments for their respective country's future policy course. Not only is this impeded by the need to agree on the position with the national government and obtain the approval of parliament, but – depending on the situation – there may be strong political incentives to renege on a commitment previously entered into in the framework of coordination. This risk would always arise, for example, if the central bank, counting on a restrictive fiscal policy stance, committed itself to an expansionary monetary policy. Even if *some* governments kept their 'promises', it would be most unlikely that *all* governments (and parliaments) would do so. There would, at any rate, be a high risk of moral hazard. To judge from the experience with the Stability and Growth Pact, it would most certainly be unwise to subject the ECB's monetary policy to such 'tests'. In the end, monetary policy would be blamed for having sacrificed its own objective of price stability to the interests of the other stakeholders. There would be much too great a risk of the central bank losing credibility.

The same objections can be raised against the proposal to create a 'European economic government' as a 'counterpart' or 'counterweight' to the ECB, as called for not least in the 2007 presidential campaign in France, and as reiterated by the winning candidate.

What, if anything, does this mean? Can it really mean that the governments of the member states should willingly cede their responsibility for economic policy to a European institution and subordinate it to the common interest? Just how little credence can be given to this idea is obvious from the fact that the very politicians who call most vociferously for a 'European economic government' are those who forget the European dimension as soon as their own national interests are at stake. This reveals the true purpose behind the proposal, namely to pressure, if not to force, the ECB to pursue a less stability-oriented policy. Quite apart from the fact that any attempt to exert political influence on the monetary policy of the ECB is a clear breach of the Treaty provisions, such ideas mean hindering the ECB in its endeavour to fulfil its sovereign mandate, namely to ensure price stability.

That these demands have little objective justification is also evident from the fact that arrangements already exist to enable a mutual exchange of opinions. To mention only the official or obligatory contacts: the representative of the finance ministers (and the responsible European Commissioner) is invited to every meeting of the ECB Governing Council. The ECB President takes part in the consultations of the Eurogroup as well as in the macroeconomic dialogue aimed at fostering an exchange of views with the representatives of industry and the trade unions. One can scarcely complain of a lack of information-sharing opportunities.

### Assignment of responsibility and implicit coordination

However, disputing the necessity for *ex ante* coordination and questioning what it could achieve by no means implies putting the case for the individual stakeholders to act as they please. The conception of EMU is founded on a clear assignment of policy responsibility. *Monetary policy* has a clear mandate to ensure price stability. The task of *fiscal policy* – entirely a national responsibility – is to take care of the relationship between the public and private sectors, that is, to determine how macroeconomic resources are allocated across the two sectors, and to implement policy in matters of income distribution. The task of stabilisation, centred on the operation of the automatic stabilisers, is a national responsibility, subject to the rules of the Stability and Growth Pact aimed at ensuring that national policies are compatible with the requirements of EMU. *Employers* and *labour*, finally, bear the primary responsibility for employment. Employment is fostered if wage growth takes account of regional, sectoral and quality-specific requirements. Productivity growth, adjusted for the effects of job creation measures, provides a basis for an appropriate rate of growth of real wages insofar as wage formation is not left to the market. In the nominal component of wage growth, it is important in the wage-bargaining process – especially for the conclusion of longer-term wage agreements – that employers and labour can rely on the stability-oriented monetary policy and that negative inflation surprises are avoided wherever possible.[10] Here the central bank plainly has an obligation to 'deliver' vis-à-vis the other stakeholders. It cannot, for example, prevent the immediate impact on inflation of increases in indirect taxes and a deterioration in the terms of trade (e.g. an oil price rise). Conversely, if the path of wage growth is to be supportive of employment, workers must be prepared to tolerate such effects via a lower rate of increase in real wages.

There is an obvious linkage between the pursuit of an appropriate policy by the central bank on the one hand, and employers and labour on the other. If all stakeholders do what is required of them, policy coordination occurs virtually automatically.

In the same way, fiscal policy must be able to judge how the ECB will act. Thanks to its clear mandate, its monetary policy strategy and the transparency of its communication, the ECB's 'reaction function'

---

[10] This also applies with regard to fiscal policy, where the future inflation rate is an important factor in budgetary planning.

is well known. In other words, it is possible to predict how the ECB will react to exogenous shocks and strive to re-establish price stability in the medium term.

Conversely, the information from the governments' budget plans is an important parameter in the ECB's assessment of the risks to price stability: the available fiscal policy data, from budgeted expenditure and revenue to tax policy measures, are incorporated as exogenous factors in the projections made by the staff of the ECB and the Eurosystem.

This *implicit coordination* presupposes that all stakeholders – the central bank, governments, and employers and labour – fulfil their respective responsibilities. If they do, the overall result will correspond to the outcome that many wrongly expect *ex ante* coordination to yield. Frequently, calls for advance in policy coordination fail to clearly assign the respective responsibilities. For example, price stability is regarded as (also) being the responsibility of employers and labour and/or of fiscal policy, while employment is (also) the responsibility of the central bank. This is not the way to achieve favourable policy outcomes. These can only be attained if responsibilities are clearly assigned, and if they can be fulfilled by the respective stakeholders using the instruments at their disposal. If everyone is supposed to be responsible for everything, in the end no one is really responsible for anything. In such a jumbled situation, what is more, it is highly likely that monetary stability and the central bank's credibility will be the first to fall by the wayside.

The ECB has been given a clear mandate. It cannot therefore allow itself to get involved in any kind of experiments that could hinder it in the pursuit of its stability-oriented policy. In order not to give rise to misconceptions and unrealistic expectations, the central bank must not only convincingly explain its policy to the public, but also continually point out the *limits* to monetary policy. Monetary policy cannot have any lasting effect on employment or growth over and above the contribution made by stable money. This needs to be spelt out. Part of this involves warning against wage developments that would negatively impact employment and prices.

Vis-à-vis fiscal policy as well, the central bank has a role to play as guardian of macroeconomic stability. Not infrequently, politicians react to urging by the central bank not to depart from, or to return to, a sound fiscal policy course by saying: if the central bank comments on fiscal policy, it must obviously allow politicians to comment on, and possibly criticise, the stance of monetary policy. Quite apart from the fact that, as repeatedly needs to be emphasised, seeking to influence the ECB is prohibited by statute, any such retort can be countered by the following argument. As a non-political and thus a 'neutral' authority, the task of watching over macroeconomic stability is bound to accrue to the central bank in a monetary union with numerous national governments. The citizens expect the central bank to play this role, especially in those countries where the national central banks fulfilled this function in the past and continue to do so. This does not mean that the central bank should express an opinion on all aspects of fiscal policy. While it is certainly not easy to define where responsibility for the stable development of the macroeconomy in the monetary union ends, it does not include commenting on and criticising, for example, individual tax policy measures in a member state.

But political demands that the ECB do one thing (lower interest rates) or not do another (raise interest rates) impair the effectiveness of monetary policy and hence cause harm to society. They may lead to higher financial market volatility and partly or wholly negate the effect of a monetary policy measure.[11] This would occur, for instance,

[11] In this connection, the comments by former US Treasury Secretary Robert Rubin are noteworthy: 'Before 1993, Presidents and Treasury Secretaries had sometimes opined on what the Fed should be doing with regard to interest rates and sometimes tried to lean on the Fed chairman in various ways. Bill Clinton, by contrast, always adhered to the principle of not commenting publicly on Fed policy. Whenever the contrary suggestion was made inside the White House, I argued that commenting was a bad idea for several reasons. First, and most fundamental, the Fed's decisions on monetary policy should be as free from political considerations as possible. Second, evident respect for the Fed's independence can bolster the President's credibility, economic

if politicians were to put strong verbal pressure on the central bank to lower interest rates. If in these circumstances interest rates actually are reduced, because the central bank considers it appropriate, doubts might nonetheless arise as to whether the central bank really is independent, resulting in rising inflation expectations.

Only a central bank that is immune to any such suspicion thanks to its unwavering pursuit of a stability-oriented monetary policy can prevent such potential adverse side-effects.

## Does one size fit all?

Does the *one size* of the single monetary policy fit all? The question reflects fundamental concerns as to the workability of monetary union and even scepticism about its continued existence.[12] What lies behind these doubts, which predate monetary union and have accompanied it to this day?

### *Causes of divergences*

In EMU, there is only one single monetary policy course. The central bank takes action after weighing up the risks to price stability in the single currency area as a whole, with the Harmonised Index of Consumer Prices (HICP) as the most important variable.

In the individual member states, however, economic conditions can diverge to varying degrees. As a result, monetary policy that is appropriate for the euro area as a whole may be (excessively) 'tight'

confidence, and confidence in the soundness of our financial markets. Third, the bond market might be affected by any belief that the Fed chairman was under political pressure that could affect the Fed's actions. There was also another factor I came to recognize after moving to Treasury: we advised other countries around the world, such as Mexico during the peso crisis, that their central bank governors should be insulated from political pressure. Attempting to put political pressure on our own central bank would undermine that prescription.' R. E. Rubin, *In an Uncertain World: Tough Choices from Wall Street to Washington* (New York, 2003), p. 193.

[12] See O. Issing, 'The single monetary policy of the European central bank: one size fits all', *International Finance*, 4:3 (Winter 2001).

or 'loose' from the 'national' perspective. But the ECB cannot take account of such *divergences*, and hence 'one size does not fit all'. There will always be some differences. Only in exceptional situations would one expect economic conditions to be in perfect harmony. This is true for regions within a single country with its own currency, and all the more true for a large currency area covering many countries. However, whether and to what extent this leads to major problems depends, firstly, on the nature, duration and magnitude of the divergences. A second decisive factor is the flexibility of markets and the ability of national policy to support necessary adjustments.

The primary cause of a sizeable divergence in economic developments is a so-called *asymmetrical exogenous shock* affecting one or more countries. One example would be where a country that specialises in exporting one product or group of products experiences a sharp decline in foreign demand. The subsequent slump in exports could lead – depending on the importance of the sector in the country's overall economy – to an economic downturn, and in the extreme case even trigger a recession, while other countries are largely unaffected by the shock.

In a less pronounced form, an exogenous shock can be said to be asymmetrical if, while affecting all countries, it does so to differing degrees. An example would be a sharp rise in energy (e.g. oil) prices on the world market that affects all countries, but chiefly those which are especially dependent on that form of energy. Since the single monetary policy cannot react to such differences, such divergences may even be magnified in a monetary union.

How vulnerable is EMU to the risk of asymmetric shocks? In the economic structure of the EMU member countries, the similarities outweigh the differences, so that severe asymmetric shocks are unlikely to occur. It is true that the steep rise of the oil price (and of other energy prices in its wake) did not affect the individual member countries in the same way, but the shock itself outweighed country-specific idiosyncrasies.

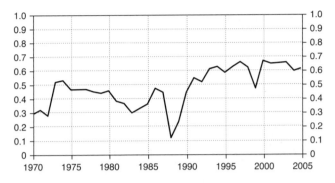

Source: ECB computations based on European Commission data.
Note: Data for Germany refer to West Germany up to 1991.
[1] The trend-cycle decomposition has been obtained by using the Baxter King band pass filter over the period 1960–2008. For the period 2006–08, European Commission forecasts of real GDP have been used.
[2] Eight-year rolling correlations of pairs of euro area countries were first computed and the unweighted average of these correlations calculated subsequently.
**Figure 14** Average of eight-year rolling correlations of output gap across euro area countries[1,2] (in unweighted terms)

What is remarkable is the high degree of synchronisation in the *business cycle*. Figure 14 shows that the degree of synchronisation of business cycles across the euro area countries has increased since the early 1990s and is currently at a historically high level. From the business cycle perspective, the ECB's single monetary policy poses no major problems.

There are only limited differences in *growth rates* across euro area member countries, a finding that is borne out by a comparison with growth in different regions of the USA. As can be seen from figure 15, the dispersion of growth rates in the euro area (measured by the unweighted standard deviation) is not significantly different from that across regions of the United States. This dispersion basically reflects differentials in trend growth rates; to the extent that these represent a catching-up process in countries with below-average living standards (in terms of per capita income), they are a welcome phenomenon. The position of the eleven 'old'

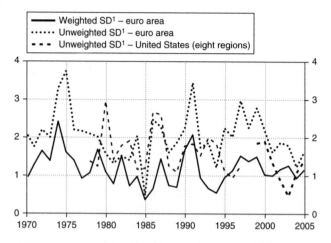

*Source:* ECB computations based on European Commission and US Bureau of
Economic Analysis (BEA) data.
*Note:* Data for Germany refer to West Germany up to 1991. The euro area
excludes Slovenia. There is a statistical break in the US regional data in 1998.
For the US states and regions, data refer to gross state product. The eight regions
are defined by the BEA and cover the whole country.
[1] SD = standard deviation.
**Figure 15** Dispersion of real GDP growth across the euro area countries

euro area countries reveals remarkable changes in this respect.
Greece and Spain have made considerable progress (see figure 16),
but remain below the average in terms of per capita income.
Ireland has been remarkably successful: starting from a very low
level, its per capita income is meanwhile well above the euro area
average.[13]

Growth differentials may, however, also be related to divergent
price developments. Their causes can be explained, inter alia, by

---

[13] The ECB has regularly conducted in-depth analyses of economic developments in
EMU as a whole and in the individual member countries. The findings of a conference
on 'What Effects is EMU Having on the Euro Area and its Member Countries?' are
summarised in a series of papers; see ECB Working Papers, nos. 594–9.

See also the comprehensive study by the European Commission: *The EU Economy,
2006 Review*, Commission of the European Communities, Directorates General for
Economics and Financial Affairs.

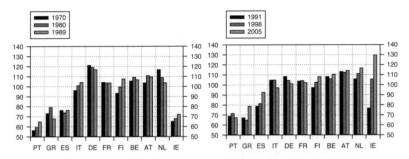

*Source:* ECB computations based on European Commission data.

*Note:* Data for Germany refer to West Germany up to 1991.

[1] In both charts the countries have been ranked in ascending order of the year 2005. Luxembourg is excluded as per capita GDP computations are distorted by the high number of cross-border workers. Such a computation for Luxembourg would show a per capita GDP in purchasing power standard of close to 230 relative to the euro average in 2005.

**Figure 16** Per capita GDP in purchasing power standard[1]

the so-called Balassa–Samuelson effect.[14] Productivity growth is generally high(er) in the sectors that manufacture traded goods. If wages in these sectors rise accordingly, labour will tend to desert the sectors that produce non-traded goods – and which are therefore not exposed to competition across borders. To prevent this, wages will also be increased in these sectors, by more than is matched by an increase in productivity. The result is a corresponding increase in prices that affects the overall development of prices in the economy and leads to higher (national) inflation. Prices can therefore be expected to rise faster in countries that are in the process of catching up. Nonetheless, empirical studies show that this effect has been limited in EMU in its current composition.[15]

---

[14] The name originates from two papers that were published in the same year: B. Balassa, 'The purchasing-power parity doctrine: a reappraisal', *Journal of Political Economy*, 72 (1964); P. A. Samuelson, 'Theoretical notes on trade problems', *Review of Economics and Statistics*, 46 (1964).

[15] ECB, 'Inflation differentials in a monetary union', *Monthly Bulletin*, October 1999.

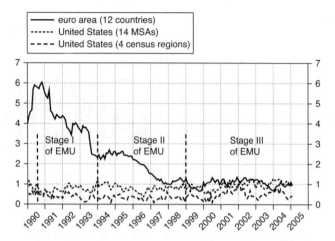

Sources: Eurostat, US Bureau of Labor Statistics and ECB calculations.
[1] Data up to February 2005.

**Figure 17** Dispersion of annual inflation in the euro area, fourteen US metropolitan statistical areas (MSAs) and the four US census regions[1]

Figure 17 shows that inflation differentials across the later euro area countries narrowed considerably during the convergence process in the 1990s. Following the introduction of the euro, they stabilised at a low level not very different from the figure for fourteen metropolitan areas in the USA.

### Real interest rate, real exchange rate, risk-sharing

Quite a few observers regard inflation differentials as a serious problem for EMU. Since the ECB sets its (nominal) policy interest rates at the same level for the entire currency area, the *real interest rate*, that is, the interest rate adjusted for domestic inflation, differs across countries: the higher the domestic inflation rate, the lower the real interest rate (and vice versa). This 'real interest rate argument' has been adduced, for example, to point out that the ECB's monetary policy was (too) tight for Germany, in particular in the first few years, because of the higher real interest rate implied by the country's low inflation rate relative to the EMU average, whereas in countries such as Spain or Ireland with significantly higher inflation, a low, predominantly negative (short-term) real interest rate contributed to overheating. On this view, therefore, one size does not fit all, and the single monetary policy creates divergences in economic growth that are extremely damaging and could, in the long run, even jeopardise the continued existence of EMU.

On closer analysis, however, this real interest rate argument becomes a lot less persuasive. Firstly, the single nominal interest rate is simply an unalterable characteristic of monetary policy in the single currency area. If it leads to difficulties, other mechanisms and instruments at national level are needed to remedy or at least alleviate them. Secondly, a particular point of criticism is the use of the current rate of inflation to calculate the real rate of interest. Real interest rates determine the cost of capital and thus play a role in investment decisions. In this calculation, however, what is important is not the *current* rate but the *expected* future rate of inflation (as well as the expected rate of return on real capital).

Studies have shown that differentials in *expected* inflation across euro area member countries are very small, with expectations largely in line with the ECB's target. In any case, a large proportion of investment takes place not, or not only, at home but (also) in other EMU countries, in which case calculating the real interest rate by reference to 'domestic' inflation ceases to have any justification.

In a monetary union, nominal exchange rates between member countries are permanently fixed. Hypothetically, it is possible to calculate a *real exchange rate* that takes account of inflation differentials across the countries concerned. Changes in the real exchange rate thus reflect, inter alia, changes in a country's price competitiveness within the monetary union. If one country's inflation rate is persistently lower than the average of the monetary union, its exports will become more competitive, especially against those of countries whose prices (and costs) are growing at an above-average rate.[16]

Changes in the real exchange rate are therefore a mechanism that over the longer term counteracts the influence of real interest rates insofar as this is relevant. In terms of the single monetary policy and the cohesion of the currency area, the interaction of these two mechanisms leads to a correction of deviations and a convergence of growth rates. The more flexibly markets and prices (wages) react to the respective situation, the faster this adjustment proceeds.

Within a monetary union there is a further mechanism that affords a degree of protection against the effects of asymmetric shocks: *risk-sharing* in financial investments. If an investor distributes his or her assets across different countries within the currency area, this portfolio *diversification* can at least partly offset differences in returns due to varying economic conditions in the individual countries. While in principle the option of diversifying exists everywhere, the irreversible fixing of parities eliminates the exchange rate risk and hence removes a major uncertainty in cross-border investments within EMU. The result is increased financial linkages and greater risk-sharing. Thus financial market integration helps improve the functioning of monetary union.

In this connection, it is also apparent that the financing of current account balances among the individual member states becomes easier and generally takes place smoothly. The magnitudes involved can be seen from figure 18. This figure shows, inter alia, a considerable deterioration in the current account balance for Greece and Spain, a persistently high deficit for Portugal and a marked improvement for Germany and the Netherlands.

---

[16] Since its inflation rate has been below average since the start of EMU, Germany has recorded considerable competitiveness gains. See also Deutsche Bundesbank, 'Current account balances and price competitiveness in the euro area', *Monthly Report*, June 2007.

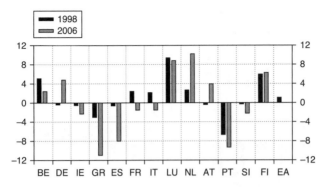

*Source:* ECB computations on European Commission data.
*Note:* Slovenia is not included in the euro area figures. Current account balances for individual euro area countries refer to the balance of current transactions with the rest of the world including other euro area countries.
**Figure 18** Current account balances (percentages of GDP)

However positive the greater ease of financing of current account balances in EMU may be considered in principle, the fact remains that the risk of devaluation of the national currency and the related risk premium on interest rates no longer exist, which means that an important warning signal of undesirable developments with adverse repercussions is lost or becomes harder to discern.

### The responsibility of national policy

Persistent, large net current account positions may be an indicator of a macroeconomic imbalance. In EMU there are certainly grounds for supposing this to be the case for certain countries. Spain and Portugal, for example, have had large intra-EMU current account deficits for many years. One reason is the persistent divergence across member countries in developments in *unit labour costs*. In countries such as Spain, this trend has been reinforced by the strong increase in domestic demand.

Shifts in price and cost competitiveness tend to be reflected in the current account balance. Figure 19 shows this relationship for twelve euro area countries. Over the years since the start of monetary union

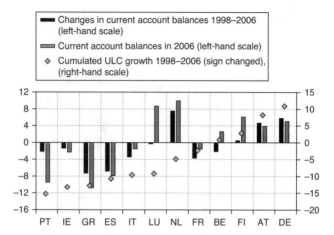

Source: ECB computations on European Commission data.
Note: Slovenia is not included in the euro area figures. Current account balances for individual euro area countries refer to the balance of current transactions with the rest of the world including other euro area countries.
[1] A negative sign of cumulated unit labour costs (ULC) indicates an increase relative to the euro average, i.e. a relative deterioration in cost competitiveness. Countries are ranked in ascending order according to changes in cumulated ULC compared with the euro area average.
**Figure 19** Current account balances and cumulated ULC (percentage points; percentages of GDP; percentages)[1]

the cumulated divergence for some countries has reached extremely worrying dimensions. The associated sizeable changes in price competitiveness are bound to lead to tensions over time.

As already mentioned, inflation differentials across EMU countries have been relatively moderate from one year to the next. What is a cause for concern, however, is that it is basically always the same countries whose inflation has been either *above* or *below* the average. These differentials largely coincide with the divergences in unit labour costs. The inflation differentials are also markedly greater than implied by the above-mentioned Balassa–Samuelson effect, which reflects the catching-up process and can be regarded as less problematic from the competitiveness perspective.

The differences in the development of unit labour costs chiefly reflect divergences in *wage growth*. This reveals one aspect of EMU that economic policy stakeholders have sometimes failed to recognise, and sometimes ignored or at least underestimated. Simply put, while in the past individual countries frequently compensated for a loss of competitiveness by devaluing their currency, this instrument is no longer available within EMU. If employers and labour disregard this radical change in macroeconomic conditions, the result, as has been described, will be a loss of competitiveness leading to tensions within EMU.

Precisely from this perspective, numerous observers have put part of the blame for the divergences within EMU on restrained wage growth in Germany. But one need only consider the high level of unemployment in Germany over this period to see that this line of argument has no basis in reality. There is no convincing reason why a country with high, largely structural unemployment should follow an economically inappropriate path of wage growth in the interests, as it were, of cohesion within EMU. Wage moderation over a period of many years was a major factor in reducing unemployment and (from 2005) increasing employment in Germany, confirming that this was the right course to follow. At the same time, it lowered inflation pressures across the euro area and thus contributed to a relatively low level of nominal interest rates. All the countries in the euro area benefited as a result. Adjustment, therefore, has to come from those countries in which wage growth has led over the years to a loss of competitiveness.

For EMU to function optimally, the policy areas that remain a *national responsibility* need to play their part. This applies not only to wage policy but also to other areas, in particular fiscal policy, for which the Stability and Growth Pact sets out the appropriate course.

A look at a completely different area provides a vivid illustration of the responsibility of national authorities. There have been wide divergences in the development of real-estate prices, with some countries having recorded double-digit rates of increase for many years. To the extent that this reflects a catching-up process and the relative scarcity of the 'housing' good, this is a necessary shift in relative prices. But, even if it is difficult to draw the line precisely, there are clear signs that the rise in real-estate prices in some countries has been excessive and hence a cause for concern on account of the associated distortions – misdirected investment, overheating – and the probability of a correction (which has in fact already started).

The ECB can take account of real-estate prices only at the level of EMU as a whole. Indeed, the monetary aspect of these processes (money supply, lending) is taken into account in the monetary analysis under its strategy, and hence reflected in monetary policy-making. The single monetary policy cannot, however, give consideration to developments in individual countries. Responsibility for correcting such processes lies with national policy. In particular, it should refrain from any measures (e.g. tax relief) that further fuel a boom in the property sector, and reduce or eliminate incentives. Other instruments, such as affecting the supply of land, changing zoning laws, etc., and not least banking regulation (above all, rules on mortgage lending), can also help counter overheating by means of national policy measures.

Within EMU, the single monetary policy and national policy need to work together, a task made all the easier if the fundamental conditions for the proper functioning of a monetary union are fulfilled, namely flexible markets and unimpeded competition within the monetary union. The more flexibly prices in labour, goods and services markets react to changes and facilitate the process of adjustment, the less need there will be for corrective economic policy action.

It is all the more crucial for policy to meet these requirements because one tool, which in the context of a nation state normally plays a major role in offsetting divergent economic developments in individual regions, is lacking within EMU. This tool is *revenue sharing*, whereby public funds are channelled from the central government or other area authorities to regions where the economy is relatively weak(er). This generally involves large amounts of money. Although some EU funding fulfils a similar role, neither its scale nor its focus are comparable with revenue equalisation in a national context. This is unlikely to change in the foreseeable future. The huge sums required for such revenue sharing would probably far exceed what citizens would be prepared to pay. Any attempt to move in this direction would be likely to create serious political tensions. Quite apart from that, it would most likely be difficult if not impossible to develop a system that did not create considerable negative incentives (moral hazard, the free-rider problem) and invite abuse.

This line of reasoning leads us back to the conditions for an *optimal currency area*, which may serve as a pointer to the necessary changes. There is accordingly no static answer to the question of whether 'one size fits all'. Rather, what policy needs to do is to create the conditions whereby the single monetary policy does fit all. To begin with, this involves a thorough examination of whether a country is 'ready' for EMU and the single monetary policy. Premature accession runs the risk that a low real rate of interest due to higher inflation will lead first to elements of overheating (construction boom, etc.) and subsequently to a painful correction. After accession, the work of implementing the required reforms needs to continue.

## The enlargement of the euro area

### The European Union and monetary union

With the accession of ten and then a further two new members, the European Union meanwhile comprises twenty-seven countries with a population of over 490 million people. Although the economic weight of even the larger new member states is modest, in terms of GDP the EU is now the world's largest economic area. It will doubtless take time for the single market to become a reality in this area, but on the other hand the huge potential should not be underestimated. If the dynamism of the new member states can be sustained, or even boosted, economic growth in the EU overall, and not least also in the 'old' member countries, could be raised to a new level. For this to happen, however, the established members need to face up to competition from the newcomers and take the opportunity provided by enlargement to make their own economies more flexible.

None of the ten (twelve) new EU members even considered an 'opt-out clause', meaning that all of the countries are committed to joining the euro area in due course. Slovenia was the first of the new EU members to introduce the euro, on 1 January 2007, with Malta and Cyprus following suit from the beginning of 2008, while the large countries (among the ten) – the Czech Republic, Hungary and Poland – have repeatedly postponed their plans for accession.

With each new member country that joins, the monetary union becomes (even) more heterogeneous. The question of whether 'one size fits all' thus takes on a new dimension. Not least, the inflation pressure associated with the necessary catching-up process provides a clear warning to each individual country not to aim to join EMU too soon.

Flexible markets, in particular an adaptable labour market, are important prerequisites that must be fulfilled if the single monetary policy is not to become a problem for a new member country after joining monetary union. The well-known *convergence criteria* point the way to preparing for participation in EMU.[17] At the same time, they represent the entrance examination that has to be passed if the candidacy is to be successful.

Criticism has been levelled chiefly at the price stability criterion. The Treaty stipulates that the average of (at most) the three EU countries with the lowest inflation rate is to be taken as the initial value, which is then 'marked up' by 1.5 percentage points. In terms

---

[17] On this topic, see the regular convergence reports of the ECB and the European Commission.

of purely economic logic, this way of arriving at the figure for the price stability criterion is certainly open to question. Firstly, the wording of the Treaty clearly specifies three (at most) EU countries. But why should the rate of inflation in countries that may not even belong to EMU be the rate that determines whether a country can join the euro?

Secondly, a country's inflation rate (averaged over the last twelve months) may be heavily influenced by special factors and be correspondingly less meaningful as a basis for determining an appropriate stability criterion.

By way of a solution or alternative, there have been repeated calls for the adoption of either the rate of inflation in the 'best-performing' euro area countries or the ECB's quantitative definition of price stability (an annual rise in the HICP of less than 2 per cent) as the yardstick.

From the economic standpoint, there is very little to object to in this approach. However, the 1.5 percentage point 'mark-up' would cease to have any justification if the ECB definition were to be used, so that the end result would not be too dissimilar to the status quo. But it is the statutory – and hence ultimately political – argument that remains crucial. The Treaty clearly refers to EU member countries. Any infringement of clear Treaty provisions would be bound to weaken the sense of what is, or is not, permissible under the law and ultimately to call the whole statutory framework into question. The discussions surrounding the Stability and Growth Pact may serve as a warning in this regard.

In fact, the Treaty does provide for a degree of flexibility. The ECB made use of this in its 2004 Convergence Report, where it explained why the inflation rate in Lithuania (−0.2 per cent) was influenced by special factors and hence, as an 'outlier', was not included in the calculation of the 'best three'.[18]

---

[18] ECB, *Convergence Report 2004*, chapter I.

For the progressively expanding monetary union to be successful, it is crucial that accession does not take place prematurely, but that it is based on adequate advance preparation by the country concerned. One of the most important elements is a sound fiscal policy. With the persistent problems in its public finances, Italy provides something of a cautionary example of how little weight attaches in reality to promises to solve outstanding fiscal problems later, i.e. after accession to EMU. If the prospect of being admitted to the euro area, meanwhile an established area of stability, is not sufficient to induce a country to follow a sound fiscal policy course, how can one expect it to 'mend its ways' after accession to EMU, made possible only by a 'political rebate' on the fiscal policy criteria?[19] Nor should one overlook in this context the responsibility of the 'old' members, who should, to encourage discipline, set a good example by adhering to the rules of the Stability and Growth Pact. Non-compliance with the Pact, by contrast, undermines efforts by the new member states and threatens the whole foundation of EMU.

Not least, the process of drawing closer to EMU also involves participation in the exchange rate mechanism without tensions for a period of at least two years. Every new member of the EU should begin by examining at what stage in the frequently uncompleted process of transformation (from decades of socialist central planning to a free-market economy) and of catching up it should enter into a fixed exchange rate arrangement. Participation in the ERM is the last test, intended to show how ready a country is ultimately to participate successfully in monetary union, that is, in a system of irreversibly fixed exchange rates and a single monetary policy.

---

[19] Years before the start of monetary union, I drew the following analogy. The tendency of the public sector to spend can be compared to a drinker's habit. If the future monetary union regards itself as a community of teetotallers or at most highly disciplined drinkers, all candidates seeking admission to the club should demonstrate that they have forsworn their bad habits *beforehand*. One should not rely on a promise to do so only *afterwards*. O. Issing, 'Europe: political union through common money?', The Institute of Economic Affairs, Occasional Paper, no. 98 (London, 1996), p. 26.

## The ECB and the single monetary policy

The convergence reports also include an assessment of the extent to which a country's national legislation is compatible with the EU Treaty. As regards the provisions of relevance to monetary policy, the central question is how far the statutes of the national central bank guarantee independence – in all its aspects. Political attacks against the incumbent central bank governor and (party-)politically motivated disputes over a reappointment or the appointment of a new governor are worrying signs that, in certain cases, acceptance of the principle of central bank independence still has some way to go.

Even before the event, the opening-up of EMU to new members raised the question of whether an ever-larger *ECB Governing Council* would still be able to function effectively. To facilitate a future amendment to the Statute of the ECB, the Treaty of Nice accordingly included an *enabling clause*, whereby Article 10 (2) of the Statute may be amended by unanimous decision of the EU Council, meeting in the composition of the heads of state or government, and acting:

1. either on a recommendation from the ECB, based on a unanimous decision by the Governing Council, and after consulting the European Parliament and the Commission,
2. or on a recommendation from the European Commission and after consulting the ECB and the European Parliament.[20]

This clause gave the ECB Governing Council a great opportunity to present a convincing model of its own for the future voting modalities in the Governing Council. By requiring a unanimous decision, however, the Treaty of Nice also set the bar very high, since it was a question of reconciling widely diverging interests, notably between 'large' and 'small' countries. Following extensive and – to begin with,

---

[20] See ECB, 'The adjustment of voting modalities in the Governing Council', *Monthly Bulletin*, May 2003. Article 10(2) of the Statute does not relate to decisions taken by weighted vote (e.g. on the ECB's capital, etc.).

not surprisingly, tense – discussions, the Governing Council unanimously adopted its recommendation on 3 February 2003. Following the procedure provided for under the enabling clause, the European Commission presented its opinion, in which it proposed a number of enhancements (including a lower number of national central bank governors with voting rights), while recognising that the limits imposed by the enabling clause clearly restricted the scope for reforms. At its plenary session on 13 March 2003, the European Parliament rejected the ECB's recommendation, the proposed model having been criticised as overly complex. In the Parliament's view, the status quo should be maintained for the time being (with all members of the Governing Council retaining voting rights); the Convention on the future of Europe should prepare a more comprehensive reform. However, the resolution of the European Parliament had no practical effect.

On 21 March 2003, the EU Council (meeting in the composition of the heads of state or government) adopted the ECB's recommendation, giving effect to the amendment of Article 10 (2) of the ECB Statute.

Under the revised Article 10 (2), a *rotation system* for the national central bank governors comes into operation as soon as their number exceeds 15.[21] The participating countries are divided initially into two groups (16 to 21 governors) and finally, as numbers increase, into three (22 to 27 governors). The number of governors with voting rights is limited to 15 at any time. This means that the larger the total, the more governors are temporarily barred from voting. To implement this, a system of rotating voting rights is put in place.

The criteria for allocation to the three groups (from 22 central bank governors upwards) are the share of the respective member state in euro area GDP at market prices, with a weight of five-sixths,

---

[21] By a majority of two-thirds of all the members, the ECB Governing Council can postpone introduction until such time as the number of governors exceeds 18.

TABLE 8: *Three-group rotation system (second stage) – voting frequencies of governors in each group*

| | | | Number of governors in the Governing Council | | | | | | |
|---|---|---|---|---|---|---|---|---|---|
| | | 16–21 | 22 | 23 | 24 | 25 | 26 | 27 |
| 1st group | No. of voting rights/ No. of governors | | 4/5 | 4/5 | 4/5 | 4/5 | 4/5 | 4/5 |
| | *Voting frequency* | *First stage:* | 80% | 80% | 80% | 80% | 80% | 80% |
| 2nd group | No. of voting rights/ No. of governors | *Rotation system* | 8/11 | 8/12 | 8/12 | 8/13 | 8/13 | 8/14 |
| | *Voting frequency* | *with two* | 73% | 67% | 67% | 62% | 62% | 57% |
| 3rd group | No. of voting rights/ No. of governors | *groups* | 3/6 | 3/6 | 3/7 | 3/7 | 3/8 | 3/8 |
| | *Voting frequency* | | 50% | 50% | 43% | 43% | 38% | 38% |
| Σ voting rights | | 15 | 15 | 15 | 15 | 15 | 15 | 15 |

*Source:* ECB, *Monthly Bulletin*, May 2003, p. 79.

and the relative size of its financial sector, with a weight of one-sixth.[22]

The first group comprises the five countries with the highest overall weight, and shares four votes; the second group shares eight voting rights, and the third three. The size of these groups varies according to the number of central bank governors (see table 8). The precise implementing provisions specifying the rotation of voting rights in each group (such as the time interval between rotations) will be adopted by the Governing Council on the basis of a provision contained in the revised Article 10 (2) of the Statute.

This system means that the frequency with which a central bank governor is entitled to vote depends on which group the country belongs to. In the first group, the central bank governors have a voting right 80 per cent of the time. As numbers increase, the voting frequency in the second and third groups is progressively

[22] Only the 'final position' is described here. For details, and concerning the transitional phase with two groups, see the above-mentioned ECB *Monthly Bulletin* of May 2003.

reduced to 57 per cent and 38 per cent respectively. The six members of the Executive Board retain permanent voting rights. The Governing Council considered this appropriate because, unlike the national central bank governors, the members of the Executive Board are appointed following a 'European' procedure under the Treaty and operate solely in the context of the euro area and of the ECB which is responsible for it. The President of the ECB retains a casting vote.

This rotation system ensures that the composition of the overall group of Governing Council members with voting rights is always representative of the euro area. It also ensures that, among the members with voting rights, the principle of 'one member, one vote' continues to apply. The system is characterised by transparency and automaticity. The rules make it possible to ascertain precisely which central bank governors will be entitled to vote at what point in the future. This avoids any possibility of the allocation of voting rights being a subject of internal dispute and, above all, any attempt at outside political influence.

Numerous papers, notably from academia, have addressed the question of how the problem of a growing number of members in the ECB Governing Council can best be solved.[23] Unsurprisingly, the proposals predominantly call for the number of votes to be reduced as far as possible and concentrated largely, if not exclusively, among the members of the Executive Board.

The principal criterion underlying such thinking is that of efficiency: a significantly smaller group than the Governing Council, which was regarded as too big from the start, would facilitate decision-making and improve the quality of monetary policy.

This perspective ignores two crucial conditions for the success of the single monetary policy. Firstly, the broad distribution of

---

[23] For an overview see, for example, A. Belke and B. Styczynska, 'The allocation of power in the enlarged ECB Governing Council: an assessment of the ECB rotation model', *Journal of Common Market Studies*, 44:5 (June 2006).

Governing Council membership across the euro area can yield important insights and contributions towards appropriate policy-making, not in pursuit of national interests – a risk which restricted voting rights and representativeness already serve to exclude – but through the opportunity for an extensive exchange of opinions. Secondly, this perspective reduces monetary policy to mere decision-making. A critical factor in the success of monetary policy, however, is its proper communication. Unless its monetary policy decisions find support in all the countries of the euro area, the ECB will remain a foreign body without hope of public backing for its policy. To achieve this, active communication by the national central banks is needed, with their governors at their head. It is difficult to imagine how this could take place with the requisite degree of personal commitment in the long run if the persons concerned were excluded on principle from the decision-making process.

This personal inclusion is also safeguarded under the Statute, which enshrines the right of participation in meetings of the ECB's Governing Council. (All proposals that ignore this condition thus have no basis in reality.) Obviously, the meetings of a group comprising – in an extreme case – thirty-three members (six Executive Board members and twenty-seven central bank governors) would pose major organisational problems. It will be up to the members of the future Governing Council to make sensible arrangements for this – doubtless an extremely challenging task. The question of voting rights, however, needed to be resolved *ex ante* and given a legal foundation in the Statute.

## Monetary union without political union?

'Europe' is one of the major issues of our time. There is a vast literature that addresses a broad spectrum of questions, ranging from geography to western Christian roots. There are not a few who regret the path of economic integration that has been taken since the Second World War, since it was bound to lead the economic aspects to predominate. Would it not have been much better, much more in accordance with the European ideal, to strive for European unity through culture? Whether this or any other way would have been a realistic option, and whether it would have succeeded, is of course eminently debatable. This is not an attempt to reduce the broader issue of Europe to an economic perspective. Today's reality does, however, reflect a process of integration that, while initiated with political intentions, has nevertheless been implemented largely at the economic level. The introduction of the single currency and the establishment of monetary union marked a further radical change in the structure of Europe.

It is from this vantage point, in short on the basis of the status quo, that I should now like to address the question of political union.

### The euro – a currency without a state

In 'normal' circumstances, the currency area is identical with the national territory. The introduction of the euro created a situation without historical precedent: on the one hand, a currency – the euro – and a supranational monetary authority – the ECB – charged with conducting a single monetary policy for a stable currency; on the other hand, a group of countries and national governments – eleven at the outset, and now fifteen – whose authority ends at the respective national borders.

The euro is a currency for a large number of countries, but at the same time it is actually stateless. What this might imply for its viability was already the cause of a great deal of debate and concern before the event. Since the start of monetary union the question has been: is this institutional arrangement sustainable? Can *monetary union* survive without *political union*? To judge by the number of warning voices, the euro's chances of survival are rather poor.

For example, the then German Federal Chancellor Helmut Kohl emphasised in his government statement on 6 November 1991: 'It cannot be repeated often enough. Political union is the indispensable counterpart to economic and monetary union.' (The minutes of the Bundestag session indicate applause at this point from all sides of the house, that is, from the Christian Democrats (CDU/CSU), the Liberal Democrats (FDP) and the Social Democrats (SPD).) 'Recent history, and not just that of Germany, teaches us that the idea of sustaining an economic and monetary union over time without political union is a fallacy.'

On this view, monetary and political integration need to go hand in hand. Judging by history, political unity as a rule comes first. A new state, be it the German Reich in 1871 or the large numbers of former colonies upon gaining independence, introduces a national currency *after* its establishment.

But might the introduction of a single currency not actually foster the process of political integration or even make it inevitable? The political discussion is rich in such hopes. In a debate in the European Parliament in November 1966, for example, MEP Hans Dichgans spoke of the symbolism that would attach to a European coin that would serve to strengthen a European awareness.

The French monetary policy-maker Jacques Rueff had declared as early as in 1950 that 'L'Europe se fera par la monnaie ou ne se fera pas' – Europe will be created through the common currency or it will not be created at all.

The idea that the currency could play such a *pacemaker role* found little support among economists.[24] After nine years of the euro, experience seems to bear out such scepticism. The countries participating in monetary union are still far removed from any structure that would merit the name of political union. It should not be forgotten,

---

[24] On the discussion that took place prior to monetary union, see O. Issing, 'Europe: political union through common money?', *Economic Affairs*, 20:1 (March 2000).

nevertheless, that the transfer of monetary policy responsibility to the supranational institution ECB represents a significant relinquishing of national sovereignty. This was nowhere more keenly appreciated than in Germany, where the Deutsche Bundesbank was held to be the guarantor of stability – and not just of the monetary kind – in the postwar state.

A central bank does not make a state, but every state has a central bank. That is the normal state of affairs. In the context of EMU, the ECB is an important element in the formation of a state – no less, but also no more.

### Political risks

One avenue along which monetary union could actually function as a pacemaker towards political union does not, to put it mildly, augur well. In the words of former German President Richard von Weizsäcker, the message is (*Focus*, 28 November 1994):

> Put the other way round: if this common foreign policy comes about, it will only be via monetary union. Monetary union will naturally take time in coming. It will also not be cheap. If the currencies of areas at different stages of economic development can no longer fluctuate against each other, equalisation payments will be needed. Getting people used to the idea of monetary union is the only way I can see of ultimately also achieving a common foreign policy.

It is questionable whether a common foreign policy of the member states can be achieved as it were through the back door of monetary union or can be 'bought' by means of large transfer payments. Without the political will on the part of all the governments and parliaments concerned, and not least without support from the citizens, this cannot be expected to produce a stable mandate. Large transfer payments, which ultimately have to be raised via taxes, would be likely to seriously overstrain 'European-mindedness' in the countries that had to pay them – currently at any rate, and also for the more distant future – and would tend rather to foment scepticism or even hostility towards 'Europe'.

Along similar lines, there are proposals for supplementing 'monetary Europe' with a *social union*. This idea played an important role in the deliberations of the European Convention and was reflected in provisions aimed at enshrining a 'European social model' in the Treaty. The same thinking is behind the French President's (successful) attempt to water down the EU's commitment to free competition.

'Harmonising' or 'Europeanising' social rights would indeed bring the members of EMU closer to political union. Rigid labour market rules, etc. would put increased pressure on intra-Community transfer payments. Such a social union would in any event be associated with a rising burden of taxes and contributions to finance welfare payments.

A move in the direction of a European welfare state would, however, divert the EMU economy from the course that is essential to the success of the single monetary policy. As has already been explained in detail, 'one size fits all' can only work if markets generally, and labour markets in particular, become more flexible. But Community-level social legislation, etc. goes in completely the opposite direction – the wrong direction from the point of view of a successful monetary union. Obviously, the principle of policy primacy always applies. But one cannot pursue policy successfully against the laws of the market.[25]

One should guard against interpreting any step towards greater political integration as also representing a step towards ensuring the long-term success of the single market and monetary union. Quite

---

[25] This inevitability was elaborated by E. von Böhm-Bawerk in a famous essay: 'Macht oder ökonomisches Gesetz?', *Zeitschrift für Volkswirtschaft, Sozialpolitik und Verwaltung* (Vienna, 1914, reprinted by Wissenschaftliche Buchgesellschaft, Darmstadt, 1975).

the reverse: any measures that run counter to the proper functioning of the single monetary policy and the stability of the euro undermine the foundations of EMU and, with them, important building blocks in the integration that has been achieved to date.

These considerations do not, fundamentally, have any bearing on ambitions for a common foreign or defence policy. Whether Europe agrees to move in this direction or not, it will have at most a marginal effect on EMU and the success of its monetary policy. This does not mean that over time the common currency may not also foster a sense of identification.

Not only central bankers, however, feel queasy when reading the words with which the then Portuguese Prime Minister Antonio Guterres inflated the role of the euro at the Madrid summit of heads of state or government in 1995: 'When Jesus resolved to found a church, he said to Peter "You are Peter, the rock, and upon this rock I will build my church." You are the euro, and upon this new currency we will build our Europe.'

Beyond their religious fervour, these words do contain a grain of truth. 'Europe', or at any rate that part of it that is now under the umbrella of EMU, is indeed founded not least on the common currency. With the introduction of the single currency, monetary union represents on the one hand a continuation of the process of so-called functional integration, in other words the dismantling of all barriers to achievement of the free exchange of goods, services and capital and the free movement of persons. But on the other hand, with the establishment of a supranational central bank, EMU goes well beyond purely economic integration.

As has been described in chapter 2, after the failure of political ambitions, Europe sought to integrate via the economy – with outstanding success. It remains to be seen whether, now that the military threat associated with the division of Europe has disappeared, the time is ripe for energetic efforts to further political integration. But in any case, political intentions must not be detrimental to the currency and the economy if 'Europe' is to be advanced.

Economic integration is a success story without parallel anywhere in the world. Nowhere has this been more apparent than in the attraction exerted first by the European Economic Community (EEC) and then the EU, with candidates queuing up, then as now, to gain admission. The prosperity of European countries is due in large measure to the dismantling of trade barriers and the opening-up of markets. Germany, for example, has profited more than any other country from this development. Its reintegration into the international community, including transatlantic relations, was facilitated not least by its economic resurgence. The shared success of economic integration has yielded benefits to Europe that go beyond the economic. It cannot be denied that the Community has also helped to secure the peace.

There is no reason to downplay the success of economic integration. If one speaks of the 'economic trap' in which the Community is caught, what lies behind it is criticism of how the economic aspect has come to dominate.[26] But it was economic dynamism that won the day over political hesitancy. If politicians are now hoping to regain via 'Brussels' competences that they have actually or only purportedly lost, this does not augur well – not just in economic terms, but also politically.

One can argue till one is blue in the face how far Europe has already progressed beyond the status of 'special-purpose association', and what the future may hold.[27] Nobody can predict today what form Europe will take in the future, all the more as past models such as confederations, 'l'Europe des patries', etc. can offer no blueprint for the architecture of tomorrow's Europe. There is absolutely no point

[26] See O. Sievert, 'Europa – Dominanz des Wirtschaftlichen?', in Konferenz der Deutschen Akademien der Wissenschaften, Akademie der Wissenschaften and der Literatur, Mainz (ed.), *Europa – Idee, Geschichte, Realität* (Mainz, 1996).

[27] See in the same volume the contribution by J. Isensee, 'Europäische Union – Mitgliedsstaaten. Im Spannungsfeld von Integration and nationaler Selbstbehauptung, Effizienz und Idee'.

in pursuing some utopian vision of a 'United States of Europe'. 'Europe' draws its strength from its cultural and linguistic variety, from its countries' history. Historians such as D. North have shown clearly that the roots of Europe's modern resurgence are to be found here, not least in the competition between institutions and systems. This should serve to caution against following any grand design towards some form of unified state but rather to embark on a process of discovery à la Hayek.

It may be doubted whether the political mechanisms are favourable to a 'trial and error' approach. The urge to centralise, the shifting of responsibilities to the Community level, has become virtually unstoppable. The principle of subsidiarity for the most part exists only on paper, and exerts practically no restraining influence. Has 'Brussels' ever returned a responsibility to the lower levels, even when the centralised arrangement has manifest shortcomings?

## Political prerequisites for the success of EMU

Let us return to the opening question: can monetary union function and prosper without political union? Reducing it to its essence, one could also express the problem thus: since its inception, monetary union has been seeking a congruent political complement. The prerequisites for the success of EMU are easy to describe: they are the Statute of the ECB founded on the pillar of independence, the mandate to give priority to price stability and the prohibition of monetary financing. Simply put, this means: the euro represents *depoliticised* and hence stable money. Monetary policy is removed from the political process of parties and elections, and it is left to the independent central bank to safeguard price stability.

There is only one answer to the often-repeated disparaging remark that such an important task cannot be left to 'technocrats' who are not answerable to the electorate: this was precisely what the Maastricht Treaty intended and was implemented through ratification in

European law. Political attempts to regain part or all of the responsibility for monetary policy undermine the very foundation of the currency and thus of what has been achieved in European integration to date. It should, moreover, be constantly brought to the mind of politicians just what pre-EMU monetary policy actually meant. Where member states had espoused the cause of monetary stability, they followed the course mapped out by the Bundesbank. Insisting on monetary policy 'autonomy', by contrast, essentially meant facing the necessity of repeatedly devaluing the national currency. The countries concerned paid a heavy price for investors' consequent mistrust in the form of correspondingly high interest rate risk premia.

The monetary policy of the Bundesbank itself, on the other hand, was immune from domestic political influence thanks to the central bank's *de facto* unassailable independence.[28]

Monetary union, which was launched – not, to be sure, driven by the central banks – under the pressure of the 1 January 1999 deadline, needs politicians to make the contribution they owe it to ensure its success. This means, for one thing, committing to achieve the degree of market flexibility that the single monetary policy does indeed require. (Not that this would not be a matter of urgency, even without monetary union, in order to foster growth and employment.)

Politicians have freely acknowledged this obligation to 'deliver' in droves, both before the start of EMU and afterwards. One need only read, for instance, the agenda approved by the heads of state or government in Lisbon in 2000.

In the case of the second institutional pillar of EMU, the Stability and Growth Pact, it will be perfectly sufficient if member states actually fulfil the obligations solemnly agreed to and enshrined in treaties.

---

[28] In his address on the occasion of the sixty-fifth birthday of Bundesbank President Hans Tietmeyer, the then German Chancellor Helmut Kohl remarked aptly: 'As a politician, I have often been annoyed at the decisions of the Bundesbank. As a German citizen, I am pleased and thankful that we have a central bank free from political influence.'

Not by chance, the area where the currency and politics rub up against each other is that of public finances. Control over public finances goes to the heart of western democracy. If this were to be transferred from the national to the European level, one would *de facto* have largely attained political union – and that will not happen soon. The national parliaments are not willing to renounce sovereignty in this regard, and the national governments in turn are accountable to their national parliaments and ultimately to the voters 'at home'.

How can one resolve the dilemma whereby the same national governments have control over the European procedure for applying the Stability and Growth Pact? Over time, non-compliance with its rules undermines the foundations of a currency union based on stable money. Logically, monetary union requires European commitments to take precedence over national sovereignty.

Naturally, this is true only for that aspect of fiscal policy that is reflected in budget balances and the level of indebtedness. The logic of monetary union by no means entails harmonising tax rates and so forth.

Put very simply, in requiring balanced budgets in the 'good times', the rules of the Pact are founded on a principle that has universal validity. If countries take this to heart, the tension between the European commitment and national sovereignty disappears. One should not give up hoping that this 'reconciliation' will be achieved, and on a lasting basis; but nor, perhaps, should one bet on it actually happening.

# SIX

# Europe at the crossroads

It undoubtedly required political courage to fix the beginning of monetary union definitively for 1 January 1999. To date, the euro's success has proved the confraternity of 'economic doubters' wrong. The single currency has brought the member states monetary stability: internally, with a low rate of inflation; and externally, with the protection the common currency affords against the foreign exchange market repercussions of exogenous shocks that were repeatedly experienced in the past.

The political decision did not, however, remove all justification for the reservations entertained by many economists about a premature start to EMU. The economies of the member states still have some way to go to satisfy the conditions necessary for monetary union to function properly. The political courage at the beginning needs to be complemented by the resolve to pursue the necessary reforms.

Fiscal policy has yet to demonstrate convincingly its full compliance with the self-imposed rules of the Stability and Growth Pact. Confidence in stability is certainly not fostered if, over and over again, governments solemnly promise to follow a sound budgetary policy in the future, as they did for instance in Berlin in the spring of

2007, only to see one or the other distancing themselves from such promises a few months later. And how credible are commitments if, many years after accession to EMU, countries still have debt levels of over 100 per cent of GDP – and that despite the 'gift' of markedly lower interest rates associated with entry into EMU?

An especially serious long-run threat to EMU arises from the ambitions to develop the EU in the direction of a welfare state with far-reaching social rights. Once these are given legal force, it will be virtually impossible to amend them even if glaring problems arise, since there will always be a group of countries that will benefit from the status quo.

There is no skirting the conclusion that the concept of a European *social union*, with wide-ranging rights that cement labour market rigidities rather than removing them, is not compatible with the principles of a stability-oriented monetary union. Under such circumstances, the single monetary policy would be unable to yield its potential benefits, and macroeconomic tensions would inevitably arise. This risk is all the greater, the more that structural unemployment – due precisely to such a lack of labour market flexibility – increases. Even leaving these consequences aside, enshrining extensive social rights at the Community level would inherently tend to be associated with transfer payments between member states, with the risk of creating deep-seated political tensions.

In reality, the opposition between social concerns and a policy of stable money that is repeatedly talked up in political debate does not exist. Inflation always affects the disadvantaged most – those who are unable to protect themselves against its arbitrary distributive effects. A free society can only endure on the basis of trust in the state and its institutions. Not least, this also includes having confidence in the stability of the currency. To take but one example: how can citizens reliably make their own private provision for old age if they cannot be confident that the currency they invest in will still retain its value after ten, twenty or thirty years?

The fact is that European integration, starting in the west, and extending eastwards following the fall of the Iron Curtain, is built on an economic foundation, that is, on dismantling international barriers and guaranteeing free competition. This is where its great successes lie. The introduction of the single currency raises economic integration to a new level that, whether one wants it or not, has far-reaching repercussions on other, politically highly sensitive areas. Whether in fiscal policy or in the reforms needed to make markets more flexible, monetary union exacts its price. For any country interested in stability and growing prosperity, it is a price worth paying, given the return on that investment – notably also in welfare terms.

In debating the possibility of a country's *exit* from EMU, moreover, it quickly becomes clear that, after weighing up all the pros and cons, no country would conclude that it would be better off outside than in. Were a member state, in the context of a major crisis, actually to give serious consideration to the question of whether or not to remain in EMU, such a situation might even act as a catalyst in the implementation of long-needed reforms. There is an obvious comparison with the efforts undertaken with the aim of gaining access to monetary union. The members of EMU can therefore regard any threat to leave by one of their number with equanimity. The Statute of the ECB rules out solving the problem of public debt through an inflationary monetary policy, as was known from the outset. This certainty for investors in euro-denominated securities constitutes the major difference compared with national arrangements, which in principle leave this way of escaping from national debt open as a last resort.

As regards the relationship between the European Union and EMU, there remain two options for those countries that do not join the monetary union. One, which would seem to be attractive for smaller countries in particular, is to link the national currency to the euro as a stability anchor. With the exchange rate 'tied down', as it were, the country becomes a 'monetary policy satellite', which, as the example of Denmark shows, can certainly yield stable conditions. The other option for an EU country outside EMU is to do what is necessary to ensure macroeconomic stability on its own.

The United Kingdom has shown that this can be done, given an appropriate monetary policy regime. After a decade of growth and stability, it is not surprising that the question of a possible UK accession to EMU is currently completely off the agenda. In the light of the much-vaunted British pragmatism, one can fairly safely predict that thought will only be given to such a step if two conditions materialise: firstly, the UK experiences a sizeable and persistent macroeconomic disturbance; and secondly, a glance at 'Europe' shows EMU to be thriving or at least functioning properly. At all events, for any country 'going it alone' – not just for the United Kingdom and the pound sterling – the risk remains that, at some point in the future, international capital movements may have a considerable impact on the exchange rate.

Nine years after the start of EMU, Europe is at the crossroads. With the establishment of the single market, economic integration is in principle complete, even if its implementation in important areas – services, free movement – still has major obstacles to surmount. In the monetary field, the success of the euro is beyond doubt. Hence ambitions and hopes are being pinned on progress in political integration. In a sense, politics is picking up where it left off following the Second World War and the failure of the European Defence Community project.

European integration has never been a linear process. Over and over, crises had to be overcome, fresh starts were made and progress was achieved. The image of a cyclist who falls over if he comes to a stop has been used to describe the need constantly to move forwards. In the meantime, monetary union has reached a stage where this 'bicycle theory' carries a lot of risks. 'Europe' has perhaps come closer to a 'final state' (in the words of Udo di Fabio) than many would admit. Failure to acknowledge this is more and more a source of risk.

Not everything that actually or purportedly serves the end of closer political integration leads us in the right direction. The difficulties that such endeavours may create for the functioning of the single monetary policy have been pointed out in several places in this book.

The ECB is well equipped to continue pursuing its policy to safeguard the stability of the euro in the future. There are two sources of vulnerabilities. Firstly, since the remarkable agreement that was reached on the stability-oriented Statute of the ECB, policy-makers have so far failed to play their part in ensuring the lasting success of monetary union, a failure that is manifest in the violations of the Stability and Growth Pact and the unfulfilled promises to make markets more flexible. Secondly, the 'social orientation' of many efforts towards greater political integration is at variance with the successful pursuit of the single monetary policy.

What will the future bring? It is of course easy to speculate. Based on the status quo and visible intentions, various scenarios might offer pointers to conceivable developments.

### 1. Strengthening of EMU

With the Statute of the ECB, the monetary policy for a stable euro is on a firm footing. Following the successful start and the stability demonstrated in all the years since, this scenario would see policy-makers making every effort to secure the full benefits of the single currency. To this end, there would be full compliance with the rules of the Stability and Growth Pact. The internal market would be quickly completed and the reforms committed to under the Lisbon Agenda would be fully implemented. The resultant greater market flexibility, especially labour market flexibility, would vastly improve the ability to adjust to economic shocks. Under such circumstances, the single monetary policy would yield its full benefits, with the principle of 'one size fits all' applying to the fullest extent possible. Over and above the active shaping of the environment in which monetary policy operates, this scenario presupposes that policy-makers desist from pursuing any projects – of the 'social union' sort – that would jeopardise the success of EMU.

Monetary union based on this model, thanks to stable money, sustained economic growth and high employment, would be underpinned internally by the trust of its citizens, and would become even more attractive to those outside, in particular for the 'not-yet-members' of the EU. The euro would further strengthen its position as an international currency and, owing to its internal stability, also make a major contribution to international monetary and financial stability.

## 2. Conflict-free extension of political union

In this scenario, the EU would progress further towards political union, without coming into conflict with the conditions necessary for a stability-oriented monetary union. In the areas that have long been at the centre of efforts towards that end, the member states would agree to transfer national responsibilities to the Community. Ideas and proposals would cover areas ranging from foreign policy to defence policy and even internal security. This development towards political union could proceed more or less in parallel with scenario 1, the strengthening of EMU. There remains the question of whether all twenty-seven EU member states would end up also being members of EMU.

The caveat to this scenario is how the EU institutions would be funded in order to enable them to implement the proposed measures. For such a plan to succeed, it would need the backing of EU citizens not just for the political objectives but also for their financing.

## 3. Political union in conflict with EMU

While scenario 2 largely leaves aside economic aspects, a third scenario would cast a cloud over future developments in Europe. This

would see the EU moving in the direction of a welfare state with cod-
ified social rights, welfare entitlements harmonised at a high level,
and still tighter regulation of the labour market. Monetary union
founded on the stable value of money and a European social union
of this sort would be an utterly incompatible mix.

In such circumstances, monetary policy would be unable to produce
its hoped-for positive effects. The 'single-size' monetary policy would
simply not fit all. Exogenous shocks and internal imbalances would
have a marked impact on employment and growth in individual countries. Across the euro area, the economy, and hence employment and
real wages, would lag behind the potential and outcomes in comparable regions. In such a situation, the ECB would still do its utmost to
fulfil its mandate of monetary stability, but it would be increasingly
exposed to political attack. With the economy underperforming,
EMU would confirm the sceptics' predictions. Confidence in the euro
would be diminished, not just among the citizens of the euro area,
even if the unsatisfactory state of affairs could not be laid at the door
of the ECB.

In such a scenario, the single currency would risk straining cohesion within the Community rather than fostering a sense of identification. However, it is not just that the foundations of EMU would be
undermined – in itself a disastrous outcome; there would in addition
be political tensions. High-level European welfare norms and social
rights enshrined at EU level and therefore enforceable across
'Europe' would put the Community to a critical test, not least owing
to the calls for substantial intra-Community transfer payments that
would unavoidably result. Even within a nation state, persistent large
transfer payments between regions can create considerable tensions.
Such an increase in transfer payments between EU (or EMU)
member states is highly unlikely to find approval among those who
would have to fund it through the taxes they pay, all the more so as
transfer arrangements of this kind almost inevitably create wrong
incentives. It might in the end be tempting to create or amplify a

'transfer need', or in any case to do nothing that would mean becoming a 'giver' rather than a 'taker'.

The threat that such a scenario would pose to European cohesion resides not least in the fact that, once set in stone in EU legislation, entitlements are very difficult if not impossible to revoke. In this regard, therefore, Europe would be well advised not to adopt a trial-and-error approach.

Naturally, one can conceive of any number of ways in which elements from these three scenarios might combine to shape the further integration of Europe. The respective outcomes would be determined by whichever of the elements came to dominate. Monetary union, the stability of the single currency, is at any rate an asset one should not risk losing. Of course, the currency is not everything, but without a stable currency one cannot predict a rosy future for European integration. European monetary union, the pre-eminent project of recent integration policy, is after all built upon the promise of stable money, a promise that, all scepticism notwithstanding, has hitherto been fulfilled.

In the end, one needs constantly to recall just how much today's Europe differs from that of the twentieth century, especially the first half of the twentieth century. The more remote the year 1945 becomes, the more the memory of war and destruction and Europe's subsequent resurgence risks being lost. It is one of the reasons why I should like to end this book with a small personal recollection.

In the ECB's first year, I happened to be sitting at lunch one day with the then Vice-President Christian Noyer for company. Swapping personal experiences, we discovered that his father, a French soldier, had been interned in a German prisoner-of-war camp at the same time as my own father was in France with the German occupying forces. Over fifty years later, the sons of these two combatants were working together at the ECB to help make the euro, the common currency, a success, and not just in France and Germany.

# Index